The Law of Charitable Status

This in-depth commentary on the Charities Act 2006 outlines the new requirements for qualifying as a charity and examines the concept of 'public benefit'. The author, a former Charity Commission lawyer who has practised in charity law for twenty years, conducts a theoretical and empirical analysis of the reasons that charitable status might be removed by the Charity Commission, looks at the position of charitable property when institutions cease to be charitable and examines the likely effect of the independent Charity Tribunal on the appeals process. The post-Act treatment of controversial charities is also explored.

ROBERT MEAKIN is a partner at the London and Cambridge offices of Stone King Sewell LLP Solicitors, having previously been a lawyer with the Charity Commission. He holds a PhD in charity law and is a visiting lecturer at Cambridge University.

The Law of Charitable Status: Maintenance and Removal

ROBERT MEAKIN

CAMBRIDGE
UNIVERSITY PRESS

CAMBRIDGE
UNIVERSITY PRESS

Shaftesbury Road, Cambridge CB2 8EA, United Kingdom

One Liberty Plaza, 20th Floor, New York, NY 10006, USA

477 Williamstown Road, Port Melbourne, VIC 3207, Australia

314–321, 3rd Floor, Plot 3, Splendor Forum, Jasola District Centre, New Delhi – 110025, India

103 Penang Road, #05–06/07, Visioncrest Commercial, Singapore 238467

Cambridge University Press is part of Cambridge University Press & Assessment, a department of the University of Cambridge.

We share the University's mission to contribute to society through the pursuit of education, learning and research at the highest international levels of excellence.

www.cambridge.org
Information on this title: www.cambridge.org/9780521516037

First published 2008

A catalogue record for this publication is available from the British Library

ISBN 978-0-521-51603-7 Hardback

Contents

Table of Cases

Table of Statutes

1

Introduction

Introduction

The author's interest in the Commission's powers of removal arises from acting for a majority of the School Fee Planning Charities[1] from 1993 onwards. It appeared at the time that the Commission was not confident about its powers to remove these charities from the register. The author's subsequent involvement in the Charity Law Association's Working Party Review of the consultation document *Maintenance of an Accurate Register of Charities*, which was eventually published as RR6-*Maintenance of an Accurate Register of Charities*,[2] reinforced the view that this subject had received little academic or professional attention. This is surprising because a decision by the Commission that an institution is not a charity is just as important as a decision that an institution is a charity. Much has been written about charitable status in the context of registration but there is a dearth of research on removal from the register or the removal of charitable status.

Basic propositions

There are five basic propositions.

First, the Commission's powers of removal are limited. It should rarely be the case that charities are removed from the register. If charities are removed too often then the public and the Government will lose confidence in the process.[3]

It is the need to maintain confidence in charities which underpins Lord Simmonds dictum that *'once a charity always a charity'*.[4] If an institution ceases to be a charity due to the passage of time or a change in social circumstances then it is argued[5] in this book that the appropriate course of action is a *cy-pres* scheme.[6] The principle that a charity never dies is subject to some

[1] [1996] Ch.Com.A.R. paras. 187–191. [2] November 2000.
[3] See p. 7 of this chapter. [4] *National Anti-Vivisection Society* v. *IRC* [1948] AC 31 at 74.
[5] Chapter 3, pp. 71–73.
[6] S. 13(1)(e)(ii) Charities Act 1993. A *cy-pres* scheme is a legal document made by the Commission which updates the purposes of a charity.

exceptions but, for the reasons outlined above, it is important that they are limited.[7]

Second, there is a distinction between the governing instrument of a charity and its property.[8] The distinction is between form and substance. A charity's property can be schemed[9] for new charitable purposes where those purposes have become dated, leaving the governing instrument to be removed from the register. Whether property is held charitably will not always depend on the objects set out in the governing instrument. The intention of the donors will be paramount[10] and this may result in property being applied *cy-pres* even where the institution was never charitable.[11] The effect of removal, in such circumstances, will not be as drastic as might at first appear because the property will continue to be applied for charity and only the governing instrument removed from the register.

Third, the Commission has a problem of legality when removing charities because of its inability to make law in the field of charitable status. As a public body, it may not act outside its powers.[12] Its powers derive from the Court or legislation. There is no power in the Charities Act 1993, the Charities Act 2006 or any other enactments which authorises the Commission to judicially decide questions of charitable status. Its role is to register[13] charities and in doing so it must follow the general law but there are so few decisions of the Court and legislation that the Commission is forced into becoming a *de facto* law-maker.[14] Its dilemma is that its duty to obey the existing law clashes with its need to respond to social change so that charitable status does not become irrelevant. The theoretical need to follow decisions of the Court and legislation and the lack of such decisions and legislation to follow appears to have restrained the Commission from removing or attempting to remove too many charities from the register. The Charity Tribunal does not greatly assist in this respect as it too must follow the general law.[15] It will be shown in this book that, through necessity, the Commission is becoming more like a legislator than a regulator.[16]

Fourth, there is a need for greater clarity about the extent of the Commission's powers of removal. Related to this is the doubt surrounding the essential indicia of charitable status.[17] Logic dictates that what disqualifies an institution from being a charity is just as important as what qualifies it to be a charity.

Fifth, there is a need for charities removed from the register to have access to justice. Although this book shows that charities can rarely be removed from the register, Chapter 8 shows[18] that the appeal process is unfairly weighted in favour of the Commission. Removed charities meet obstacles of judicial review

[7] See pp. 4–7 of this chapter. [8] Chapter 5, pp. 104–5.
[9] S.13 Charities Act 1993. [10] Chapter 5, pp. 104–5. [11] Ibid.
[12] *Boddington* v. *British Transport Police* [1999] 2 AC 143 at 171 *per* Lord Steyn.
[13] S. 3 A(1) Charities Act 1993. [14] This is explained in Chapter 3, pp. 65–67.
[15] See Chapter 8, pp. 171–5. [16] Chapter 3, pp. 65–67.
[17] See Chapter 2, pp. 12–18. [18] Chapter 8, pp. 171–5.

and common-law remedies, and are also deterred by the high costs in appealing. This makes reform of the appeal system crucial.[19]

Summary of the book

The extent of the Commission's powers of removal is presently unclear. Little research has been carried out in this area. This book seeks to clarify the position. One of the purposes of this book is to clarify the limits of the power in which the Commission could remove an institution from the register.

In Chapter 2 the essential indicia[20] of charitable status are analysed. Being a charity in law is a necessary requirement for registration[21] and a loss of one or more of the essential indicia will oblige the Commission to remove an institution from the register.[22] It is shown in this chapter that the essential indicia of charitable status are not clear and that this lack of clarity supports the basic proposition[23] that the Commission's powers of removal need clarification. The Commission cannot be confident about its powers of removal if it cannot be certain that an institution is not a charity.

In Chapter 3 it is shown that each of the grounds for removal under section 3 (4) of the Charities Act 1993 – '*no longer considers is a charity*'; has '*ceased to exist*' or '*does not operate*' – are limited.[24] Furthermore, where rectification of the register is concerned, it is argued[25] that institutions will retain their tax reliefs until the date of removal, except where they were never charitable or where they are removed because they have amended their 'trusts'.[26] It is argued that this interpretation further limits the effect of removal.

Chapter 4 applies three of the basic propositions[27] to controversial charities: the Commission's powers of removal are limited; the Commission can only legally remove charities from the register in limited circumstances; and its powers require clarification. These are charities connected to the state either through funding agreements or trusteeship,[28] schools which charge fees[29] and new religious movement charities.[30]

Chapter 5 points out[31] that a distinction needs to be made at the outset between the governing instrument of a charity and property held for charitable purposes. While a charity might be removed from the register, it does not necessarily mean that its property will be lost to charity. It is argued that it will rarely be the case that property will be lost to charity when the charity is removed from the register because charitable property will be applied *cy-pres*[32] for charitable purposes.

Chapter 6 explores the extent to which the Commission's powers of investigation lead to the removal of charities from the register under section 3(4) of the

[19] See Chapter 9. [20] Chapter 2, pp. 12–18. [21] See pp. 12–13 of this chapter.
[22] S.3(4) Charities Act 1993. [23] Pp. 1–4 of this chapter. [24] Chapter 3, pp. 45–50.
[25] Chapter 3, p. 52. [26] S.3(5) Charities Act 1993. [27] Pp. 1–4 of this chapter.
[28] Chapter 4, pp. 85–89. [29] Chapter 4, pp. 89–93. [30] Chapter 4, pp. 94–102.
[31] Pp. 1–4 of this chapter. [32] Chapter 5, pp. 108–12.

Charities Act 1993. The chapter illustrates, through documentary analysis of the Commission's published inquiry reports[33] that the Commission's powers of removal are limited and charities will rarely be removed from the register.

Chapter 7 looks at the Human Rights Act 1998 and the Charities Act 2006. Some of the provisions of these acts broaden the scope of charitable status, making it harder for the Commission to remove charities from the register. The implications for charities on the register are discussed. This chapter supports the basic proposition[34] that there is a problem of legality when interpreting the law of charitable status because the Commission has so few decisions of the court and legislation to follow. When interpreting the law in the light of the Human Rights Act 1998 the Commission must second-guess what the Court would decide or what Parliament intended. Although the Charities Act 2006 sets out a list of charitable purposes[35] it is not definitive and in time will date. The Charities Act 2006 does not solve the Commission's problem of legality because in these instances the Commission must try again to establish what might be the law.

Chapter 8 shows that legal appeal processes put the Commission in a position of strength when using its powers to remove charities from the register. This is in spite of the constraints of the Commission when considering grounds for removal.

Chapter 9 makes suggestions about reforming the law.

Why the power to remove charities from the register is important

There are a number of reasons why the power to remove charities from the register is important. First, government policy on the delivery of public services by charities means that there is an increased need to ensure that the register is accurate and that those charities which do not qualify for registration are removed. Second, there is a need to ensure that tax reliefs are properly applied.[36] Third, there is a need to ensure that donors are not discouraged from giving. This will be discussed further in the next paragraph.[37] Fourth, the law is changing and it is important to understand the foundations of the law which underpin the new legislation so that there can be a correct analysis of the Commission's powers of removal. All of these reasons will now be explored.

The importance of the charity sector in the delivery of public services

At present there is no definitive source of information about the charity sector as a whole.[38] However, for registered charities the definitive source is the Commission. The Commission records that there are 190,000 registered charities in England and

[33] Chapter 6, pp. 121–4. [34] Pp. 1–4 of this chapter. [35] S.2(2) Charities Act 2006.
[36] P. 12 of this chapter. [37] Pp. 12–13 of this chapter.
[38] *The Role of The Voluntary and Community Sector in Service Delivery: A Cross Cutting Review*, September 2002, p. 9 (www.hm-treasury.gov.uk).

Wales with £38 billion annual income representing 3.4 per cent of total GDP.[39] The number of registered charities is growing by about 1,800 per annum.[40]

It is estimated that there are between 500–700,000 organisations registered or unregistered in the charity not-for-profit sector.[41] The National Council for Voluntary Organisations (NCVO) estimated in July 2005 that there were 169,249 'general charities' in the UK[42] which had a total income of £26.3 billion in 2003/4.[43] Two-thirds of the total income was generated by 3,200 organisations equating to 2 per cent of the sector.[44] The NCVO estimates that almost 38.1 per cent of the income of general charities in the UK in 2003/4 came from government.[45] For the first time, contract income from the public sector is now worth more than grant income from the same source.[46] As a source the only type of income to increase as a proportion of total income between 1995–2003/4 was the public sector from 28 per cent to 38.1 per cent of the sector's income. To illustrate the growing importance of charities in this area it was estimated that between 1991 and 1995, contract income from government increased by over 50 per cent in real terms.[47]

The Government wants to enable the charity sector to become a more active partner in shaping state policy and the delivery of public services.[48] This was recently emphasised by the government's White Paper *Higher standards, better schools for all more choice for parents and pupils*[49] which proposed the introduction of self-governing charitable foundation schools run as not-for-profit organisations, including charities now provided for by the Education and Inspections Act 2006. It is also illustrated by a Home Office document, *Working Together: Co-operation between Government and Faith Communities*,[50] which proposed that there should be a partnership between faith communities, including faith-based charities to deliver public services. In the health sector, the National Strategic Partnership between the NHS and charities means that charities will play a bigger role in supplementing the NHS.[51] The role of charities delivering public services is a theme that has been reiterated since the government's compact with charities in 1998.[52]

[39] [2005/6] Ch. Com. A.R. p. 1. [40] Ibid. [41] Ibid. para 2.10.

[42] Wainwright, Clark, Griffith, Jochum and Wilding, *The UK Voluntary Sector Almanac 2006* (London: NCVO, 2006) p. 43.

[43] Ibid. p. 51. [44] Ibid. p. 53. [45] Ibid. p. 59.

[46] Ibid. p. 2. See also *The Future Role of the Third Sector in Social and Economic Regeneration: Final Report*, July 2007, Cm 7189.

[47] [2005/6] Ch. Com. A.R. p. 1.

[48] See *The Future Role of the Third Sector in Social and Economic Regeneration: Final Report*, July 2007, Cm 7189.

[49] Cm 6677 (2005). See www.dfes.gov.uk. See para 2.11.

[50] Home Office Faith Communities Unit, February 2004.

[51] *New Agreement between NHS and Voluntary Sector*, 20 September 2004, ref number: 2004/0339. See www.dh.gov.uk.

[52] *Compact Getting It Right Together*, November 1998, Cm 4100. See also *The Role of the Voluntary and Community Sector in Service Delivery: A Cross Cutting Review*, September 2002 (www.hm-treasury.gov.uk).

An increasing reliance on charities to deliver public services can be traced back to the 1980s with the emergence of what has become known as the 'contract culture'.[53] Prior to this charities relied on grant-aid for funding. Grants tended to represent a general contribution to a charity which was not linked to an identifiable service.[54] Now there is a purchaser / provider relationship in the delivery of public services.[55] Therefore, the government has an interest in ensuring that charities are *bona fide*, have good governance and are efficient. The statistics and government reports show that charities and not-for-profit organisations now have an important role in the delivery of public services. It is because charities are far more central to the delivery of public services that the accuracy of the register and the issue of removal from the register has gained in importance.

Tax reliefs

The government will also have an interest in the removal of charities from the register because charities also receive government-funded tax reliefs which are available to both charities and their donors.[56] The value of tax reliefs to charities was estimated in 2003/4 as almost £3 billion.[57] Anything which damages the reputation of the charity sector and its regulation will not be good news for a government which relies so much on the charity sector to deliver public services.

Donors

It is part of the government's policy to encourage more people to give to charity.[58] Despite an increase in public funding to 38.1 per cent of the charity sector's income, donations from the public in 2003/4 were 35.4 per cent.[59] Without such income the work of charities would be significantly restricted. An important source of information for potential donors is the register of charities.

[53] Morris, D., 'Charities and the Contract Culture: Partners or Contractors? Law and Practice in Conflict', Charity Law Unit, Liverpool University, 1999.

[54] Ibid.

[55] The implications arising from this relationship are explored in Morris, D., 'Charities and the Contract Culture'. The contract culture in the field of health and social services is explored in R. Meakin, *Charity in the NHS: Policy and Practice*, 1st edn (Bristol: Jordans, 1998).

[56] Inland Revenue: information for charities. www.inlandrevenue.gov.uk/stats/charities/menu.htm.

[57] See Wainwright, Clark, Griffith et al., *The UK Voluntary Sector Almanac 2006*, p. 43. For a commentary on charity tax reliefs see J. Kessler QC, *The Taxation of Charities*, 5th edn (2005).

[58] See *Getting Britain Giving: Inland Revenue Guidance Note for Charities* (2001) (www.hmre.gov.uk) and *The Giving Campaign* (www.givingcampaign.org.uk).

[59] Wainwright, Clark, Griffith, et al., *The UK Voluntary Sector Almanac 2006*, p. 61.

Law reform

Following the Charities Act 2006[60] it is likely that the issue of removal will become more relevant. There are a few reasons for this. First is the abolition of the presumption of public benefit[61] in the case of the old first three heads of charity.[62] In addition, the Commission now has a duty to issue guidance on public benefit.[63] In doing so it will be obliged to follow the general law where there is little analysis of public benefit. This is partly because the court has rarely considered public benefit in respect of the old first three heads of charity because it has been presumed. Now that the Commission has to issue public benefit guidance, it will be forced to second-guess Parliament or the court.[64] This might lead to the removal of more charities from the register.

Second, the Charities Act 2006 provides for a Charity Tribunal.[65] Although the Tribunal must follow the general law because there are so few decisions by the Court or legislation on charitable status, the Charity Tribunal will have to second-guess the court in much the same way as the Commission. Decisions by the Charity Tribunal might lead to more charities being removed from the register if the Commission is prepared to test its powers generally.[66]

Therefore it is important that the foundations which underpin the law are clarified so that the law can be understood and the Charities Act 2006 is correctly interpreted and applied.[67]

60 Prior to the Charities Act 2006 there was a *Review of the Register* which included an examination of the Commission's power of removal, and, prior to the publication of the Charities Bill [HL], the Strategy Unit Report *Private Action, Public Benefit A Review of Charities and the Wider Not-for-Profit Sector*; The Government response to the Strategy Unit Report: *Charities and Not-for-Profits: A Modern Legal Framework* (Home Office, 2003) and the Draft Charities Bill [2004]. Following the publication of the Draft Charities Bill a Joint Committee of the whole House published a report, *Report from the Joint Committee on the Draft Charities Bill*, HL Paper 167-I HC 660-I, 30 September 2004 and the Government's response, *Government's Response to the Committee's Report*, Cm 6440, 21 December 2004.

61 See *National Anti-Vivisection Society* v. *IRC* [1948] AC 31 *per* Lord Simonds at pp. 66–67.

62 S. 3(2) Charities Act 2006.

63 S. 4(1) Charities Act 2006. To date the Commission have issued the following guidance: *Public Benefit – The Charity Commission's Approach* (January 2005), *Public Benefit – The Charity Commission's Position on how Public Benefit is Treated in the Charities Bill* (July 2005), *The Charity Commission's Approach to Public Benefit, Appendix to Parliamentary Briefing* (October 2006) and *Charities and Public Benefit: The Charity Commission's General Guidance on Public Benefit* (January 2008).

64 See for example Chapter 2, pp. 34–42 and Chapter 4, pp. 94–95.

65 S. 8 Charities Act 2006.

66 See Chapter 8, pp. 171–5 and Chapter 4, pp. 86–87 for statements made by the Commission.

67 See Chapter 7, pp. 126–8 *et seq.* for an examination of the changing face of charitable status following the Human Rights Act 1998 and the Charities Act 2006.

Introduction to the general law

Why is there a register of charities? What is the effect of registration and removal? What are the Commission's current powers of removal?

The register of charities

Section 3 A (1) Charities Act 1993 places a duty on charities to register. The register was introduced by the Charities Act 1960. The idea behind the register was to provide information to the public and social workers so that charitable resources could be accessed for the benefit of those in need.[68] A secondary purpose was to enable the Commission when using its *cy-pres*[69] powers to alter the objects of obsolescent charities so that their funds could be put to better use.[70] Registration provides a conclusive presumption that an institution is charitable for all purposes other than rectification.[71]

Some charities are exempt[72] or excepted[73] from registration. Excepted charities may elect to be registered if they wish.[74] Charities which are exempt or excepted from registration and not registered cannot, of course, be removed from the register. However, the Inland Revenue might consult the Commission as to whether these institutions are charitable, and if the Commission advises that they are not then this might lead to the loss of tax reliefs. If this happens the practical effect will be the same as being removed from the register. The grounds for removal from the register, apart from the ground that the charity does not operate[75] will be relevant to the question of whether the institution is charitable. Therefore the book has a wider relevance than simply looking at the powers of removal from the register.

The Commission's powers of removal

The relevant legislation is contained in the Charities Act 1993. The power to remove charities[76] from the register is contained in section 3(4) Charities Act 1993:

> The Commission shall remove from the register –
>
> (a) any institution which it no longer considers is a charity, and
> (b) any charity which has ceased to exist or does not operate.

[68] Nathan, *The Charities Act 1960*, 1st edn (London: Butterworths, 1962) p. 20.
[69] S. 13 Charities Act 1993. [70] Nathan, *The Charities Act 1960*, p. 20.
[71] S. 4(1) Charities Act 1993. [72] S. 3 A(2), Schedule 2 Charities Act 1993.
[73] S. 3 A(2)(b) & (c) Charities Act 1993. [74] S. 3 A(6) Charities Act 1993.
[75] S. 3 (4) Charities Act 1993.
[76] For a summary of the grounds for removal see pp. 4–7 of this chapter.

The wording 'no longer considers is a charity' would include the following grounds for removal:

(A) The institution never had the essential indicia of charitable status. It is submitted in this book that the essential indicia of charitable status are being subject to a legal obligation to carry out charitable purposes,[77] being within jurisdiction,[78] having charitable purposes,[79] which includes the requirement of public benefit,[80] and being viable in the sense that if the charitable purposes are impossible from the outset that a general, rather than a specific, charitable intention is expressed by the settlor so that the property is applied *cy-pres*.[81] It is arguable that a lack of independence from the state is part of the essential indicia of charitable status, although this argument is not supported in this book.[82]

(B) Sham charities.[83]

(C) Where there is a change in the law that confirms that the institution was never charitable.[84]

(D) Charities registered by the Commission under a mistaken understanding of the law.[85]

(E) Change in the trusts.[86] This would happen when the trustees exercised a power of amendment to cause the loss of one or more of the essential indicia of charitable status.[87]

'Ceased to exist' includes the exercise of a power of dissolution in the case of incorporated and unincorporated charities[88] where the property is exhausted by being expended on the charitable purposes in the case of unincorporated charities,[89] or is transferred,[90] but arguably not where it is transferred by way of a scheme[91] of the Commission, reverts,[92] where the charity comes to an end in the case of a time charity,[93] or where the objects are dependant on a particular institution which closes, or a particular property which is no longer available.[94]

It is submitted[95] that a charity 'does not operate' if it does not qualify for registration[96] because its gross income does not exceed £5,000 a year[97] or £100,000 in the case of an excepted charity[98] and yet still legally exists. It is arguable that the Commission can use its power to remove charities from the register where they do not carry out charitable activities. However, this argument is not supported in this book.[99]

[77] Chapter 2, pp. 14–18. [78] Chapter 2, p. 23. [79] Chapter 2, pp. 23–31.
[80] Chapter 2, pp. 34–42. [81] Chapter 2, p. 42. [82] Chapter 2, p. 43.
[83] Chapter 3, pp. 54–57. [84] Chapter 3, pp. 57–59. [85] Chapter 3, pp. 59–65.
[86] Chapter 3, pp. 73–75. [87] Chapter 2, pp. 12–18. [88] Chapter 2, pp. 20–22.
[89] Chapter 3, pp. 75–83. [90] Ibid. [91] Ibid. [92] Ibid. [93] Ibid. [94] Ibid.
[95] Chapter 3, pp. 50–52. [96] S. 3 A (1) Charities Act 1993.
[97] S. 3 A(2)(d) Charities Act 1993. [98] S. 3 A(2)(b) & (c) Charities Act 1993.
[99] See Chapter 3, pp. 50–52 for arguments rejecting this interpretation.

Under Section 4(2) Charities Act 1993:

> *Any person who is or may be affected by the registration of an institution as a charity may, on the ground that it is not a charity ... apply to the Commission for it to be removed from the register*

Section 4(1) Charities Act 1993 refers to rectification of the register but does not set out grounds for rectification.[100]

The Commission also has protective powers under sections 18 and 19 Charities Act 1993 which might lead it to use its power of removal under section 3(4) Charities Act 1993. These powers are discussed in Chapter 6.[101] They include, *inter alia*, the appointment and removal of trustees and the appointment of an interim manager. Sometimes, after using its power to institute an inquiry[102] and to call for documents and search records,[103] the Commission may conclude that a charity should be removed from the register because it has 'ceased to exist'[104] or 'does not operate'[105] without the need to exercise any of its protective powers under sections 18 and 19 Charities Act 1993.

General approach to writing the book

There is surprisingly little written about the removal of charities from the register. There have been three spurts of interest by legal practitioners and academics. First, when the charitable status of the Gun Clubs was examined by the Commission;[106] second, when the *Review of the Register* was announced[107] and third, following the publication of the Strategy Unit Report[108] and the Charities Act 2006 which led to much discussion on the effect of the abolition of the presumption of public benefit, some of it consisting of serious analysis, but most of it flowing from superficial commentary from various national newspapers.[109]

This book mainly draws on the common law of charitable status. This sometimes involves an exploration of what is charitable which, in turn, leads to the deduction of what is not charitable. Decisions of the Commission and its publications[110] (such as the *Review of the Register*) are critically examined against relevant legislation and the common law. The author's experience as a lawyer at the Commission between 1988 and 1993, and subsequently in private

[100] Chapter 3, p. 52. [101] Chapter 6, pp. 114–16.
[102] S. 8 Charities Act 1993. [103] S. 9 Charities Act 1993.
[104] S. 3(4) Charities Act 1993. See Chapter 3, pp. 75–83 and Chapter 6, p. 123.
[105] S. 3(4) Charities Act 1993. See Chapter 3, pp. 50–52 and Chapter 6, pp. 121–3.
[106] See Chapter 3, pp. 60–65. [107] See Chapter 3, pp. 65–67.
[108] Cabinet Office, *Private Action, Public Benefit: A Review of Charities and the Wider Not-for-Profit Sector* (2002).
[109] See Chapter 4, p. 89. The focus has mainly been on fee-paying independent schools with charitable status.
[110] These can be accessed on the Commission's website: www.charity-commission.gov.uk.

practice to the present day, is also drawn upon when discussing points of practice and unreported cases. Where information is obtained, other than from public sources, client confidentiality is respected. During this time the author has been exclusively involved in the practice of charity law as it applies to a broad range of charities falling within each of the heads of charity. The author's legal practice in charity law is varied but includes a considerable volume of applications for charity registration and representing charities subject to Commission inquiries.

In Chapter 6 the issue of removal is supported by documentary analysis of published Commission inquiry reports over a two-year period between 2003 and 2004.[111]

The techniques employed help provide an up-to-date objective analysis of the law as it relates to the removal of charities from the register and an analysis of the Commission's approach to removal.

[111] See Chapter 6, pp. 121–4.

2

Essential indicia of charitable status

Introduction

At this stage it is necessary to explore the essential indicia of charitable status because this is a crucial issue in the context of the Commission's powers to remove charities which it 'no longer considers is a charity'.[1]

It is submitted that the essential indicia of charitable status are being subject to a legal obligation to carry out charitable purposes,[2] being within jurisdiction,[3] having charitable purposes,[4] which includes the requirement of public benefit[5] and being viable in the sense that, if the charitable purposes are impossible from the outset, that a general, rather than a specific, charitable intention is expressed by the settlor so that the property is applied *cy-pres*.[6] It is arguable that a lack of independence from the state is part of the essential indicia of charitable status, although this argument is not supported in this book.[7]

It is submitted that an institution which lacks one or more of the essential indicia of charitable status[8] from its inception cannot be a charity[9] for the purposes of the Charities Acts 1993 and 2006 and will therefore have been mistakenly registered.[10] It is argued that an institution could have the essential indicia of charitable status at its inception, but might subsequently lose some by the exercise of an express power in the governing instrument,[11] or because its objects have ceased to be charitable in law due to a change in social circumstances or the passage of time.

Where indicia are lost through the exercise of a power of amendment, the Commission must remove an institution from the register under section 3(4) Charities Act 1993 on the basis that it no longer considers that the institution is a

[1] S. 3(4) Charities Act 1993. [2] Pp. 14–18 of this chapter. [3] P. 23 of this chapter.
[4] Pp. 23–34 of this chapter. [5] Pp. 34–42 of this chapter. [6] P. 42 of this chapter.
[7] P. 43 of this chapter.
[8] For express powers which can have the effect of removing the essential indicia see pp. 14–17 of this chapter and for sham trusts which can become lawful see Chapter 3, pp. 54–57.
[9] S. 1(1)(a) & (b) Charities Act 2006.
[10] For the other grounds for mistaken registration see Chapter 3, pp. 54–65.
[11] Pp. 20–22 of this chapter.

charity. If this happens, the original property would be held on charitable trusts in the case of an unincorporated charity,[12] and arguably in the case of an incorporated charity.[13] Where institutions no longer have charitable objects due to the passage of time or a change in social circumstances, it is argued that the Commission will need to apply the property *cy-pres*[14] for charitable purposes.[15] In either case, the survival of charitable property supports the proposition that the Commission's powers of removal are limited.

One of the basic propositions of this book is that the Commission's powers of removal need clarification.[16] It is argued in this chapter that a lack of certainty over the essential indicia contributes to a lack of certainty about the Commission's powers of removal. If the Commission cannot be certain about whether an institution is a charity in law then it will be uncertain about whether it can remove it because it no longer considers it to be a charity.[17]

The essential indicia for charitable status are not clear in a number of respects. First, it is not clear whether the mere inclusion of powers in an unincorporated charity's governing instrument, which, when exercised, could remove one or more of the essential indicia, would have the effect of preventing an institution from being a charity.[18]

Second, 'charitable purposes'[19] are defined as purposes falling within the list of purposes listed in section 2(2) Charities Act 2006 or existing charity law[20] or by virtue of section 1 Recreational Charities Act 1958,[21] any purposes reasonably analogous to, or within the spirit of, those purposes,[22] and any purposes as reasonably analogous to, or within the spirit of, any purposes recognised under charity law[23] to be analogous to those purposes.[24] This chapter[25] argues that this statutory definition is unhelpful because it does not entirely explain what charitable purposes are. To discover what constitutes charitable purposes there is a need to refer to the general law.[26] The problem is that there are so few decisions of the court setting out what is charitable that the Commission is forced into becoming a *de facto* lawmaker when deciding questions of charitable status.[27] As a result, in practice, charities are often registered by the Commission on the basis of its own decisions on charitable

12 *Baldry* v. *Feintuck* [1972] 1 W.L.R. 552 *per* Brightman J at 557. See Chapter 3, pp. 19–22 and Chapter 5, pp. 108–12.

13 *Re Vernon's Will Trusts* [1972].

14 S. 13(e)(ii) Charities Act 1993.

15 See Chapter 3, pp. 45–52.

16 Chapter 1, pp. 1–4.

17 S. 3 (4) Charities Act 1993.

18 See pp. 20–22 of this Chapter.

19 S. 2 (1) Charities Act 2006.

20 S. 2(8) Charities Act 2006 defines *'existing charity law'* as *'the law relating to charities in England and Wales'*.

21 S. 2(4)(a) Charities Act 2006.

22 S. 2(4)(b) Charities Act 2006.

23 S. 2(8) Charities Act 2006 defines *'charity law'* as *'the law relating to charities in England and Wales.'*

24 S. 2(4)(c) Charities Act 2006.

25 See pp. 23–24 of this chapter.

26 *'Charitable purposes'* are defined in section 2(1) Charities Act 2006. See pp. 23–24 of this chapter.

27 Chapter 3, pp. 45–52.

status which do not have the force of law and therefore leave a doubt about the charitable status of institutions.[28]

Third, the definition of 'charity'[29] for the purposes of the Charities Acts 1993 and 2006 requires there to be an 'institution'[30] which is defined as 'an institution whether incorporated or not, and which includes any trust or undertaking', but there is no such requirement for there to be an 'institution' for the purposes of the common law. There is, therefore, a distinction between the requirements for charitable status set by the common law and the requirement that an institution is a charity for the purposes of registration.[31]

Fourth, it is unclear when the court or the Commission can look at activities to determine charitable purposes.[32]

Fifth, there are often fine distinctions made by the court between what is charitable and what is non-charitable. To take but one example, it is unclear what qualifies as charitable research in the field of literary and cultural studies.[33]

Sixth, related to the question of whether purposes are charitable in law is the question of whether such objects are for the benefit of the public. There is a dearth of decisions of the court on charitable status including public benefit.[34] Furthermore, an examination of the decisions of the court on public benefit reveal a complex, confusing and at times illogical picture.[35]

Seventh, where the viability of a charity from its inception is in question, an institution's charitable status will turn on whether the court can construe a general rather than a specific intention to further charitable purposes.[36] Whether there is a specific or a general intention is not always clear.

Eighth, it needs to be made clear that independence from the state is not a requirement of charitable status.[37]

A legal obligation to carry out the charitable purposes

The first element of charitable status that needs to be discussed is the requirement for there to be a legal obligation to carry out charitable purposes. In order to see what constitutes a legal obligation to carry out charitable purposes one needs to examine the statutory definition of 'charity'.

'Charity' is defined in the Charities Act 2006[38] as:

> an institution which –
>
> (a) is established for charitable purposes only, and
> (b) falls to be subject to the control of the High Court in the exercise of its jurisdiction with respect to charities.

This definition requires further explanation.

[28] Chapter 3, pp. 59–65.
[29] S. 1(1) Charities Act 2006.
[30] S. 78(5) Charities Act 2006.
[31] Pp. 14–18 of this chapter.
[32] Pp. 27–31 of this chapter.
[33] Pp. 32–34 of this chapter.
[34] Pp. 35–36 of this chapter.
[35] Pp. 35–42 of this chapter.
[36] P. 42 of this chapter.
[37] P. 43 of this chapter.
[38] S. 1(1) Charities Act 2006.

An 'institution' is defined in the Charities Act 2006 [39] as 'an institution whether incorporated or not, and includes any trust or undertaking'. Trusts are defined as:

> *the provisions establishing it as a charity and regulating its purposes and administration, whether those provisions take effect by trust or not, and in relation to other institutions has a corresponding meaning.*[40]

'Special trusts' are defined as:

> *property which is held and administered by or on behalf of charity for any special purposes of the charity, and is so held and administered on separate trusts relating only to that property*[41]

Even though 'trusts' are defined[42] widely as including provisions which take effect by trust or not it is submitted in this book that where the Commission no longer considers an institution to be a charity[43] due to any change in its trusts[44] that in this context 'trusts' must equate to the essential indicia of charitable status.[45] One of the essential indicia is a legal obligation to carry out charitable purposes which would include a trust and which is now explained.

A charitable trust can be created orally in the case of an *inter vivos* trust of personalty.[46] In contrast a trust of land or interest in it must be evidenced by some writing signed by some person who is able to declare such trust or by his will[47] and where property is devised or bequeathed to charity under a will the formalities under section 9 Wills Act 1937, as amended by the Administration of Justice Act 1982, must be complied with. Usually, charitable trusts are created by a settlor or a testator who transfers or bequeaths or devises funds or property to trustees upon trust for charitable purposes. Although a trust is usually created in this way it can arise by way of presumption by the court where there is no record of a trust deed and there is evidence that property has been dedicated for charitable purposes over a long period of time.[48]

There are three essential requirements for a charitable trust.[49] First, there must be certainty in the words used to create it.[50] Second, the subject matter must be certain.[51] Third, there must be certainty that all the potential objects are charitable.[52] If any one of these three certainties is lacking there will not be a

[39] S. 78(5) Charities Act 2006. [40] S. 97(1) Charities Act 1993. [41] Ibid.
[42] Ibid. [43] S. 3(4) Charities Act 1993. [44] S. 3(5) Charities Act 1993.
[45] See Chapter 3, p. 53. [46] *M'Fadden* v. *Jenkyns* (1842) 1 Ph 153.
[47] Section 53(1)(b) Law of Property Act 1925.
[48] *Goodman* v. *Mayor of Satash Corp* (1882) 7 App Cas 633, HL.
[49] *Knight* v. *Knight* (1840) 3 Beav 148 *per* Lord Langdale at 172. See Warburton J 'Charitable Trusts-Unique' (1999) 63 Conv, Jan/Feb 20–31.
[50] *Tito* v. *Waddell* (No 2) [1977] 3 All ER 129.
[51] *Palmer* v. *Simonds* (1854) 2 Drew 221.
[52] *Chichester Diocesan Fund and Board of Finance (Incorporated)* v. *Simpson* [1944] Ch 253 *per* Lord Greene MR at 259.

charitable trust, consequently there will be no legally binding obligation to carry out charitable purposes and as a result there will not be a charity. This is discussed in more detail later in this Chapter.[53]

'Incorporated'[54] is not defined in the Charities Acts 1993[55] and 2006 but this legal expression would include companies incorporated under the Companies Act 2006, corporations incorporated by Royal Charter and Charitable Incorporated Organisations.[56]

It is not clear what is meant by 'undertaking'.[57] What therefore constitutes an 'undertaking' for the purposes of registration as a charity? In the absence of any statutory guidance it is submitted that there is a need to look to the general law for what constitutes an 'undertaking'. A contextual interpretation of 'undertaking' would lead to the conclusion that 'undertaking' means a legal obligation to carry out charitable purposes because the definition of 'institution'[58] includes the words 'corporate' and 'trust' both of which place legal obligations on trustees to carry out charitable purposes. Following the rule of construction *noscitur a sociis*[59] it would follow that 'undertaking' involves a legally binding obligation to carry out purposes. This interpretation is reinforced by Lord Nathan[60] who chaired the Committee which published the Nathan report.[61] The findings and recommendations of the Nathan report led to the Charities Act 1960, including the original statutory reference to 'undertaking'.[62] Lord Nathan commented that the term 'trust or undertaking' means property held on charitable trusts.

It is submitted that an 'undertaking' could include a contractual 'undertaking'. A contractual undertaking could be oral or created by conduct.[63] Most conveyances of land or of any interest therein must be transferred by deed.[64] Most contracts for the sale or disposition of an interest in land must be made in writing.[65] An unincorporated association is a contract between members.[66] Yet a gift to an unincorporated association with charitable purposes tends to be construed by the court as a gift on trust for the charitable purposes of the

[53] P. 11 of this Chapter. [54] Ibid.

[55] Section 97(1) Charities Act 1993 defines a 'company' as '*a company formed and registered under the Companies Act 1985 or to which the provisions of that Act apply as they apply to such a company*'.

[56] S. 34, Schedule 7 Charities Act 2006. [57] S. 78(5) Charities Act 2006. [58] Ibid.

[59] A word is known by the company it keeps. See Maxwell, *Interpretation of Statutes*, 12th edn (London: Sweet and Maxwell, 1969) pp. 64 *et seq*.

[60] Nathan *The Charities Act 1960*, 1st edn (London: Butterworths, 1962) p. 25.

[61] The Nathan Report Cm 9538. [62] S. 46(1) Charities Act 1960.

[63] *Hart* v. *Mills* (1846) 15 L.J. Ex 200; *Steven* v. *Bromley & Son* [1919] 2 KB 722.

[64] S. 52(1) Law of Property Act 1925.

[65] S. 2 Law of Property (Miscellaneous Provisions) Act 1989.

[66] *Re Koeppler's Will Trusts* [1985] 2 All ER 869 *per* Slade LJ at 874.

association.[67] It is therefore submitted that where a charitable 'undertaking' is contractual the court would probably construe property as also held subject to charitable trusts. This is probably what Lord Nathan meant when he concluded that the term 'trust or undertaking' means property held on charitable trusts.[68] The court has never made it a requirement that there is an 'undertaking' to carry out charitable purposes.[69] In fact the court will give effect to charitable intention where property is given to the charity upon charitable trusts by way of a scheme where the trust machinery has not been provided for by the donor or has failed.[70] Furthermore, where property is given to charity without being constituted as a corporate body or as a trust then the court will have no jurisdiction[71] and the Crown as *parens patriae* will act as the constitutional trustee[72] and apply the property by way of Royal Sign Manual. Therefore, there is a distinction between the requirements for charitable status under the general law and the requirement that an institution is a charity for the purposes of the Charities Acts 1993 and 2006 and registration.

It is theoretically possible that an institution could be removed from the register[73] because it is not subject to an 'undertaking' to carry out charitable purposes but on appeal from the Charity Tribunal[74] the court could decide that the institution is a charity for the purposes of the common law. This could then lead to the bizarre situation that the Commission then refuses to register the institution because it is not a charity[75] for the purposes of the Charities Acts 1993 and 2006. In practice this will not happen because the Commission insists on charities applying for registration having a governing instrument which will fall within the definition of an 'institution'.[76]

It is clear, however, that there is no requirement for a charity to have a formal governing instrument.[77] A charitable trust of personalty is enforceable without any evidence in writing of the terms of the trust.[78] Furthermore, where funds

[67] *Re Vernon's Will Trusts* [1972] Ch 300 *per* Buckley J at 303; *Re Morrison* (1967) 111 SJ 758; *Re Finger's Will Trusts* [1972] Ch 286 *per* Goff J at 294 and *Neville Estates Ltd* v. *Madden* [1962] Ch 832 *per* Cross J at 849–850. These decisions indicate the recent trend, but for an example of an unincorporated association which was construed by the Court to hold its property for its members absolutely see *Re Ogden* [1933] Ch 678 *per* Lord Tomlin at 681–682.

[68] Nathan *The Charities Act 1960*, 1st edn (London: Butterworths, 1962) p. 25.

[69] By way of illustration see *AG* v. *Mathieson* [1907] 2 Ch 383; *Re Bennett* [1960] Ch 18.

[70] *Paice* v. *Archbishop of Canterbury* (1807) 14 Ves 36, 83; *Re Burley* [1910] 1 Ch 205.

[71] *Re Bennett* [1960] Ch 18 *per* Vaisey J at 26.

[72] *Paice* v. *Archbishop of Canterbury* (1807) 14 Ves 36 *per* Lord Eldon at 372.

[73] S. 3(4) Charities Act 1993. [74] S. 2 Charities Act 2006. [75] S. 1(1) Charities Act 2006.

[76] S. 78(5) Charities Act 1993 defines an 'institution' as 'incorporated or not' and including 'any trust or undertaking'. For examples of model governing instruments see www.charitylawassociation.org.uk.

[77] See *Re North Devon and West Somerset Relief Fund Trust* [1953] 1 WLR.1260 but note that it is the responsibility of those who receive funds for charitable purposes to execute a trust deed declaring precise trusts. See *AG* v. *Mathieson* [1907] 2 Ch 383. See Picarda H *The Law and Practice Relating to Charities*, 3rd edn (1999) Chapter 16, p. 209.

[78] *Lyell* v. *Kennedy* (1889) 14 App Cas 437 at 457.

have been raised on appeal without a governing instrument the trustees have an implied authority to put in place a governing instrument which will clarify the objects and set out the administrative powers to enable those objects to be carried out.[79] The Charities Act 1993 (as amended by the Charities Act 2006) recognises that charities can be created without governing instruments.[80] With the notable exception of Charitable Incorporated Organisations[81] the Charities Acts 1993 and 2006 do not prescribe what must be contained in a governing instrument. They simply say there must be 'charitable purposes'.[82] The relative unimportance of governing instruments to the question of what is a *charity* is discussed further in Chapter 5.[83]

Where charities do have a written governing instrument, there are three possible reasons why there might not be a legally binding obligation to carry out charitable purposes. First, in the case of a charitable trust, one or more of the three certainties might be lacking.[84] Second, express clauses in a governing instrument may prevent charitable status.[85] Third, the charitable objects are too widely drafted.[86]

One or more of the three certainties is lacking

There are three essential requirements for a charitable trust.[87] If one of these requirements is missing then there cannot be a charitable trust and, as a result, there cannot be a legally binding obligation to carry out charitable purposes. It follows that the institution must be removed from the register unless one of the exceptions explained later in this chapter applies.[88] Each of these three certainties is now discussed.

Certainty of words

The words used by the settlor or the testator should imply the imperative.[89] For example, if a person deposits money with a bank in their own name 'as trustee for charitable purposes' without the charitable trust having been communicated to anyone this test will not be satisfied.[90] This is a matter of construction for the Court.[91] Although it is theoretically possible for a charitable trust to be created orally[92] most charitable trusts will be in writing and most registered by the Commission will have a trust deed in a standard form,[93] and will have certainty

[79] *AG* v. *Mathieson* [1907] 2 Ch 383 at 394.

[80] S. 3B(1)(b) Charities Act 2006 refers to 'required documents' which include 'copies of the charity's trusts or (if they are not set out in any extant document) particulars of them'. See section 3B(2)(a) Charities Act 2006.

[81] S. 34 Charities Act 2006. [82] S. 1(1)(a) Charities Act 2006. [83] Chapter 5, pp. 104–5.

[84] P. 18 of this chapter. [85] Pp. 20–22 of this chapter. [86] Pp. 22–23 of this chapter.

[87] *Knight* v. *Knight* (1840) 3 Beav 148 *per* Lord Langdale at 172.

[88] P. 25 of this Chapter. [89] *Knight* v. *Knight* (1840) 3 Beav 148 *per* Lord Langdale at 172.

[90] Sinnett v. Herbert (1872) 12 Eq. 201 at 206.

[91] For example *AG* v. *Leigh* (1730) 3 P. Wms. 146 n. [92] *AG* v. *Mathieson* [1907] 2 Ch 383.

[93] For example see the Charity Law Association model trust deed: www.charitylawassociation.org.uk.

of words. It is unlikely that the Commission would, in practice, remove a charity from the register on the basis that it lacked certainty of words.

Certainty of subject matter

The second requirement for a charitable trust is that the subject matter of the charitable gift must be capable of being ascertained. For example, a charitable gift failed where blanks were left in a will for the amounts to be given to charity.[94] The question of whether a trust is void for uncertainty of subject matter where gifts are made for partly non-charitable and partly charitable purposes will fall into three categories.[95]

First, where a fund is to be divided between charitable and illegal or impossible purposes so that that neither part of the gift takes precedence over the other the court will uphold the charitable part by apportioning the fund between the two types of objects.[96]

Second, where the gift to a charity is residuary upon a void gift, the general rule is that it fails if the court finds that the precedent gift is of an unascertainable amount[97] unless the court, following inquiry, can ascertain that the subject matter is certain.[98]

Third, where the gift is construed as devoting the whole fund to charitable objects subject to the payment for a void object, the failure of the void object will result in the whole fund being available for charity.[99]

With the use of model trust deeds,[100] which usually provide for an initial nominal fund to be held on charitable trusts, it is unlikely that a trust will be void for uncertainty of subject matter. It will, therefore, rarely be the case that there will be no legal obligation to carry out charitable purposes.

Certainty of objects

A charitable trust requires not certainty of objects but certainty that all potential objects are charitable.[101] If a trust is charitable then, unlike a non-charitable trust,[102] the absence of an individual beneficiary who can prove that he is interested in a share of the trust property does not matter. Here the court dispenses with the requirement that there must be a beneficiary because the Crown, as *parens patriae*, can enforce the charitable trust by way of a scheme.[103]

94 *Hartshorne* v. *Nicholson* (1858) 26 B 58.

95 J Warburton *Tudor on Charities*, 9th edn (London: Butterworths, 2003) pp. 138–140.

96 For example *Doyley* v. *AG* (1735) 4 Vin. Abr. 48; *Sallesbury* v. *Denton* (1857) 3 K & J 529.

97 *Chapman* v. *Brown* (1801) 6 Ves 410.

98 *Mitford* v. *Reynolds* (1841) 1 Ph 199.

99 *Kelly* v. *AG* [1917] 1 Ir.R.183.

100 For example see the Charity Law Association model trust deed: www.charitylawassociation.org.uk.

101 *Chichester Diocesan Fund and Board of Finance (Incorporated)* v. *Simpson* [1944] Ch 253 *per* Lord Greene MR at 259.

102 *Bowman* v. *Secular Society Ltd* [1917] AC 406 at 441.

103 *Re Diplock* [1941] Ch 253 *per* Lord Greene MR at 259.

Examples of objects which are not certain are discussed later[104] along with exceptions to the rule that a failure to express charitable purposes will lead to non-charitable status.[105]

It is possible that objects expressed in a charity's governing instrument will not be in a charitable form. In such cases, unless certain exceptions apply,[106] these institutions must be removed.[107] However, in practice, the Commission will follow the court[108] in assisting those institutions which are in substance charitable to adopt charitable objects and remain on the register.[109]

Express clauses in a governing instrument which prevent charitable status

A number of court decisions held that where administrative powers enabled the trustees to carry out non-charitable purposes, the institution could not be a charity.[110] Much the same conclusion could be reached about unfettered amendment and dissolution clauses. It could be argued that any power of amendment must be circumscribed so that it cannot be used to convert charitable objects into non-charitable objects, or at least only allow the power to be exercised with the prior consent of the Commission or the High Court.[111] Without such a restriction, it could be argued that the institution would not be subject to a legally binding obligation[112] to carry out charitable purposes. This means that powers of amendment tend to be expressed so that they must be exercised in direct furtherance of the charity's objects.[113] In practice, the Commission insist that the power of amendment to change objects, the dissolution clause or the power of amendment itself cannot be exercised without its consent.[114]

The same principle applies to powers of dissolution which are not expressly restricted to transferring property for charitable purposes. There is a potential problem because the trustees have the option to pass the assets to a non-charitable institution. Note the judgment of Cross J in *Neville Estates* v. *Madden*:[115]

104 Pp. 32–34 of this chapter. 105 P. 25 of this chapter.
106 *Ibid.* 107 S. 3(4) Charities Act 1993.
108 *Incorporated Council of Law Reporting for England and Wales* v. *AG* [1972] Ch 73.
109 For example see *Concordis International Trust* 23 July 2004: see www.charity-commission.gov.uk 'Decisions of the Commission.'
110 For example, *Karen Keymouth be Jisroel Ltd* v. *IRC* [1932] AC 650; *Oxford Group* v. *IRC* [1949] 2 All ER 537. See, for example, the Charity Law Association's model governing instruments: www.charitylawassociation.org.uk.
111 This is a statutory requirement for charitable companies. See section 64(2) (2A) Charities Act 1993.
112 S. 78(5) Charities Act 2006 defines an 'institution' as including 'any trust or undertaking'.
113 For example, *Karen Keymouth be Jisroel Ltd* v. *IRC* [1932] AC 650; *Oxford Group* v. *IRC* [1949] 2 All ER 537.
114 For example see the Charity Law Association model trust deed: www.charitylawassociation.org.uk.
115 *Neville Estates* v. *Madden* [1962] Ch 832 at 849.

> If the gift is one of the second class, i.e. one which the members of the association for the time being are entitled to divide among themselves, then, even if the objects of the association are in themselves charitable, the gift would not, I think, be a charitable gift. If, for example, a number of persons formed themselves into an association with a charitable object – say the relief of poverty in some district – but it was part of the contract between them that, if a majority of members so desired, the association should be dissolved and its property divided between the members at the date of dissolution, a gift to the association as part of its general funds would not, I conceive, be a charitable gift.

This is why, in practice, the Commission insist that dissolution clauses are restricted to transferring the property to similar charitable purposes.[116]

Alternatively, it could be argued that until the powers of amendment or dissolution are exercised, the institution is subject to a legally binding obligation[117] to carry out charitable purposes. This analysis accords with time charities and charities which hold property subject to a reverter provision. Time charities exist for a set period during which time the income is applied for charitable purposes and the capital is divided amongst persons or charities.[118] At the end of the set period of time, the time charity distributes property, ceases to exist and must then be removed from the register of charities.[119] In the case of a reverter, property is usually given subject to a condition that should the property cease to be used for the purposes of the charity it will revert back to the donor or his heirs in law.[120] Unlike a time charity, in the case of a reverter, the charity holding the property which reverts can continue unless the property was part and parcel of the objects.[121] Both examples demonstrate that the existence of charity for a finite time can be accommodated in law. A logical extension of this principle is that unfettered powers of amendment or dissolution do not prevent charitable status until they are exercised to render the property non-charitable.

One can distinguish these situations from those where the charitable objects are not separated from non-charitable powers. Here the institution does not have exclusively charitable purposes.[122] In contrast, where there are exclusively charitable purposes, it is submitted that the court will enforce the legally binding

[116] For example see the Charity Law Association model trust deed: www.charitylawassociation.org.uk.

[117] S. 78(5) Charities Act 2006 defines 'institution' as 'incorporated or not' and including any 'trust or undertaking'.

[118] *Re Rymer* [1895] 1 Ch 19. For a commentary on time charities see J. Claricoat and H. Phillips, *Charity Law A-Z: Key Questions Answered*, 2nd edn (Bristol: Jordans, 1998).

[119] S. 3(4) Charities Act 1993.

[120] See for example the rights of reverter under the School Sites Act 1841 and the Reverter of Sites Act 1987.

[121] *Re J W Laing Trust* [1984] Ch 143.

[122] For example, *Karen Keymouth be Jisroel Ltd* v. *IRC* [1932] AC 650; *Oxford Group* v. *IRC* [1949] 2 All ER 537.

obligation to carry out those purposes until such time as they cease to be charitable because of, say, amendment or dissolution.[123] This appears to be the better analysis and is consistent with the Court of Appeal decision in *Construction Industry Training Board* v. *AG*[124] where the court made no objection to a provision in a charity's governing instrument allowing the Minister to wind up the charity and determine where the funds should be distributed without any restriction on his power to allow funds to be applied on dissolution for non-charitable purposes.

It seems that if there is no legally binding obligation[125] upon trustees to carry out charitable objects even on a temporary basis, then the institution will not be a charity. Alternatively, if there was a legal obligation on the trustees to carry out charitable objects but at a later stage the trustees exercised an express power[126] removing one of the essential indicia of charitable status then the charity would cease to be charitable in law. In each case removal from the register would be the appropriate course of action.[127]

The charitable objects are too widely drafted

If objects are drafted too widely so that they allow charitable property to be applied for non-charitable purposes then the Court will, save in exceptional circumstances, hold that the institution is non-charitable.[128] Where property was conveyed for such Roman Catholic purposes 'as the Trustees with the consent of the Bishop may prescribe' the Court held that the trustees could lawfully, without committing any breach of trust, exercise their powers and devote the trust fund to objects which were not charitable.[129] Such a form of wording could have enabled the Bishop to establish an enclosed contemplative order of nuns which would lack the public benefit required to be charitable.[130]

In another case, *Oxford Group* v. *IRC*,[131] objects were held to be non-charitable because, *inter alia*, one of the objects was expressed in the following terms:

> To do all such other things as are incidental, or the association may think conducive, to the attainment of the above objects or any of them.

The court held that this wording would force it to opine on whether the association thought something was conducive to the charitable objects rather than whether the activity was conducive to the main charitable object.[132]

[123] See pp. 14–18 of this chapter.
[124] *Construction Industry Training Board* v. *AG* [1973] Ch 173. See Chapter 4, pp. 87–88.
[125] Pp. 14–18 of this chapter. [126] Chapter 3, pp. 73–75.
[127] S. 3(4) Charities Act 1993. See Chapter 5, pp. 108–12.
[128] See p. 25 of this chapter. [129] *Ellis* v. *IRC* (1949) 31 TC 178.
[130] *Gilmour* v. *Coats* [1949] AC 426. [131] *Oxford Group* v. *IRC* [1949] 2 All ER 537.
[132] Ibid. at 545.

The Commission has followed the approach of the Court when registering charities. An example of this is the application by the Animal Abuse, Injustice and Defence Society[133] which was rejected because, *inter alia*, its objects were too widely drafted and could be construed as permitting the promotion of an object (in this case anti-vivisection) which would be contrary to the public benefit.[134]

It will be shown later in this chapter that the court can, at its discretion, apply the doctrine of severance to save the charitable part of the fund where the objects are a mixture of charitable and non-charitable.[135]

Jurisdiction

The next component of the essential indicia of charitable status is that the charity must be subject to the jurisdiction of the High Court in the exercise of its jurisdiction with respect to charities.[136] It is settled law that an institution will not be regarded as a charity if it is governed by a governing instrument subject to foreign law.[137] It will not be a charity because the court will have no means of controlling it and there will be no guarantee that its funds would be applied for exclusively charitable purposes.

An institution which does not fall within the jurisdiction of the High Court in the exercise of its jurisdiction with respect to charities must have been registered by mistake or have subsequently amended its governing instrument in such a way as to cease to be within jurisdiction.[138]

Charitable purposes

This paragraph explains what charitable purposes are and sets out the problem areas in the field of charitable status. First, the Commission does not have any lawmaking powers when deciding questions of charitable status. There are so few decisions of the Court dealing with the question of charitable status in contemporary society that even following the Charities Act 2006 it is expected

133 [1994] Ch. Com. Dec. Vol. 2 pp. 1–4.

134 See *National Anti-Vivisection Society* v. *IRC* [1948] AC 31.

135 *Salisbury* v. *Denton* (1857) 3 K & J 529. See pp. 20–24 of this chapter.

136 S. 1(1)(b) Charities Act 2006. See *Construction Industry Training Board* v. *AG* [1973] Ch 172. See Chapter 4, pp. 7–8.

137 See *Camille and Henry Dreyfus Foundation Inc* v. *IRC* [1954] 2 All ER 466 (CA) and *Gaudiya Mission and others* v. *Brahmachary and others* [1997] 4 All ER 957. See also *His Beatitude, Archbishop Torkom Manougian, Armenian Patriarch of Jerusalem* v. *Yolande Sonsin and Others* [2002] EWHC 1304 (Ch) where Jacob J commented, *obiter*, at paras. [35]-[38] that, contrary to the Commission's views it was not essential for a charitable trust that there should be a trustee within jurisdiction because the court could still exercise its jurisdiction. Although note that the European Commission has sent a formal request to the UK government to end discrimination of foreign charities in respect of tax reliefs. See www.europa.eu/rapid/pressReleasesAction.do?

138 P. 23 of this chapter and Chapter 3, pp. 73–75.

that many charities will be registered on the basis of the Commission's decisions.[139] Second, it is not clear when the court and the Commission can look at activities rather than objects to determine charitable status.[140] Third, the court has made many fine distinctions between what is charitable and what is non-charitable which could allow the Commission to revisit its decisions.[141] This is illustrated later in this chapter with reference to research into literary or cultural subjects.[142]

What are charitable purposes?

The statutory definition of 'charity'[143] makes it a condition that an institution is 'established for charitable purposes only'. 'Charitable purposes'[144] are defined as those purposes listed in section 2(2) Charities Act 2006 or existing charity law,[145] or by virtue of section 1 Recreational Charities Act 1958[146] and any purposes reasonably analogous to, or within the spirit of, those purposes,[147] and any purposes as reasonably analogous to, or within the spirit of, any purposes recognised under existing charity law[148] to be analogous to those analogous purposes.[149]

To explain the full extent of all charitable purposes one has to look beyond the statutory definition to the Preamble to the Statute of Charitable Uses Act 1601[150] which reads:

> The relief of aged, impotent, and poor people; the maintenance of sick and maimed soldiers and mariners, schools of learning, free schools and scholars of universities; the repair of bridges, havens, causeways, churches, sea banks and highways; the education and preferment of orphans; the relief, stock or maintenance of houses of correction; marriages of poor maids; supportation, aid and help of young tradesmen, handicraftsmen and persons decayed; the relief or redemption of prisoners or captives and the aid or ease of any poor inhabitants concerning payments of fifteens, setting out of soldiers, and other taxes.

The various instances of charitable purposes set out in the preamble were classified by Lord MacNaughton in *Pemsels* Case[151] as falling into four categories: the relief of poverty; the advancement of education; the advancement of religion; and other purposes beneficial to the community. The Charities Act 2006 now sets out a list of twelve specific charitable purposes[152] and accepts the

[139] Pp. 26–27 of this chapter. [140] Pp. 27–31 of this chapter. [141] Pp. 32–34 of this chapter.
[142] Ibid. [143] S. 1(1)(a) Charities Act 2006. [144] S. 2(1) Charities Act 2006.
[145] S. 2(8) Charities Act 2006 defines 'existing charity law' as 'the law relating to charities in England and Wales'.
[146] S. 2(4)(a) Charities Act 2006. [147] S. 2(4)(b) Charities Act 2006.
[148] S. 2(8) Charities Act 2006 defines 'existing charity law' as 'the law relating to charities in England and Wales'.
[149] S. 2(4)(c) Charities Act 2006. [150] 43 Eliz. 1 C. 4 (repealed).
[151] *Income Tax Purposes Commissioners* v. *Pemsel* [1891] AC 531.
[152] S. 2(2) Charities Act 2006.

existing law of charitable status and purposes analogous to either the statutory list or the existing law of charitable status.[153]

For charitable purposes not expressly listed in the Charities Act 2006,[154] the Preamble to the Statute of Charitable Uses Act 1601[155] is the starting point for determining charitable status.[156] The court has regarded the Preamble as guide-posts to interpreting charitable status according to the needs of contemporary society.[157] Within an overall broad approach to the Preamble, the court has adopted two different routes.[158] The first assumes a new purpose which is beneficial to the community to be charitable unless reasons can be found to deny charitable status.[159] The second requires a new purpose to be analogous to charitable purposes as decided by the court. How specific the analogy must be has varied from the narrow approach adopted by Dillon J in *Barralet* v. *AG*[160] as needing to find an analogy from what is stated in the Charitable Uses Act 1601[161] or from what has already been held to be charitable within the fourth head of charity to the wider approach which draws a broad analogy with the kinds of purposes already accepted as charitable.[162]

An institution with objects which are not charitable in law will not be a charity.[163] There are exceptions to this rule.[164] First, if the wording of the trust permits the property to be applied for both charitable and non-charitable purposes the court may apply the doctrine of severance, saving the charitable part of the fund.[165] Second, a trust with some non-charitable purposes which came into operation before 16 December 1952 may be saved by the Charitable Trusts (Validation) Act 1954. Third, what is apparently a non-charitable purpose may be construed as charitable if conjunctive words have been used when listing the purposes of the trust.[166] Fourth, if the main purpose of an institution is charitable then non-charitable powers expressed as incidental or subsidiary to it will not be a bar to charitable status.[167]

[153] S. 2(4)(a) (b) & (c) Charities Act 2006. [154] S. 2(2) Charities Act 2006.

[155] 43 Eliz. 1 C. 4 (repealed).

[156] *Scottish Burial Reform and Cremation Society Ltd* v. *Glasgow Corporation* [1968] AC 138 at 151 *per* Lord Upjohn. See generally J. Warburton, *Tudor on Charities*, 9th edn (London, Butterworths, 2003) pp. 4–7.

[157] *Incorporated Council of Law Reporting for England and Wales* v. *AG* [1972] Ch 73 at 87, *per* Russell LJ.

[158] J. Warburton, *Tudor on Charities*, 9th edn (London: Butterworths 2003) pp. 5–7.

[159] *Incorporated Council of Law Reporting for England and Wales* v. *AG* [1972] Ch 73 at 87, *per* Russell LJ.

[160] *Barralet* v. *AG* [1980] 3 All ER 918 at 926.

[161] The Charitable Uses Act 1601 43 Eliz. 1 C. 4 (repealed).

[162] *Re Strakosch* [1949] Ch 529 *per* Lord Greene MR at 538. [163] *Ante.*

[164] For commentary on these points see J Warburton, *Tudor on Charities*, 9th edn (London: Butterworths, 2003) pp. 12–13.

[165] See *Salisbury* v. *Denton* (1857) 3 K &J 529. [166] See *Blair* v. *Duncan* [1902] AC 37.

[167] See *IRC* v. *Glasgow (City) Police Athletic Association* [1953] AC 380.

When deciding novel purposes the Commission takes a constructive approach. Where a specific analogy to the Preamble or a decision of the court cannot be found they will look at the Preamble and the principles applied by the court to find a broad analogy.[168] The Commission has made it clear[169] that it will try progressively to meet the evolving needs of society, not restrict itself to close analogies and adopt a generous as opposed to a restrictive view[170] with a general approach of deciding in favour of charity.[171]

An example of this approach is *Public Concern at Work*[172] which was established to promote ethical standards in the workplace including advice to potential whistle blowers. An analogy was drawn with charities with purposes tending to promote the mental or moral improvement of the community and to charities promoting compliance with the law. Another example is *Business in the Community*[173] which was registered with objects to advance industry and commerce for the benefit of the public through making advice, training and support available to local bodies which assisted individuals setting up businesses, particularly in areas of high unemployment. This was accepted by the Commission as charitable on the basis that it was itself analogous to the accepted charitable purpose of promoting craft and craftsmanship[174] which was analogous to the charitable purpose of promoting commerce and industry.[175]

The Review of the Register, which is discussed in Chapter 3,[176] indicates a more proactive approach by the Commission to the question of charitable status. Now the Commission will announce new charitable purposes rather than wait until an application with novel purposes.[177]

The Commission's dilemma

It is one of the basic propositions in this book that there is a fundamental problem with the Commission removing an institution from the register because it does not have charitable objects.[178] As a public body it must not act outside its powers.[179] The Commission only has the powers conferred on it by the Charities Acts 1993, 2006 and other enactments.[180] It does not have the statutory powers to decide questions of charitable status and therefore it must follow decisions of

[168] RR1 a-*Recognising New Charitable Purposes* (2001), para. 23.

[169] [1985] Ch. Com. A.R. paras. 24–27. [170] *Ibid.* para. 27.

[171] *Ibid.* [172] *Public Concern at Work* Ch. Com. Dec., Vol. 2 (1994) at pp. 9–10.

[173] *Business in the Community* [1987] Ch. Com. A.R. paras. 15–17.

[174] See *IRC* v. *White and AG* (1980) 55 TC 651.

[175] [1987] Ch. Com. A.R. paras. 15–19. [176] Chapter 3, pp. 65–67.

[177] See RR1-*The Review of the Register of Charities* (Version – September 2001) and RR1 a-*Recognising New Charitable Purposes* (Version – October 2001).

[178] See Chapter 1, pp. 1–4.

[179] See *Boddington* v. *British Transport Police* [1999] 2 AC 143 at 171 *per* Lord Steyn for an authority for the proposition that public authorities must act within their powers.

[180] As for other enactments see, for example, the Charities Act 1992.

the court or legislation. Its role is simply to register charities and in doing so it must follow the general law.[181]

Ultimately the question of what are 'charitable purposes' is one for Parliament or the Court to resolve. Prior to the Charities Act 2006[182] there was so little legislation[183] and so few cases[184] that charitable status was shaped by the process of registration conducted by the Commission. Although the Charities Act 2006[185] lists twelve specific charitable purposes and provides for a Charity Tribunal[186] which can decide questions concerning the registration and removal of charities from the register[187] this does not help the Commission decide novel questions of charitable status.

When registering institutions with novel purposes and with no clear legal authority to look to for guidance the Commission in practice widens the boundaries of charitable status. Because it has no law-making powers[188] it can only 'create law' for the purposes of registration. Chapter 3 argues that the legal basis upon which the Commission registers institutions with novel purposes is open to question.[189] There may be thousands of charities on the register which the court might at a later date decide are not charitable. In the meantime, the Commission is forced to second-guess the court. It follows that there is a need for greater clarity about the Commission's powers of removal.[190]

Objects or activities?

It is unclear when the court and the Commission can look at the activities of a charity to determine whether the objects are charitable. Although the general rule[191] is that it is the objects of an institution which determine charitable status, there are so many exceptions that substance[192] is equally as important as form. It is important to note that where non-charitable activities are carried on outside the scope of the charitable purposes then the analysis is usually one of breach of trust.[193] However, if the Commission decides to look at the substance of registered charities rather than their form then this could lead to the removal of charities from the register, rather than the Commission seeking to use its protective powers.[194]

181 *'Charitable purposes'* are defined in section 2(1) Charities Act 2006.
182 S. 2(2) Charities Act 2006 lists 12 specific charitable purposes.
183 For example the Recreational Charities Act 1958 and the Charities Act 2006.
184 A search of Westlaw over the last 3 years did not reveal any decisions by the Court specifically on the issue of charitable status.
185 S. 2(2) Charities Act 2006. 186 S. 8 Charities Act 2006.
187 Schedule 1 C Charities Act 1993.
188 They only have the powers conferred on them by the Charities Act 1993 and other enactments. See Chapter 3, pp. 45–52.
189 Chapter 3, pp. 45–52. 190 S. 3(4) Charities Act 1993.
191 *AG* v. *Ross* [1986] 1 WLR 252 at 264. 192 *Ibid.* per Scott J at 263.
193 *Ibid. per* Scott J at 264. 194 Ss. 18 & 19 Charities Act 1998.

The general rule of law[195] is that where the objects of a charity are in a clear charitable form then the Court is not entitled to look at extrinsic evidence. This was expressed in the House of Lords by Lord Brown-Wilkinson, prior to the Charities Acts 1992 and 1993, when debating a clause in the Charities Bill which would have enabled the Commission to look into an institution's likely future activities when determining whether it should be registered as a charity:

> under existing law the legal status of a charity is determined once and for all by what is set out in its written constitution. If the words state the purpose to be a charitable purpose that is the end of the matter: it is a charity ... Clause 2 changes the substantive law of charity. I am anxious as to what its consequences might be, not in relation to those charities that might be called dodgy, but in relation to bona fide charities. I am anxious that there should not be a wide-ranging investigation in the case of every charity, not only of what it has done in the past, but of what it intends to do in the future. I am sure that your Lordships are aware that there is nothing more difficult than to establish effectively what a person's future intentions are. I am sure that the Charity Commissioners accept that they are not an ideal fact-finding body such as would be required to conduct those difficult findings of fact in order to decide whether a charity should or should not be registered.[196]

The problem with this general rule was summarised by Scott J in *AG* v. *Ross*:[197]

> The skill of Chancery draftsmen is well able to produce a constitution of charitable flavour intended to allow the pursuit of aims of a non-charitable or dubiously charitable flavour.

There are a number of exceptions to this general rule which give the court greater scope for looking at activities to determine whether purposes are charitable. The objects could be ambiguous. It might be unclear whether objects are charitable, pass the public benefit test or the court might suspect that the charity is a sham.[198]

The objects are ambiguous

In *McGoven* v. *AG*[199] Slade J looked at Amnesty International's constitution and handbook to construe the objects of an associated trust which claimed to

[195] *The Incorporated Council of Law Reporting for England and Wales* v. *AG* [1972] Ch.73 *per* Buckley LJ at 99.

[196] Hansard HL Deb 5th series Vol. 532, col. 836.

[197] *AG* v. *Ross* [1986] 1 WLR 252 at 263. See J. Warburton, *Tudor on Charities*, 9th edn (London: Butterworths, 2003) p. 186.

[198] See also Chapter 3, pp. 28–31.

[199] *McGovern* v. *AG* [1982] Ch 321. See also *IRC* v. *City of Glasgow Police Athletic Association* [1953] AC 380 *per* Lord Normand at 395–396.

have charitable status although the objects were of an ambiguous nature. He commented that:

> It is common ground that, in construing the ambiguous wording of Clause 2C and, indeed, any other ambiguous wording contained in the trust deed, the Court is at liberty so far as it can, to derive assistance from the statute of the unincorporated association, Amnesty International. Not only does the trust deed borrow the name 'Amnesty International' as the name of the trust, it specifically refers to Amnesty International in Clauses 9(b) and 16. The statute of this association is manifestly part of the factual matrix accompanying the execution of the trust deed.[200]

Amnesty International was held not to be a charity because of its political aims and objectives.[201]

There is a doubt about whether the objects are charitable

The Court can look behind objects where there is some doubt whether the objects are in a charitable form. In *Southwood* v. *AG*[202] the objects of an institution called the Project on Disarmament ('Prodem') were, *inter alia*, the advancement of the education of the public in the subject of militarism and disarmament and related fields by all charitable means including the promotion, improvement and development for the public benefit of research into this subject and the publication of the useful results thereof. Carnwath J[203] noted that the Commission had looked at the surrounding facts including the activities of the promoters before and after the execution of the trust deed and approved of the approach. The background material made it clear that the purpose of Prodem was specifically to challenge the current politics of western governments. These intended non-charitable activities provided evidence that Prodem had a political object and as a result Prodem could not be a charity.

In *Re Hopkinson*[204] the court held that a charity with educational objects, which made reference to a memorandum headed *A Note on Education in the Labour Party*, was not charitable, because it was really concerned with how the cause of the Labour Party could be advanced by improving its methods of propaganda, and was therefore masquerading as an educational charity. This decision should be contrasted with *Re The Trusts of the Arthur McDougall Fund*[205] where it was held that a trust with unambiguous and clear charitable

200 *McGovern* v. *AG* [1982] Ch 321 *per* Slade J at 348.

201 Note that the Commission has now accepted that institutions with charitable objects to promote human rights are capable of being charitable. See RR 12-*The Promotion of Human Rights* (version January 2005). See also Chapter 7, pp. 157–66 for a discussion on the possible effect of Article 10 of The European Convention on Human Rights on the law of charitable status.

202 *Southwood* v. *AG* The Times, 26 October, 1998 upheld on appeal in *Southwood* v. *AG* [2000] W.T.L.R.1199.

203 *Southwood* v. *AG* The Times, 26 October, 1998.

204 *Re Hopkinson* [1949] 1 All ER 346.

205 *Re The Trusts of the Arthur McDougall Fund* [1957] 1 WLR 81.

educational objects was a charity even though the governing instrument provided that the trustees had to be members of a political organisation. It will be shown again later in this chapter that the line between charitable and non-charitable objects is often fine.[206]

The court will look at activities where it wishes to ascertain the scope of objects particularly when determining whether novel purposes are charitable. The case of *The Incorporated Council of Law Reporting for England and Wales* v. *AG*[207] considered whether the publication and dissemination of law reports was charitable. In holding that this was a charitable purpose the court also held that it could look at extrinsic evidence to determine whether objects were charitable. There was no existing authority on this particular charitable purpose. Buckley LJ said:

> To ascertain for what purposes the Council was established one must refer to its memorandum of association and to that alone. It is irrelevant to enquire what the motives of the founders were, or how they contemplated or intended that the Council should operate, or how in fact operated ... But in order to determine whether an object, the scope of which has been ascertained by due processes of construction, is a charitable purpose it may be necessary to have regard to evidence to discover the consequences of pursuing the object. It would be immediately evident that a body established to promote the Christian religion was established for a charitable purpose, whereas in the case of a body established to propagate a particular doctrine it might well be necessary to consider evidence about the nature of the doctrine to decide whether its propagation would be a charitable activity.[208]

The Commission can rely on these decisions to look at the real purposes of an institution where there is a doubt over the real objects. However, where it looks at activities and extrinsic evidence it must be certain that the real purposes are non-charitable before it removes an institution from the register.[209]

The objects do not pass the public benefit test

The court can examine the activities of a charity where it is not certain whether the charity passes the public benefit test. In *IRC* v. *Oldham Training and Enterprise Council*[210] the objects of Oldham TEC were examined. Although the Court accepted that, in the main, the objects were charitable for the relief of unemployment, some of the objects potentially allowed Oldham TEC to promote the interests of individuals engaged in trade, commerce or enterprise and to provide benefits and services to them. Oldham TEC could not be regarded as a

[206] Pp. 32–34 of this chapter.
[207] *The Incorporated Council of Law Reporting for England and Wales* v. *AG* [1972] Ch.73.
[208] *Ibid. per* Buckley LJ at 99. [209] See Chapter 4, pp. 85–89.
[210] *IRC* v. *Oldham Training and Enterprise Council* [1996] STC 1218.

charity because the objects were not exclusively charitable. Lightman J conceded that it might be necessary to:

> *have regard to evidence to discover the consequences of pursuing the object ... what the body has done in pursuit of its objects may afford graphic evidence of the potential consequences of the pursuit of its objects. It is for that reason that para. 4 of the statement of agreed facts is admissible and potentially relevant.*[211]

Sham charities

The court can look at extrinsic evidence where it is faced with a sham charity.[212] A sham charity will be created where there is an intention to deceive third parties or the court as to the real intention of the promoters.[213] This is discussed in more detail in Chapter 3.[214]

Objects or activities: Conclusion

Given the number of exceptions to the general rule that the objects, as expressed in the governing instrument, rather than activities, determine charitable status, the position is unclear. There are two particular problems for the Commission when it examines activities.

First, the Commission can only look at activities as a means of determining whether the objects are charitable at the inception of a charity.[215] Where there is no evidence of activities at inception the Commission can read post-formation activities back to inception.[216] However, most charities apply for registration shortly after their inception.[217] Therefore in most cases the Commission will have evidence of charities' activities at the time of their inception and unless that evidence can be challenged by the Commission it will not be able to read post-formation activities to determine charitable intent at inception. However, the position is far from clear.

Second, where the objects of an institution are exclusively charitable then non-charitable activities, which are not carried out in furtherance of the

211 *Ibid.* at 1234.

212 *Snook* v. *London and West Riding Investments* [1967] 2 QB 786 *per* Diplock LJ at 802.

213 *Ibid.* 214 Chapter 3, pp. 54–57.

215 AG v. Ross [1986] 1 WLR 252 *per* Scott J at 263; *IRC* v. *Oldham Training and Enterprise Council* [1996] STC 1218 *per* Lightman J at 1234.

216 *Southwood* v. *AG The Times*, 26 October 1998.

217 The Commission has been asking about the activities of some charities at the registration stage since 1966 and in respect of all charities since 1996. See [1966] Ch. Com. A.R. para. 34. Note that when the register was originally established in 1961 by section 4(1) Charities Act 1960 the Commission did not ask any questions about the activities of a charity: see Nathan, *The Charities Act 1960*, 1st edn (London: Butterworths, 1962) pp. 44–45. From 1966 where a governing instrument was obscurely drafted and allowed room for doubt whether its future activities would be exclusively charitable. See also [1996] Ch. Com. A.R. para 79 and form App 1: see www.charity-commission.gov.uk.

charitable purposes,[218] will be evidence of a breach of trust.[219] As Scott J said in *AG* v. *Ross*:

> If the organisation is formed with an exclusively charitable purpose but with a constitution that permits ancillary non-charitable activities it is, on authority, charitable. If subsequently the managers of the organisation transform the ancillary non-charitable purpose into the main purpose of the organisation, the conclusion does not, in my view, follow that the organisation loses its charitable status. The right conclusion, in my opinion, would be that the managers are in breach of their fiduciary duties of management.

Where the trustees have committed a breach of trust, the correct course of action would be for the Commission to use its protective powers[220] rather than its powers of removal.

However, an increase in non-charitable activities post-formation could arguably be construed as evidence of original non-charitable purposes rather than a breach of trust.[221] In CC-9 *Campaigning and Political Activities by Charities*,[222] the Commission indicated that it was aware of this argument:

> Where political activities do begin to dominate the activities of the charity, an issue will arise as to whether the charity trustees are acting outside their trusts. In exceptional circumstances this might also lead us to reconsider whether the organisation should ever have been registered as a charity, or whether it was in fact established for non-charitable political purposes.[223]

This lack of clarity helps create uncertainty about the Commission's powers of removal and it is one of the propositions of this book that this point needs clarification.

Fine distinctions

When it comes to charitable status the court has made fine distinctions between what is charitable and what is non-charitable. To take but one example, the court has looked at research into literary or cultural subjects. In *Re Shaw*[224] George Bernard Shaw bequeathed funds for pursuing inquiries into the advantages to be gained from and the feasibility of introducing a new forty-letter alphabet and to transliterate one of his plays into the new alphabet, disseminate the results and lobby the government, the public and the English-speaking world to adopt it. Harman J held that the gift was not charitable:

> if the object be merely the increase of knowledge, that is not itself a charitable object unless it be combined with teaching or education.[225]

[218] P. 22 of this chapter. [219] *Ibid.* [220] Ss. 18 & 19 Charities Act 1993.
[221] See Chapter 3, pp. 54–57 for a discussion of *Re Esteem Settlement* [2003] JRC 092 par 60.
[222] Version – September 2004. [223] *Ibid.* para. 24. [224] *Re Shaw* [1957] 1 WLR 729.
[225] *Ibid.* at 737.

Furthermore, Harman J, in rejecting the application for charitable status, commented that there was no element of teaching or education and that the propaganda was not education in the charitable sense.[226]

In *Re Hopkins' Will Trusts*[227] a gift for research into finding evidence to support the view that Francis Bacon was the real author of plays commonly attributed to Shakespeare was held to be for the advancement of education. Wilberforce J commented:

> In order to be charitable, research must either be of educational value to the researcher or must so be directed as to lead to something which will pass into the store of educational material, or so as to improve the sum of communicable knowledge in an area which education may cover-education in this last context extending to the formation of literary taste and appreciation.

It is difficult to see the distinction made between *Re Shaw*[228] and *Re Hopkins' Will Trusts*.[229] This lack of clarity supports the basic proposition that there is a need for the Commission's powers of removal to be clarified. Wilberforce J's requirement for research to be charitable was considered by Slade J in *Re Besterman's Will Trusts*:[230]

> (1) A trust for research will ordinarily qualify as a charitable trust if, but only if (a) the subject-matter of the proposed research is a useful subject of study; and (b) it is contemplated that knowledge acquired as a result of the research will be disseminated to others; and (c) the trust is for the benefit of the public, or a sufficiently important section of the public. (2) In the absence of a contrary context, however, the court will be readily inclined to construe a valid trust for the advancement of education, it is not necessary either (a) that a teacher/pupil relationship should be in contemplation or (b) that persons to benefit from the knowledge to be acquired be persons who are already in the course of receiving 'education' in the conventional sense. (3) In any case where the court has to determine whether a bequest for the purposes of research is or is not of a charitable nature, it must pay due regard to any admissible extrinsic evidence which is available to explain the wording of the will in question or the circumstances in which it was made.'

The more liberal approach taken in *Re Besterman's Will Trusts*[231] supports the Attorney-General's argument in *Re Shaw*[232] that Shaw's alphabet was a useful piece of research beneficial to the public because it would facilitate the education of the young and the teaching of the language to show a way to save time

[226] *Re Shaw* [1957] 1 WLR 729 at 738. [227] *Re Hopkins' Will Trusts* [1965] Ch 669.
[228] *Re Shaw* [1957] 1 WLR 729. [229] *Re Hopkins' Will Trusts* [1965] Ch 669.
[230] *Re Besterman's Will Trusts* 21 January 1980 unreported, referred to in *McGovern* v. *AG* [1982] Ch 327 at 352–353.
[231] *Ibid.* [232] *Re Shaw* [1957] 1 WLR 729 at 737.

and therefore money. Without certainty about what is charitable the Commission cannot be confident about its powers of removal.[233]

Public benefit

Introduction

It was explained earlier in this chapter[234] that one of the essential indicia of charitable status is having charitable purposes[235] which includes the requirement of public benefit.[236] This paragraph briefly examines public benefit,[237] explains why public benefit is important to the question of removal[238] and explains the problem areas in public benefit.[239] The law on public benefit is confusing and, as a result, the Commission cannot be confident of its powers to remove charities from the register.

What is public benefit?

For an institution's objects to be charitable they must be for the benefit of the public.[240] In a nutshell, the requirement for public benefit is that a charity must confer a benefit on the public or a sufficient section of the public.[241] This test differs for each of the heads of charity.[242]

Why is public benefit important to the question of removal now?

Public benefit is particularly important now, following the abolition of the presumption of public benefit by the Charities Act 2006.[243] This might lead to some charities being removed from the register on the basis that the Commission incorrectly presumed them to be charitable.[244] Furthermore, under the Charities Act 2006 the Commission is under a statutory obligation

[233] For the basic propositions that the Commission's powers of removal are limited and lack clarity see Chapter 1, pp. 1–4.

[234] P. 12 of this chapter. [235] Pp. 23–32 of this chapter. [236] P. 12 of this chapter.

[237] P. 34 of this chapter. [238] P. 34 of this chapter. [239] P. 35 of this chapter.

[240] *Jones* v. *William* (1767) Amb 651 at 652.

[241] *Verge* v. *Sumerville* [1924] AC 496. Reference can also be made to the Standard textbooks: J. Warburton, *Tudor on Charities*, 9th edn (London: Butterworths, 2003) Chapter 2; H. Picarda, *The Law and Practice Relating to Charities*, 3rd edn (London: Sweet and Maxwell, 1999) pp. 19–29 and P. Luxton *The Law of Charities*, 1st edn (Oxford University Press, 2001) Chapter 4. See also Atiyah P. S. 'Public Benefit in Charities' 21 *MLR* 138, 1958. Reference should also be made to *The Charity Commission's Approach to Public Benefit, Appendix to the Parliamentary Briefing The Charities Bill and Public Benefit* (October 2006), *Charities and Public Benefit The Charity Commission's General Guidance on Public Benefit* (January 2008).

[242] Under section 2(2) Charities Act 2006 there are twelve specific heads of charity.

[243] S. 3(2) Charities Act 2006.

[244] Para. 4.18 of Cabinet Office, Strategy Unit Report, *Private Action, Public Benefit A Review of Charities and the Wider Not-for-Profit Sector* (2002).

to issue guidance on public benefit.[245] It is one of the basic propositions of this book that the Commission has no law-making powers.[246] Therefore, the Commission must follow the common law and legislation when giving their guidance.[247] The problem is that because the law of public benefit is uncertain[248] it will be difficult for the Commission to be confident about issuing guidance which is legally correct. There are three main reasons why the Commission will have difficulty giving guidance which accurately reflects the law. First, there is little analysis of public benefit by the court.[249] Second, there are few modern decisions of the court on public benefit.[250] Third, even where there are decisions of the court, the authorities are unclear.[251] As a result, the Commission will not be confident of its powers of removal.

During the Standing Committee debates in the House of Commons[252] the government presented an ambiguous analysis of how the proposed removal of the presumption of public benefit would operate. On the one hand the government explained that the issue of public benefit would be determined by common law[253] but on the other hand it stated that the Commission would have the final say.[254] Although the Commission is bound by the common law it is submitted that there is so little modern common law guidance on what constitutes public benefit that the Commission may be forced into creating its own guidance. In doing so it will, no doubt, be mindful that the government's stated intention is that the Commission should, through its guidance, 'raise the bar of what is required'[255] and this, in turn, could lead to more removals from the register even though the Commission cannot be confident of its powers of removal.[256]

Problem areas in the law of public benefit

There are numerous problem areas of public benefit. These are:

Little analysis by the court

The court has not given much guidance on what constitutes public benefit because of the previous presumption of public benefit in respect of the old first three heads of charity.[257]

There are relatively few court decisions on charitable status and this means that there have been few opportunities to consider public benefit.[258] For

[245] Under section 4(1) Charities Act 2006. [246] Chapter 1, pp. 1–4.

[247] S. 4(1) Charities Act 2006. [248] See p. 38 of this chapter.

[249] *Ibid.* [250] *Ibid.* [251] Pp. 39–48 of this chapter.

[252] Charities Bill [HL] Standing Committee 4 July 2006 cols. 45–46. See www.publications.parliament.uk.

[253] *Ibid.* col. 45. [254] *Ibid.* col. 46.

[255] *Ibid.* col. 46 *per* Miliband, Edward (Parliamentary Secretary, Cabinet Office).

[256] But see Chapter 4, p. 85 for why this is unlikely.

[257] Which has now been abolished by section 3(2) Charities Act 2006.

[258] A search on Westlaw over the last three years showed that there had been no decisions by the court exclusively dealing with the question of public benefit.

example, the court has never resolved whether *Re Compton*[259] and *Oppenheim* v. *Tobacco Securities Trust Co Ltd*[260] apply to charities with objects for the advancement of religion.[261]

Public benefit differs from one head of charity to another

The requirement that a charity must confer a benefit on the public or a sufficient section of the public[262] differs for each of the old four heads of charity.[263] Different standards apply because the *'law of charity* … has been built up, not logically, but empirically.'[264]

In relation to charities with objects for the relief of poverty, the beneficiary class can be very limited.[265] In relation to the other old four heads of charity, the advancement of education, the advancement of religion and charities with objects beneficial to the community under the fourth head of charity, the 'public' means either the community as a whole or a sufficiently (appreciably) important section of the community.[266] This issue has been decided on a case by case basis. For example, members of a Masonic lodge are not a sufficient section of the public[267] and a class of beneficiaries within a class may or may not be a sufficient section of the public.[268] Furthermore, a class of beneficiaries may be charitable for one head of charity but not another.[269] With the exception of charitable purposes for the relief of poverty an institution cannot be a charity if it has a beneficiary class determined by a personal relationship to a particular individual or company, such as a common link through blood or contract.[270] These different standards are confusing and it can be difficult to predict whether an institution will pass the public benefit test.

259 *Re Compton* [1945] Ch 123.

260 *Oppenheim* v. *Tobacco Securities Trust Co Ltd* [1951] AC 297. 261 See pp. 42–47.

262 *Verge* v. *Sumerville* [1924] AC 496. Reference can also be made to the Standard textbooks: J. Warburton *Tudor on Charities*, 9th edn (London: Butterworths, 2003), Chapter 2; H Picarda, *The Law and Practice Relating to Charities*, 3rd edn (London: Sweet and Maxwell, 1999) pp. 19–29, and P. Luxton, *The Law of Charities*, 1st edn (Oxford University Press, 2001), Chapter 4. See also Atiyah P. S. 'Public Benefit in Charities' 21 *MLR* 138, 1958. Reference should also be made to *Charities and Public Benefit: The Charity Commission's General Guidance on Public Benefit* (January 2008).

263 Note that section 2(2) Charities Act 2006 sets out a list of twelve specific charitable purposes.

264 *Gilmour* v. *Coats* [1949] AC 426 *per* Lord Simonds at 488.

265 *Dingle* v. *Turner* [1972] AC 601. 266 *Verge* v. *Somerville* [1924] AC 497.

267 *Queensland Trustees Ltd* v. *Woodward* [1912] SR Qd 291.

268 *Re Dunlop* [1984] NI 408; *IRC* v. *Baddeley* [1955] AC 572, HL.

269 See *IRC* v. *Baddeley* [1955] AC 572, HL where a class of beneficiaries was charitable for the purposes of a charity with purposes for the advancement of religion but not for the purposes of a charity with purposes for social welfare.

270 *Re Compton* [1945] Ch 123. See pp 42–47 of this chapter. See also Chapter 3, pp. 57–9 for a review of the *Compton* test in the context of the court's reluctance to overrule its decision and Chapter 7, pp. 133–6 for a review of the *Compton* test in relation to the Human Rights Act 1998.

The balance between public and private benefit

It is often difficult to distinguish between what is a public benefit and what is a private benefit. Benefits may be private because they are, by their nature, private such as a gift of flowers for a particular grave[271] or a private chapel[272] or benefits may be private because they do not serve a sufficient section of the public.[273] A subsidiary or incidental level of private benefit will not be fatal to charitable status[274] but any private benefit which is more than subsidiary or incidental[275] to the furtherance of exclusively charitable objects will be fatal to charitable status.[276] This can lead to confusion, particularly in the case of professional bodies.[277]

Harm or benefit?

It is also difficult to determine what is 'harmful' and what is of 'benefit' because most of the decisions of the Court focus on whether there is a sufficient section of the public which benefits.[278] This lack of analysis has been due to the presumption of public benefit for the first three old heads of charity.[279]

There are some obvious illustrations of what would be considered by the Court to be 'harmful.' The suggested benefit might be incapable of proof, might cause harm to the public or might be illegal or contrary to public policy.[280] In the words of Harman LJ in *Re Pinion*,[281] 'A school for prostitutes or pickpockets would obviously fail.' Equally, in the case of an institution with objects to advance religion where the doctrines are 'adverse to the very foundations of all religion, and that they are subversive of all morality'[282] that institution's purposes will not be for the benefit of the public. Now that the presumption of public benefit has been abolished[283] the Court will need to analyse less obvious cases involving *'benefit'*. To quote Lord Greene MR in *Coats* v. *Gilmour*:[284]

[271] *Rickard* v. *Robson* (1862) 31 Beav 244. [272] *Hoare* v. *Hoare* (1886) 56 LT 147.

[273] *Re Mead's Trust Deed* [1961] 1 WLR 144. [274] *London Hospital* v. *IRC* [1976] 1 WLR 613.

[275] *IRC* v. *City of Glasgow Police Athletic Association* [1953] AC 380.

[276] *Tennant Plays* v. *IRC* [1948] 1 All ER 506.

[277] See *Royal College of Surgeons of England* v. *National Provincial Bank Ltd* [1952] 1 All ER 984 and *General Medical Council* v. *IRC* [1928] All ER 252.

[278] For examples of decisions of the court which analyse benefit in terms of whether there is a sufficient section of the public see *Re Compton* [1945] Ch 123 and *Oppenheim* v. *Tobacco Securities Trust Co Ltd* [1951] AC 297.

[279] *National Anti-Vivisection Society* v. *IRC* [1948] AC 31 at 65 *per* Lord Simonds.

[280] *Ibid. per* Lord Simonds at 74. [281] *Re Pinion* [1965] Ch 85 *per* Harman LJ at 105.

[282] *Thornton* v. *Howe* (1832) 31 Beav 13, 20. [283] S. 3(2) Charities Act 2006.

[284] *Coats* v. *Gilmour* [1948] Ch 340 *per* Lord Greene MR at 345. Note that in *Re Watson* [1973] 1 WLR 1472 Ploughman J said that if there was evidence that the purpose was subversive to all mankind then the presumption of public benefit would be rebutted. The analysis of Lord Greene MR in the Court of Appeal carries greater weight.

> The contrary of 'beneficial to the public', is not 'detrimental to the public', but 'non-beneficial to the public.'

The issue as to whether something is of 'benefit' will be more difficult to determine than where something is obviously harmful. For example, there will be a wide divergence of opinion for the court to take into account in the case of charities with objects for the advancement of religion, where some religious practices such as private intercessory prayer are regarded by the court as incapable of proof[285] even if the members of the Church regard such a practice as beneficial.[286]

Following the abolition of the presumption of public benefit,[287] all charities will have difficulty in proving that intangible benefits satisfy the requirement of public benefit. The requirement of public benefit under the old fourth head is usually satisfied by demonstrating that tangible and objective benefits will flow from the purpose in question.[288] If benefits are intangible then the court will require evidence that such benefits are approved 'by the common understanding of enlightened opinion for the time being'[289] or a 'general consensus of opinion or understanding'.[290] This will at times be difficult. For example, the court rejected arguments that the suppression of vivisection contributed to any assumed advancement of morals and therefore any tangible or intangible public benefit because these arguments were outweighed by the benefits of medical research to public health.[291]

Emphasis on form over substance

The rules which the court has devised to ensure that charities have a public character rely on form rather than substance. These rules can appear artificial when applied more generally. For example, in *Re Compton*[292] the Court of Appeal held that a trust for the education of children from named families was not a sufficient section of the public. In *Oppenheim* v. *Tobacco Securities Trust Co Ltd*[293] the House of Lords ruled that the beneficial class of a trust to provide for the education of children of employees or former employees of British-American Tobacco Co. Ltd or any of its subsidiary or allied companies would not be a sufficient section of the public even though the employees totalled in excess of one hundred thousand.

285 *Coats* v. *Gilmour* [1948] Ch. 340 *per* Lord Greene MR at 350.

286 *Ibid.* at 346. Note that the Roman Catholic Church, which regards private intercessory prayer as beneficial, has an estimated membership of 4,105,635 in England and Wales. See www.catholicchurch.org.uk.

287 S. 3(2) Charities Act 2006.

288 *National Anti-Vivisection Society* v. *IRC* [1948] AC 31 *per* Lord Wright at 49.

289 *Ibid.*

290 *Ibid. per* Lord Wright at 47.

291 *National Anti-Vivisection Society* v. *IRC* [1948] AC 31. For an example of the Commission's approach see *Promotion of Equality and Diversity for the Benefit of the Public*, 14 July 2003.

292 *Re Compton* [1945] Ch 123.

293 *Oppenheim* v. *Tobacco Securities Trust Co Ltd* [1951] AC 297.

The common feature in both cases (referred to in this book as 'the *Compton* test') was summed up in the judgment of Lord Simonds in *Oppenheim* v. *Tobacco Securities Trust Co Ltd*:[294]

> These words 'section of the community' have no special sanctity, but they conveniently indicate (1) that the possible (I emphasise the word 'possible') beneficiaries must not be numerically negligible, and (2) that the quality which distinguishes them from other members of the community, so that they form by themselves a section of it, must be a quality which does not depend on their relationship to a particular individual. It is for this reason that a trust for the education of members of a family or, as in Re Compton, of a number of families cannot be regarded as charitable. A group of persons may be numerous, but, if the nexus between them is their personal relationship to a single propositus or to several propositi, they are neither the community nor a section of the community for charitable purposes.

In his dissenting judgment Lord MacDermott concluded that the *Compton* test was 'a very arbitrary and artificial rule'.[295] It appears even more artificial when one takes into account that an institution with objects to educate a particular trade or profession is accepted as being a sufficient section of the public.[296] In the words of Lord MacDermott:[297]

> Learned counsel for the appellant sought to fortify his case by pointing to the anomalies that would ensue from the rejection of his argument. For, he said, admittedly those who follow a profession or a calling-clergymen, lawyers, colliers, tobacco-workers and so on are a section of the public; how strange then it would be if, as in the case of railwaymen, those who follow a particular calling are all employed by one employer. Would a trust for the education of railwaymen be charitable, but a trust for the education of men employed on the railways by the Transport Board not be charitable? And what of the service of the Crown, whether in civil service or the armed forces? Is there a difference between soldiers and soldiers of the King?

The artificiality of the *Compton* test becomes even more apparent when it is taken into account that a sufficient section of the public for the purposes of charitable status can be described in geographical terms.[298] It follows that a trust for the education of children of all the members of a certain profession in a certain town could be charitable. In this way a charity might be created in which the number of potential beneficiaries may be less than the 110,000 persons in *Oppenheim* v. *Tobacco Securities Trust Co. Ltd.*[299]

The weakness of this formulaic test is also shown where trustees have power in the governing instrument to select the beneficiary class. They could favour a

[294] *Ibid.* at 305. [295] *Ibid.* at 318.

[296] *Hall* v. *Derby Sanitary Authority* (1885) 16 QBD 163. [297] *Ibid.* at 305.

[298] *Springfield Housing Action Committee* v. *Commissioner of Valuation* [1983] NI 184.

[299] *Oppenheim* v. *Tobacco Securities Trust Co Ltd* [1951] AC 297. See Atiyah P. S. 'Public Benefit in Charities' 21 *MLR* 1958 138–154.

class of beneficiary which comprises a private section of the public as was the case in *IRC* v. *Educational Grants Association*[300] where a company limited by guarantee was promoted, managed and funded by Metal Box Co. Ltd. Its objects were for the advancement of education, in particular by making educational grants and creating scholarships, etc. Although the objects were not restricted to the benefit of the public, the court construed the objects as being intended to be charitable. However, distribution of 75–85 per cent of educational grants to the children of employees led the court to conclude that the company was not entitled to relief from income tax because too high a proportion of its income was being paid to preferred individuals and therefore it could not be said that the income was being applied for charitable purposes only. In *Re Koettgen's Will Trusts*[301] the court held that a direction to prefer up to 75 per cent of members of a beneficiary class connected to a company and therefore not in itself constituting the public or a sufficient section of the public would not affect charitable status. Although the correctness of this case has subsequently been doubted by the court,[302] the Commission has followed the authority when deciding three cases.[303] In these cases the relevant percentages were between 65 per cent and 75 per cent. It is uncertain what percentage would cause an institution to be non-charitable and therefore the position is confused.

Lord Cross proposed a reform of the *Compton* test in *Dingle* v. *Turner*[304] by distinguishing between trusts which are essentially for private benefit and trusts which are essentially for public benefit. As Lord Cross said:

> In truth the question whether or not the potential beneficiaries of a trust can fairly be said to constitute a section of the public is a question of degree and cannot be by itself decisive of the question whether the trust is a charity. Much must depend on the purpose of the trust

This is a far more rational approach,[305] although if this approach was adopted then there would be a need to establish where to draw the line.

The problem with form over substance also occurs in the case of institutions with purposes for the advancement of religion.[306] Lord Simonds in *Gilmour* v. *Coats*[307] acknowledged that there was a 'speciously logical appearance'[308] to the argument that members of the order of cloistered nuns were open 'to any woman in the wide world who has the necessary vocation'[309] in the same way

[300] *IRC* v. *Educational Grants Association* [1967] Ch 123; affd 997.
[301] *Re Koettgen's Will Trusts* [1954] Ch 252.
[302] See *Caffoor* v. *IRC* [1961] AC 584 and *IRC* v. *Educational Grants Association* [1967] Ch 123; affd 997.
[303] See [1978] Ch. Com. A.R. paras. 86–89. [304] *Dingle* v. *Turner* [1972] AC 601 at 624.
[305] See Chapter 7, pp. 133–6 for an argument that the *Compton* test will have to be reformed following the Human Rights Act 1998.
[306] See G. Moffat, *Trusts Law: Text and Materials*, 3rd edn (Cambridge University Press, 1999) p. 746.
[307] *Gilmour* v. *Coats* [1949] AC 426. [308] *Ibid*. at 448. [309] *Ibid*.

'as the endowment of a scholarship open to a public competition is a charity'.[310] Nevertheless, Lord Simonds rejected the analogy commenting that 'law is life not logic'[311] and that the law of charity has been built up 'not logically but empirically'.[312]

The question arose in *Neville Estates* v. *Madden*[313] whether a trust for the advancement of religion amongst members of the Catford Synagogue who were 'no more a section of the public than the members for the time being of a Carmelite priory'[314] could be charitable? Cross J reconciled these two cases by making the distinction between the members of the Catford Synagogue mixing with the local community, and thereby providing public benefit, and the nuns who lived in seclusion and who thereby displayed private benefit.[315] This explanation creates further confusion because it suggests that the crucial qualification for the religious head is access by the public, not whether there is a sufficient section of the community which benefits.

Anomalous decisions

A number of anomalous decisions of the Court further confuse the issue of public benefit. For example, charities with objects for the relief of poverty only need a small beneficiary class. This results from a number of cases commonly referred to as 'the poor relations' cases.[316] There are also some anomalous cases involving the advancement of education commonly referred to as the 'founder's kin' cases[317] which are exceptions to the rule in *Re Compton*[318] that a trust for the education of children from named families is not a sufficient section of the public.

The concept of public benefit changes with time

The court's approach to public benefit will change over time. Gifts for the Jewish and Roman Catholic faiths were once held to be unlawful[319] and without public benefit, but today this is not the case. With so few decisions[320] it is difficult to be entirely confident about how the court will decide the question of public benefit. This contributes to the confusion.

310 *Ibid.* 311 *Ibid.* at 449. 312 *Ibid.* 313 *Neville Estates* v. *Madden* [1962] Ch 832.

314 *Ibid.* at 853. 315 *Ibid.*

316 An example of one of the 'poor relations' cases is *Isaac* v. *De Friez* (1753) 2 Amb 595 where the gifts were (1) a gift of two annuities to the poorest relations of the testator and of his wife; (2) a gift of income to one poor relation of the testator 'for a portion in the way of marriage and putting him or her out in the world'; and (3) a similar gift of income to one poor relation of his wife. These gifts were held to be charitable without any reasons being given in the report.

317 *Spencer* v. *All Souls College* Wilmot's Notes of Opinions (1762) 163; *AG* v. *Sidney Sussex College* (1869) LR 4 Ch 722; In *Re Lavelle, Concannon* v. *AG* [1914] 1 IR 194.

318 *Re Compton* [1945] Ch 123. See pp. 42–47 of this Chapter.

319 See *Da Costa* v. *De Paz* (1753) Amb 228 and *Carry* v. *Abbot* (1803) 7 Ves 490, 496. The Roman Catholic Relief Act 1832 and the Jewish Relief Act 1846 validated these charitable trusts.

320 See pp. 26–27 of this chapter.

Public benefit conclusion

It has been shown in this chapter[321] that the law of public benefit is unclear. The result is that the Commission cannot be confident about its powers to remove institutions from the register on the ground that they have never satisfied the public benefit test required by law.

Viability

As a matter of law, do charities need to have achievable objects? The legal authorities are clear.[322] If a charity's objects are impossible from the outset and a specific rather than a general charitable intention is expressed by the settlor then the charity fails and the charitable gifts will revert to the donors, or in the case of a will, to other beneficiaries.[323] The court has analysed the position in the following terms: when the gift can be read as devoting the property to charity and adding a condition subsequent to the gift, then, if the performance of the condition becomes impossible the gift becomes absolute, whereas if the condition precedent becomes impossible the gift will fail.[324] In some cases the court might adopt a 'wait and see' approach where it is unclear whether there will be a practical charitable purpose which will arise in the future.[325] However, it is doubtful whether the court will allow funds paid into court to remain there indefinitely.[326]

Where a general charitable intention is expressed, the charity's property can be applied *cy-pres*.[327] Whether there is a specific or general charitable intention is a matter of construction and in certain cases where it could be argued either way, it would be open to the Commission to argue that there was a specific or general charitable intention depending on whether it wants the charity to fail or continue. However, the court leans in favour of charity and therefore the Commission must follow this approach.[328]

The question of viability, therefore, is not concerned with the question of whether the work of the charity is duplicated by other charities.[329] Whether the Commission should have the power to remove charities from the register because there are too many charities carrying out the same type of work is a question which will be dealt with in the conclusion to this book.[330]

[321] Pp. 35–41 of this chapter.

[322] *Chamberlayne* v. *Brockett* (1873) 8 Ch.App.206; *Re White's Will Trusts* [1955] Ch 188.

[323] *Re Monk* [1927] 2 Ch 197 *per* Lord Hanworth MR at 204.

[324] *Ibid.*

[325] *AG* v. *Bishop of Chester* (1785) 1 Bro.C.C. 444.

[326] *Sinnet* v. *Herbert* (1872) LR 7.

[327] *Re Monk* [1927] 2 Ch.197.

[328] *Ibid. per* Lord Hanworth MR at 207. S. 1 B(3)4. Charities Act 1993 sets out the Commission's general duty of promoting the effective use of charitable resources.

[329] See Chapter 6, pp. 120–1.

[330] See Chapter 9, pp. 196–7.

Independence from the state

The Commission claim in *RR 7 – The Independence of Charities from the State*[331] that for an institution to be charitable it must exist in order to carry out charitable purposes and not to implement the policies of a government department or to carry out the directions of a government authority.[332]

No legal authorities are cited in support of this proposition and it is argued in Chapter 4[333] that the Commission appears to confuse a charity trustee's duty[334] to act in the best interests of the charity with the question of an institution being a charity which depends on the charity having the essential indicia of charitable status.[335]

It might be argued that if a charity is established in such a way that there is a high level of involvement by the state that the trustees are not subject to a legal obligation to carry out charitable purposes because the real objects of the institution are for carrying out government policies.[336] This is a doubtful assertion for two reasons.[337] First, a high level of involvement by the state will not necessarily be fatal to charitable status.[338] Second, an institution which provides funding for a charitable purpose will still be a charity even if that purpose is already provided for by state funding.[339] This is the case, even though its property may fall to be applied *cy-pres* for other charitable purposes.[340] For these reasons it is submitted that independence from the state is not one of the essential indicia of charitable status.

Conclusion

It has been shown in this chapter that, in order for an institution to be charitable for the purposes of the Charities Acts 1993 and 2006, it must be subject to a legal obligation to carry out charitable purposes,[341] be within jurisdiction,[342] have charitable purposes,[343] which includes the requirement of public benefit[344] and must be viable in the sense that if the charitable purposes are impossible from the outset that a general, rather than a specific, charitable

331 Version 2001. 332 *Ibid.* para 5. 333 Chapter 4, pp. 85–89.
334 *Bray* v. *Ford* [1896] AC 44. 335 See p. 12 of this chapter. 336 RR 7, para 6.
337 See Chapter 4, pp. 85–89. 338 *Construction Industry Training Board* v. *AG* [1973] 1 Ch 173.
339 For example see section 96 A National Health Service Act 1977 as amended by section 222 National Health Service Act 2006 which authorises health service bodies to fund-raise for their statutory functions or research. The Commission has accepted that charities can relieve public funding but remain of the view that in doing so they must be independent from the State. See *Applications for Registration of (1) Trafford Community Leisure Trust and (2) Wigan Leisure and Cultural Trust* 21 April 2004.
340 S. 13(1)(e)(i) Charities Act 1993 provides for a *cy-pres* application of charitable property where the original purposes, in whole or in part, have since they were laid down 'been adequately provided for by other means'.
341 Pp. 12–18 of this chapter. 342 P. 23 of this chapter. 343 Pp. 23–32 of this chapter.
344 Pp. 34–42 of this chapter.

intention is expressed by the settlor so that the property is applied *cy-pres*.[345] It is argued that a lack of independence from the state is not part of the essential indicia of charitable status.[346] The loss of any of these essential indicia will mean that a charity will cease to be charitable and must be removed from the register under section 3(4) Charities Act 1993 on the basis that the institution no longer appears to the Commission to be a charity.[347]

It is a basic proposition of this book that the Commission's powers of removal need to be clarified.[348] This stems from the need to clarify exactly what the essential indicia of charitable status are. Without this clarification, the Commission cannot be confident of its powers to remove institutions from the register which it 'no longer considers is a charity'.[349]

[345] P. 42 of this chapter. [346] P. 43 of this chapter.
[347] Chapter 3, pp. 73–75. For the position of property see Chapter 5, pp. 108–12.
[348] Chapter 1, pp. 1–4. [349] S. 3(4) Charities Act 1993.

3

The powers of the Commission to remove charities from the register

Introduction

This chapter examines the statutory powers of the Commission to remove charities from the register under section 3(4) Charities Act 1993. Section 3(4) Charities Act 1993 reads as follows:

> The Commission shall remove from the register –
>
> (a) any institution which it no longer considers is a charity, and
> (b) any charity which has ceased to exist or does not operate.

Section 3(5) Charities Act 1993 reads as follows:

> If the removal of an institution under subsection 4(a) above is due to any change in its trusts, the removal shall take effect from the date of that change.

The Commission can therefore remove an institution from the register in three cases: first, 'any institution which it no longer considers is a charity'; second, where an institution has 'ceased to exist'; third, where an institution 'does not operate'. It is argued in this chapter that these powers of removal are limited.

'No longer considers is a charity'

The Commission's power to remove an institution which it 'no longer considers is a charity' under section 3(4) Charities Act 1993 allows it to remove charities which were never charitable, and have therefore been registered by mistake,[1] or institutions which were charitable but have amended their governing instrument to change their 'trusts'.[2] The Commission can only remove a charity from the

[1] *National Anti-Vivisection Society* v. *IRC* [1948] AC 31 *per* Lord Wright at 46 (overruling *Re Foveaux* [1895] 2 Ch 501 because it was incorrectly decided) and *per* Lord Simonds at 74 (*obiter* that a charity once established cannot cease to be a charity due to the passage of time, a change in social circumstances or a change in the law). See pp. 53–65 of this chapter for the grounds for mistaken registration.

[2] S. 3(5) Charities Act 1993.

register because its 'trusts' have been changed where this results in the loss of one or more of the essential indicia of charitable status. How this conclusion is reached in discussed in this chapter.[3]

It is arguable that the power to remove an institution which the Commission 'no longer considers is a charity' under section 3(4) Charities Act 1993 permits the Commission to remove charities which are no longer charitable due to the passage of time, a change in social circumstances or a change in the law. This wording appears to confer discretion on the Commission to decide what is charitable. However, this argument cannot be supported for two reasons. First, the Commission has no law-making powers.[4] Second, once a charity has been established if its purposes subsequently become outdated then the Commission has a duty to make a *cy-pres* scheme.[5] These two arguments are now explained.

The first argument supports one of the basic propositions[6] of this book that the Commission has no law-making powers,[7] and must therefore follow decisions of the court and act within the scope of its powers as set out in the Charities Act 1993[8] and other enactments.[9]

The Commission is a non-Ministerial government department.[10] Its constitution is set out in the Charities Act 1993.[11] The Commission, as a public body,[12] may not act outside its powers[13] and there is no power in the Charities Act 1993 or any other enactment which authorises the Commission to judicially decide questions of charitable status. The Commission has concurrent jurisdiction and powers with the High Court in some respects[14] but it does not have concurrent jurisdiction with the High Court to determine charitable status when it registers[15] or removes[16] charities from the register. Its role in relation to the determination of charitable status is simply to register[17] and remove[18] charities and in doing so it must follow the law of England and Wales. The statutory definition of 'charity'[19] makes it a condition that an institution is 'established

[3] See pp. 73–75.

[4] See *Rule* v. *Charity Commission* (High Court, 10 December 1979); [1979] Ch.Com.A.R. 12–16 where Fox J commented *obiter* that the Commission had no power to determine charitable status and that this was a matter for Parliament or the court.

[5] S. 13 Charities Act 1993.

[6] Chapter 1, pp. 1–4.

[7] *Rule* v. *Charity Commission* (High Court, 10 December 1979); [1979] Ch.Com.A.R. 12–16.

[8] See section 1 (A-E) Charities Act 1993.

[9] For an example of other enactments see the Charities Act 1992.

[10] S. 1A(4) Charities Act 1993. See Joint Committee on the Draft Charities Bill HL 167–1/HC 660 30 September 2004, para 172.

[11] S. 1A(2) and Sch.1 Charities Act 1993.

[12] S. 1A(3) Charities Act 1993.

[13] See *Boddington* v. *British Transport Police* [1999] 2 AC 143 at 171 *per* Lord Steyn for authority for the proposition that public authorities must act within their powers. See generally H. W. R. Wade and C. F. Forsyth *Administrative Law*, 8th edn (Oxford University Press, 2000) pp. 35–37.

[14] For example see section 16(1)(a)-(c) Charities Act 1993.

[15] S. 3 A(1) Charities Act 1993.

[16] S. 3(4) Charities Act 1993.

[17] Ss. 1 C(3) & 3 A(1) Charities Act 1993.

[18] S. 3(4) Charities Act 1993.

[19] S. 1(1)(a) & (b) Charities Act 2006.

for charitable purposes only'. 'Charitable purposes'[20] are defined as those purposes listed in section 2(2) Charities Act 2006 or existing charity law[21] or by virtue of section 1 Recreational Charities Act 1958[22] and any purposes reasonably analogous to, or within the spirit of, those purposes[23] and any purposes reasonably as analogous to, or within the spirit of, any purposes recognised under charity law[24] to be analogous to those analogous purposes.[25]

The Commission has no judicial powers when removing charities from the register and is subject to the rule of law.[26] The rule of law's primary meaning is that everything must be done according to the law. This applies to all citizens including government departments.[27] A public authority may not act outside its statutory powers.[28] An *ultra vires* act is void and without effect in law,[29] which means that institutions relying on the Commission's decisions on charitable status, if these are not supported by statute or case law, cannot successfully argue that they had a legitimate expectation that their institution was charitable and that the institution should continue to be regarded as charitable.[30] Although they might successfully argue that their property should be rescued for charitable purposes by a *cy-pres* scheme.[31]

Historically the Commission has never had the power to make decisions about charitable status. The Commissioners established under the Charitable Trusts Act 1853[32] had no such power. 'Charity' was defined[33] under that Act as meaning any 'endowed' foundation coming within the 'meaning, purview or interpretation' of the Preamble of the Statute of Charitable Uses 1601[34] or over which the Court of Chancery had jurisdiction.

The Charitable Uses Act 1601 was repealed by the Mortmain and Charitable Uses Act 1888 but the Preamble was set out in that Act:[35]

> References to such charities shall be construed as references to charities within the meaning, purview and interpretation of the said preamble.

20 S. 2(1)(a) & (b) Charities Act 2006.

21 S. 2(8) Charities Act 2006 defines 'existing charity law' as 'charity law as in force immediately before the day on which this section comes into force'.

22 S. 2(4)(a) Charities Act 2006. 23 S. 2(4)(b) Charities Act 2006.

24 S. 2(8) Charities Act 2006 defines 'charity law' as 'the law relating to charities in England and Wales'.

25 S. 2(4)(c) Charities Act 2006.

26 S. 1 Constitutional Reform Act 2005 makes reference to the Rule of Law. See A. V. Dicey, *An Introduction to the Study of the Law of the Constitution* (1885), 10th edn (London: Macmillan, 1959).

27 *Wilkes* v. *Wood* (1769) 19 St.Tr. 1406 at 1408.

28 *Boddington* v. *British Transport Police* [1999] 2 AC 143 *per* Lord Steyn at 171.

29 *Anisminic Ltd* v. *Foreign Compensation Commission* [1969] 2 AC 147 *per* Lord Reid at 170.

30 *Al Fayed* v. *Advocate General for Scotland* 2004 SLT 798. See Chapter 8, pp. 180–2.

31 S. 14 Charities Act 1993. See Chapter 5, pp. 105–8.

32 As amended by the Charitable Trusts Act 1853 and the Charitable Trusts Act 1860.

33 *Ibid.* section 66(2). 34 43 Eliz. 1 C. 4 (repealed). See Chapter 2, pp. 24–26.

35 S. 13(2) Mortmain and Charitable Uses Act 1888.

The Mortmain and Charitable Uses Act 1888 was repealed by the Charities Act 1960.[36] The Charities Act 1960 provides that any reference in any enactment or document to a charity within the meaning, purview and interpretation of the Charitable Uses Act 1601, or its Preamble, shall be construed as a reference to a charity within the meaning which the word bears as a legal term according to the law of England and Wales.[37] The Charities Act 1960, which was the predecessor to the Charities Act 1993, did not therefore change the position that the Commission had no power to make law. This remained the position under the Charities Acts 1993 and 2006.

The only limited exception to the rule of law that the Commission must follow legislation or decisions of the court in respect of charitable status is contained in section 4(5) Charities Act 1993[38] which reads as follows:

> Any question affecting the registration or removal from the register of any institution may, notwithstanding that it has been determined by a decision on appeal under Schedule 1 C to this Act[39] above, be considered afresh by the Commission and shall not be concluded by that decision, if it appears to the Commission that there has been a change of circumstances or that the decision is inconsistent with a later judicial decision, whether given on such appeal or not.

Its predecessor section in the Charities Act 1960[40] attracted a lot of controversy when debated in the House of Commons.[41] One MP called the power of the Commission to disregard decisions of the court under this section as 'an impertinence and an insult to the High Court'.[42] The Solicitor General conceded that the wording was drafted on the 'assumption that the Commissioners will act reasonably'.[43] Despite the concern expressed in Parliament, section 4(5) is currently irrelevant for a number of reasons. In the first place the *res judicata* rule will generally apply and the Commission will have to follow decisions of the court on appeal against their decisions unless 'there has been a change of circumstances or that the decision is inconsistent with a later judicial decision'.[44] Note that section 4(5) is not a power to determine charitable status but a power to take into account a material change of facts or to follow a later precedent.[45]

Theoretically, it should rarely be the case that the Commission will be able to re-examine a decision of the court. The purpose of the *res judicata* rule is to impose finality on proceedings. Unless the Commission has strong grounds for re-examining a decision of the court it could itself face an appeal with the risk that the court would merely restate its decision. Secondly, section 4(5) Charities Act 1993 only applies in relation to an appeal under Schedule 1C Charities Act

[36] S. 38 Charities Act 1960. [37] S. 38(4) Charities Act 1960.
[38] See Chapter 8, p. 172 for a discussion of section 4(5) Charities Act 1993 in relation to appeals.
[39] S. 4(3) Charities Act 1993 provides for an appeal against a decision not to register or removal.
[40] S. 5(5) Charities Act 1960. [41] Hansard, Commons 1959–60, Vol. 627, pp. 867–876.
[42] *Ibid. per* Mr. Graham Page at p. 872. [43] *Ibid.* at p. 874. [44] S. 4(5) Charities Act 1993.
[45] See pp. 60–65 of this chapter.

1993 against a decision of the Commission. It is not a general power to disregard decisions of the court. History suggests that it will be just as rare[46] for there to be an appeal under Schedule 1C Charities Act 1993 as it was under section 4(3) Charities Act 1993 and therefore section 4(5) Charities Act 1993 will have little practical relevance.

Even after the Charities Act 2006, which sets out twelve specific charitable purposes,[47] when the Commission is faced with novel questions of charitable status, there are so few decisions of the court[48] which define what is charitable that the Commission is, in the context of registration and removal, forced into becoming a *de facto* lawmaker[49] where it wishes to decide that an institution was never charitable.[50] Its dilemma is that, on the one hand it has a duty to obey and follow the existing law, but on the other hand if, in doing so, it does not respond to social needs, then charitable status will lose its relevance to modern society.

This is the best it can do in the absence of statutory authority or a specific decision of the court. It amounts to second-guessing what it thinks the court would decide by applying the general principles[51] used by the court when determining charitable status. In doing so, it is important for the Commission to make a proper analysis of those principles to avoid it running the risk of acting unlawfully. In the circumstances, the Commission can either distinguish decisions of the court on the facts or because of a change of social circumstances,[52] or select an alternative basis for removal by relying on a different decision of the court.[53] Either approach by the Commission needs to be exercised cautiously, because if the Commission exceeds its powers of removal it will be acting unlawfully. The Commission will be mindful that when an institution has been regarded as charitable by the court, the court is very reluctant to disturb the rights of donors and testators who have relied on charitable status.[54] The Commission will have to be especially cautious where it has extended the

[46] A rare example of an appeal against removal is *Holmes* v. *AG*, *The Times*, 11 February 1981. A search of Westlaw over the last three years did not reveal one appeal under section 4(3) Charities Act 1993.

[47] S. 2(2) Charities Act 2006.

[48] The rarity of decisions is demonstrated by a search of Westlaw over a three-year period which failed to reveal any decisions of the court directly on the question of charitable status.

[49] This is explained in pp. 65–67 of this chapter.

[50] Where an institution was charitable but is no longer so due to the passage of time, a change in social circumstances or a change in the law then the appropriate course of action, in the context of removal, would be for the Commission to make a *cy-pres* scheme under section 13(1)(e)(ii) Charities Act 1993.

[51] See pp. 60–65 of this chapter.

[52] See pp. 60–65 of this chapter for a discussion of *Re Stephens* [1892] 8 TLR 792 and *Statement of Reasons for the Commissioners' Decision to Disallow Applications for Charity Registration from the City of London Rifle and Pistol Club and the Burnley Rifle Club* (1993).

[53] P. 65 of this chapter for a discussion of *Re Stephens* [1892] 8 TLR 792 and *IRC* v. *City of Glasgow Police Athletic Association* [1953] AC 380.

[54] *Re Compton* [1945] Ch. 123 see pp. 57–59 of this chapter.

boundaries of charitable status and then subsequently changes its mind.[55] All of these factors will mean that the Commission's power of removal is limited on the basis that it 'no longer considers [an institution] is a charity'.[56]

Even where an institution was never a charity, its property can still be rescued by way of a *cy-pres* scheme.[57] Where an institution which was charitable but is no longer so, its property must be applied *cy-pres*.[58] Where property is applied *cy-pres* in these circumstances, there will be no need to remove the governing instrument from the register. However, where the property of an institution is applied *cy-pres*[59] for the purposes of another charity, then the governing instrument of that institution can be removed from the register, either because it 'does not operate'[60] or because it has 'ceased to exist'[61] but its property will continue to be applied for charity. Where property is rescued *cy-pres* the effect of removal will therefore be limited.

'Ceased to exist'

Even where a charity has ceased to exist there can be instances where its property and governing instrument can survive. A charitable company is restored to the register of companies and subsequently the register of charities,[62] where the Crown applies property deemed *bona vacantia cy-pres* for charitable purposes.[63] Where, in the case of incorporated or unincorporated charities, there is special trust property[64] and the Commission appoints a new trustee.[65] In these circumstances the Commission's power of removal will have limited effect.[66]

'Does not operate'

It is submitted in this book that a charity 'does not operate' where it does not qualify for registration because it does not have a gross income of £5,000[67] or £100,000 in the case of an excepted charity[68] and yet legally exists.

The power to remove charities which do not 'operate'[69] applies to both unincorporated and incorporated charities. Just because a charity does not

[55] See pp. 65–67 of this chapter.

[56] There are very few removals from the register on the basis that institutions no longer appear to the Commission to be charitable. See Chapter 6, p. 124.

[57] Under section 14 Charities Act 1993. See Chapter 5, pp. 105–8.

[58] See section 13(1)(e)(ii) Charities Act 1993. See also *National Anti-Vivisection Society* v. *IRC* [1948] AC 31 *per* Lord Simonds at 74.

[59] See *Re Vernon's Will Trusts* [1972] Ch 300.

[60] S. 3(4) Charities Act 1993. See pp. 83–84 of this chapter.

[61] S. 3(4) Charities Act 1993. See pp. 75–83 of this chapter.

[62] See p. 82 of this chapter. [63] See p. 82 of this chapter.

[64] See p. 83 of this chapter. [65] S. 16(1)(b) Charities Act 1993.

[66] For the Commission's guidance see OG17 – *Removal of Organisations from the Register* (2007) and OG 202 – *Small Charities: Dissolutions and Removal from the Register* (2007).

[67] S. 3A(2)(d) Charities Act 1993. [68] S. 3A(2)(b) & (c) Charities Act 1993.

[69] S. 3(4) Charities Act 1993.

operate does not mean that it is not a charity. This power of removal does not impinge on charitable status. The effect of removal will be limited, especially where trustees are under a duty to reapply for registration.[70]

It is arguable that the Commission can use its power to remove charities from the register where they do not carry out charitable activities. However, this interpretation is not supported for a number of reasons. First, a failure to carry out charitable activities would amount to a failure of governance[71] and in such circumstances the appropriate course of action would be for the Commission to use its powers to protect charitable property.[72] Second, it would be illogical if charities with assets above the registration threshold[73] were removed because the trustees would be under a duty to reapply for registration immediately following removal.[74] Third, it would be extraordinary if a charity with substantial assets was removed from the register because the trustees had difficulty applying the objects and had not applied for a *cy-pres* scheme.[75]

Following the rules of statutory interpretation where statutes are ambiguous reference can be made to Hansard.[76] This power of removal was not examined in Parliament when the Charities Acts 1960, 1992, 1993 and 2006 were debated. Hansard is therefore of no assistance. However, the interpretation of 'does not operate' submitted in this book is supported by Lord Nathan[77] who chaired the Committee which published the Nathan Report.[78] The findings and recommendations of the Nathan Report led to the Charities Act 1960, including the original power[79] to remove charities from the register which did not 'operate'. Lord Nathan pointed out that where a charity which qualifies for registration is not operating, the correct course of action would be for the Commission to use its powers of protection[80] rather than removing the charity from the register. Removal from the register was not intended to be a punishment.[81] Although Hansard is of no assistance in this context, the court would have regard to Lord Nathan's views,[82] as one of the architects of the Charities Act 1960 which is the source of the original power[83] to remove charities which do not 'operate'.

A contextual interpretation[84] of the words 'does not operate' would mean that a charity does not qualify for registration because it does not have a gross income of £5,000[85] or £100,000 in the case of an excepted charity[86] and yet

[70] S. 3B(1)(a) Charities Act 1993. [71] *AG* v. *Alford* (1854) 4 De G.M. & G.843 at 852.
[72] Ss. 18 & 19 Charities Act 1993. [73] S. 3A(2)(d) Charities Act 1993.
[74] S. 3B(1)(a) Charities Act 1993.
[75] As they are required to do so by section 13(5) Charities Act 1993.
[76] *Pepper* v. *Hart* [1993] AC 593.
[77] Nathan *The Charities Act 1960*, 1st edn (London: Butterworths, 1962) p. 52.
[78] The Nathan Report Cm 9538. [79] S. 4(3) Charities Act 1960.
[80] Now sections 18 & 19 Charities Act 1993. [81] Nathan Op. Cit. p. 52.
[82] The Court will have regard to authoritative texts. For example note the reference made by Lord Wright to Tyssen on *Charitable Bequests* (1st edn) p. 177 in *National Anti-Vivisection Society* v. *IRC* [1948] AC 31 at 50.
[83] S. 4(3) Charities Act 1960. [84] *Beswick* v. *Beswick* [1968] AC 58.
[85] S. 3A(2)(d) Charities Act 1993. [86] S. 3A(2)(b) & (c) Charities Act 1993.

legally exists. Reading the Charities Acts 1993 and 2006 as a whole, along with their predecessors the Charities Acts 1960 and 1992, it is clear that to qualify for registration an institution must have the essential indicia of charitable status[87] along with satisfaction of the financial criteria for registration.[88] A contextual interpretation of the words 'does not operate' would point to an interpretation of removal which is consistent with the criteria for qualification for entry onto the register. The interpretation of the power to remove charities which do not 'operate' supports the basic proposition of this book that the Commission's power of removal is limited.

Rectification

When one looks at rectification under section 4(1) Charities Act 1993, it is only where an institution was never a charity that it will lose the presumption of charitable status dating back to its inception.[89] The only exception is where under section 3(4) Charities Act 1993 the removal is on the basis that the Commission no longer considers an institution is a charity due to 'any change in its trusts'[90] in which case the date of the loss of the presumption of charitable status is the date at which the change takes place and not the date of removal. In all other cases, the presumption of charitable status will be retained by institutions along with charity tax reliefs until the date of removal. Again, this will limit the effect of removal for many institutions.

Summary

The Commission's powers of removal under section 3(4) Charities Act 1993 are limited. In the case of rectification[91] of the register under section 4(1) Charities Act 1993, it is argued in this chapter[92] that institutions will retain their tax reliefs until the date of removal, except where they were never charitable or where they are removed because they have amended their 'trusts'.[93] This interpretation of section 4(1) Charities Act 1993 further limits the effect of removal.

'No longer considers is a charity'

In this chapter when looking at the Commission's power to remove an institution which it 'no longer considers is a charity' under section 3(4) Charities Act 1993 a distinction is made between institutions which were never charities and charities which once were but have ceased to be charitable in law.

[87] See Chapter 2, pp. 12–18.
[88] S. 3A(2)(b), (c) & (d) Charities Act 1993.
[89] Pp. 69–71 of this chapter.
[90] S. 3(5) Charities Act 1993.
[91] S. 4(1) Charities Act 1993.
[92] Pp. 69–71 of this Chapter.
[93] S. 3(5) Charities Act 1993.

Never a charity

An institution which is registered as a charity but was never a charity must have been registered by mistake. There are several grounds for mistaken registration.

Never had the essential indicia of charitable status

It was argued in Chapter 2[94] that for an institution to be charitable for the purposes of registration it must have the essential indicia of charitable status. Further it was argued in Chapter 2 that the essential indicia of charitable status includes being subject to a legal obligation to carry out charitable purposes,[95] being within jurisdiction,[96] having charitable purposes[97] which includes the requirement of public benefit[98] and being viable in the sense that if the charitable purposes are impossible from the outset that a general, rather than a specific, charitable intention is expressed by the settlor so that the property is applied *cy-pres*.[99] It is arguable that a lack of independence from the state is part of the essential indicia of charitable status, although this argument is not supported in this book.[100]

There are very few decisions of the Commission involving mistaken registration and removal of an institution which lacked one or more of the essential indicia of charitable status. A review of the Commission's Annual Reports produced one example in 1967. *Scott Baden Commonwealth Ltd*[101] had objects for,

> the promotion of Christian ethics and the encouragement of Christian principles in industry with a view to ensuring good relations between management and labour in industry and the discharge by the persons engaged in industry … of their social obligations to the community and for those purposes to … exercise the powers following so far as the same may be exercised by a body of persons established for charitable purposes only.

When examining these objects the Commission interpreted the words 'with a view to' as having the effect of making the true objects of the company 'ensuring good relations between management and labour in industry and the discharge by persons engaged in industry … of their social obligations to the community'. It concluded that there was no legal authority for the proposition that either of these objects were charitable. The company was therefore removed from the register because it had been mistakenly registered. It should rarely be the case that institutions are registered on the mistaken understanding that they are charities.

[94] Chapter 2, p. 12. [95] Chapter 2, pp. 14–22. [96] Chapter 2, p. 23.
[97] Chapter 2, pp. 23–32. [98] Chapter 2, pp. 34–42. [99] Chapter 2, p. 42.
[100] Chapter 2, p. 43.
[101] *Scott Baden Commonwealth Ltd* [1967] Ch.Com.A.R. 48, App D, Pt 2. See Chapter 6, pp. 17–18.

It will be shown in Chapter 4[102] that there has never been a systematic review of the application of the public benefit test for charities on the register. The Strategy Unit[103] proposed that the Commission carry out such a review and the Commission now has a public benefit objective.[104] Although the Strategy Unit, in one part of its report, contemplates the Commission persuading under-performing charities to develop their public benefit provision, rather than losing their charitable status,[105] it also suggests that such a review might lead to the removal of charities from the register. If the Commission does remove institutions because they lack public benefit then it is important that it does so on the basis that the institutions never had sufficient public benefit.[106] If a charity has sufficient public benefit from its inception then a subsequent lack of public benefit will equate to a breach of trust.[107] It was shown in Chapter 2[108] that there is a danger that the Commission might interpret post-registration activities as evidence of a lack of public benefit at the inception of the institution rather than as a breach of trust. It is argued in this chapter[109] that if the Commission removes an institution from the register then it is important that it interprets public benefit in a way which is consistent with the principles applied by the court and in doing so this will limit the Commission's powers of removal.

Sham charities

An institution which is a sham cannot be a charity in law. Such an institution which is a sham charity must have been registered by mistake and must be removed from the register because the Commission no longer considers it to be a charity.[110]

There are no English legal authorities which expressly deal with a sham charity therefore there is a need to examine the general law. The leading case on the law of sham is *Snook* v. *London and West Riding Investments*[111] where Diplock LJ summed up a sham in the following terms:

[102] Chapter 4, pp. 94–95.

[103] Cabinet Office, Strategy Unit Report, *Private Action, Public Benefit: A Review of Charities and the Wider Not-for-Profit Sector* (2002). To date the Commission has issued the following guidance: *Public Benefit – the Charity Commission's Approach* (January 2005), *Public Benefit – The Charity Commission's Position on how Public Benefit is Treated in the Charities Bill* (July 2005) and *Charities and Public Benefit The Charity Commission's General Guidance on Public Benefit* (January 2008).

[104] S. 1B(2)2 Charities Act 2006.

[105] Cabinet Office, Strategy Unit Report, *Private Action, Public Benefit A Review of Charities and the Wider Not-for-Profit Sector* (2002) para. 4.18.

[106] *National Anti-Vivisection Society* v. *IRC* [1948] AC 31 *per* Lord Simonds at 74.

[107] *AG* v. *Ross* [1986] 1 WLR 252 *per* Scott J at 264. See Chapter 2, pp. 30–31.

[108] Chapter 2, pp. 31–32. [109] Pp. 60–65 of this chapter.

[110] S. 3(4) Charities Act 1993.

[111] *Snook* v. *London & West Riding Investments* [1967] 2 QB 786 at 802.

> It is, I think, necessary to consider what, if any, legal concept is involved in the use of this popular and pejorative word. I apprehend that, if it has any meaning in law, it means acts done or documents executed by the parties to the 'sham' which are intended by them to give third parties or the court the appearance of creating between parties legal rights and obligations different from the actual legal rights and obligations (if any) which the parties intend to create.

Diplock LJ stressed that there must be a common intention:[112]

> But one thing I think is clear in legal principle, morality and the authorities … that for acts or documents to be a 'sham' with whatever legal consequences follow from this, all the parties thereto must have a common intention that the acts or documents are not to create the legal rights and obligations which they give the appearance of creating. No unexpressed intentions of the 'shammer' affect the rights of a party whom he deceived.

Although there are no recorded decisions of the court involving sham charities there are authorities, albeit from other jurisdictions, which deal with the question of whether religions are shams. These indicate that it will only be in extreme circumstances that the court will rule that an institution claiming to be a religion is nothing of the sort. By analogy, the same should also be generally true of charities, and the lack of legal authorities on the issue appears to support this supposition. For example, Murphy J in the Australian decision of the court in *Church of the New Faith* v. *Commissioners for the Pay Roll Tax* (a case which determined whether Scientology was a religion for the purposes of tax relief) commented:[113]

> Some claims to be religious are not serious but merely a hoax, but to reach this conclusion requires an extreme case.

A further example of a sham religion may be found in an American decision *Theriault* v. *Silber*[114]. In this case there was no claim that the 'church' was a charity. The issue was whether Theriault, who was a prisoner, had had his constitutional right to free exercise of his religion violated. The Texas Court held that the church that he had founded was not a religion. The members of the church consisted mainly of fellow inmates and its services involved 'gripe sessions' of a violent and raucous nature. The church's one attempt at a paschal feast was a tongue-in-cheek request for the prison authorities to supply steak and wine. Clearly this 'religion' was a sham. The facts indicate the type of extreme circumstances when the court will take into account the nature and

[112] *Ibid.* See also *Hitch* v. *Stone* [2001] STC 214.

[113] *Church of the New Faith* v. *Commissioners for the Pay Roll Tax* (1983) 154 CLR 120.

[114] *Theriault* v. *Silber* 391 Fed Supp 578 (1975); cited in Picarda, H. 'New Religions and Ethical Movements as Charities' (1981) 131 NLJ 436.

content of religious doctrines when determining whether there is a religion or something masquerading as a religion.

The only recorded removal of a charity from the register on the ground that it was a sham is that of Oak House Charity.[115] This college was registered as a charity with objects to advance the education of the general public in the skills of bookkeeping and other related subjects. Prior to registration, the trading activities carried on by the college were carried out by one of the trustees (who was also the director of the college) as a business trading as 'The Learning Library'. As the inquiry report states, this trade continued under the guise of a charity.[116] The court came to the conclusion that the only reason for setting up the charity was to evade tax. The Commission agreed that the charity was a sham and removed it from the register.

Before leaving the subject of sham charities, an interesting problem arises from the decision of the court in *Re Esteem Settlement*.[117] Although this Jersey decision is only of persuasive value, it may have some relevance to charities. Here the original trust was valid, but later another asset was purportedly transferred to the trust on what was agreed by the parties to be sham trusts. It raises the question of whether the Commission could, in certain circumstances, argue that a charity was originally valid but property subsequently transferred to it was not held for charity as it was transferred with a sham intention.[118] For example, terrorists might take on the trusteeship of a valid charity and then transfer funds to it with the intention that they should be used to provide arms. It seems logical to divide the property up into what was intended for charity and what was not.[119] Equally, a charity might have been created as a sham, but subsequently become a valid charity. This would happen where new trustees are appointed who are not party to the sham intention and are legally bound to carry out the real purposes of the charity.[120]

Sham charities are rare [121] and it is submitted that it would be far more likely that the Commission would remove charities from the register because there is a doubt about the institution's real objects[122] or because it lacks sufficient public benefit[123] because these grounds for removal do not involve the need to show an intention to deceive.[124]

115 *Oak House* Charity Inquiry (July 2001). 116 *Ibid.*
117 *Re Esteem Settlement* [2003] JRC 092 par 60. 118 See Chapter 2, p. 31.
119 See Chapter 5, pp. 105–8.
120 *A* v. *A and St. George's Trustees Ltd* 2007 WL 1243205 *per* Munby J at 45. It would follow that the appointment of trustees by the Commission would limit its powers of removal because it would convert a sham charity into a lawful charity. For the appointment of trustees in the context of an inquiry see Chapter 6, pp. 16–17.
121 The only example on the Charity Commission's website and Annual Reports is *Oak House* Charity Inquiry (July 2001).
122 See Chapter 2, pp 28–30 and Chapter 4, pp. 85–89. 123 Chapter 2, pp. 30–31.
124 *Hitch* v. *Stone* [2001] STC 214; *Snook* v. *London & West Riding Investments* [1967] 2 QB 786 at 802.

Change in the law

The wording 'no longer considers is a charity'[125] allows the Commission to remove an institution where the court or Parliament[126] decides that contrary to a previous decision of the court that the institution was never charitable.[127] The common law authority for the removal of a charity which was previously held to be charitable by the court is *National Anti-Vivisection Society* v. *IRC*[128] where the House of Lords decided to overrule *Re Foveaux*[129] because an object for the total suppression of vivisection was not charitable, as any assumed public benefit in the advancement of morals would be far outweighed by the detriment to medical science and research, and consequently to public health, and that the main object of the National Anti-Vivisection Society was political as it promoted a change in the legislation.

At this point, an analysis of the declaratory theory of judicial decisions is required. The declaratory theory of judicial decisions is that judges do not make or change law: they discover and declare the law which is, throughout, the same. According to this theory, when an earlier decision is overruled the law is not changed; its true nature is disclosed, having existed in this form all along.[130] Although it is now accepted that this theory is a myth,[131] because judges do change the law, the retrospective effect of judicial decisions remains.[132] This means that whenever the court overrules its previous decision on a question of charitable status, the effect of its decision will be to determine that a charitable purpose was never charitable. All institutions relying on the original decision of the court for their charitable status will be determined never to have been charitable.

It will rarely be the case that the Court overrules its previous decision.[133] The effect of overruling a decision means that the law is changed retrospectively[134] and the court is very reluctant to disturb the rights of testators and

[125] S. 3(4) Charities Act 1993.

[126] There is no recorded instance of Parliament declaring a purpose to be no longer charitable in law. It is not enough to declare a purpose unlawful because the property can be rescued by way of a *cy-pres* scheme under section 13(1)(e)(ii) Charities Act 1993. See *Da Costa* v. *De Paz* (1753) Amb 228 and *Carry* v. *Abbot (1803) 7 Ves* 490, 496.

[127] *National Anti-Vivisection Society* v. *IRC* [1948] AC 31.

[128] *Ibid.*

[129] *Re Foveaux* [1895] 2 Ch 501.

[130] *Kleinwort Benson Ltd* v. *Lincoln City Council* [1999] 2 AC 349 *per* Lord Browne-Wilkinson at 358.

[131] Lord Reid described the theory as a 'fairy tale in which no one any longer believes' in his article 'The Judge as a Law Maker' 12 J.S.P.T.L. (N.S.) 22 (1972–1973).

[132] *Kleinwort Benson Ltd* v. *Lincoln City Council* [1999] 2 AC 349 *per* Lord Browne-Wilkinson at 358.

[133] The only instance of this happening is *National Anti-Vivisection Society* v. *IRC* [1948] AC 31.

[134] *Kleinwort Benson Ltd* v. *Lincoln City Council* [1999] 2 AC 349 *per* Lord Browne-Wilkinson at 358.

donors who have relied on the previous decision in good faith.[135] For example, the Court of Appeal decision in *Re Compton*[136] avoided the retrospective effect of overruling the *'poor relations'* cases[137] by distinguishing them on their own particular facts. In doing so it was able to declare a more modern rule of public benefit without disturbing the rights of those who relied on those existing precedents.[138]

This raises the key question of whether the Commission has the power to overrule the court. There is a fundamental problem of legality with the Commission deciding that an institution does not have charitable objects and should therefore be removed from the register.[139] The Commission has no law-making powers[140] and must therefore follow legislation or decisions of the court.[141] However, even after the Charities Act 2006, which sets out a list of twelve specific charitable purposes,[142] there are also likely to be so few decisions of the court interpreting charitable status that the Commission will sometimes be forced into becoming a *de facto* lawmaker when it wishes to decide that an institution was never charitable.[143] Its dilemma is that, on the one hand it has a duty to obey and follow the existing law, but on the other hand it must respond to changing social needs.

There is no recorded instance of the Commission removing a charity from the register because it says that a decision of the court is wrong. There are, however, some signs that the Commission is starting to regard itself as having the same power as the court to determine charitable status. This has become apparent through various statements made through its Review of the Register.[144] To date, the Review of the Register has involved an attempt to develop charitable status by the Commission through a process of analogy, with purposes already accepted by the court or the Commission as charitable, and through the application by the Commission of the public benefit test.[145]

135 *Re Compton* [1945] Ch 123 *per* Lord Greene MR at 139.

136 *Re Compton* [1945] Ch 123.

137 An example of one of the *'poor relations'* cases is *Isaac* v. *De Friez* (1753) 2 Amb 595 where the gifts were (1) a gift of two annuities to the poorest relations of the testator and of his wife; (2) a gift of income to one poor relation of the testator 'for a portion in the way of marriage and putting him or her out in the world'; and (3) a similar gift of income to one poor relation of his wife. These gifts were held to be charitable without any reasons being given in the report.

138 The process of distinguishing is discussed in pp. 60–65 of this chapter.

139 *Ibid.*

140 See *Rule* v. *Charity Commission* (High Court, 10 December 1979); [1979] Ch.Com.A.R. pp. 12–16. The Commission only has the powers conferred on it by the Charities Act 1993, 2006 and other enactments. See pp. 1–9 of this chapter.

141 See *Boddington* v. *British Transport Police* [1999] 2 AC 143 at 171 *per* Lord Steyn.

142 S. 2(2) Charities Act 2006.

143 This is explained in pp. 65–67 of this chapter.

144 The Review of the Register documents are available on the Commission's website: www.charity.commission.gov.uk.

145 See RR 1a – *Recognising New Charitable Purposes* (2001). For an example of this approach see RR 5 – *The Promotion of Community Capacity Building* (2000), RR 3 – *The Relief of Unemployment* (1999), RR 2 – *The Promotion of Urban and Rural Regeneration* (1999) and more recently RR 12 – *The Promotion of Human Rights* (2005).

However, there is some indication in the Review of the Register documents that the Commission regards itself as having the same powers as the court to decide that purposes are no longer charitable. For example, the Commission claims in RR 1a – *Recognising New Charitable Purposes*:[146]

> We have the same powers as the Court when determining whether an organisation has charitable status and the same powers to take into account changing social and economic circumstances-whether to recognise a purpose as charitable for the first time or to recognise that a purpose has ceased to be charitable.

If the Commission considers that it has the same power as the court then it might think that it can overrule decisions of the court even though it has no such power. When removing charities in the absence of a decision of the court, it is submitted that the Commission should have regard to the reluctance of the court to overrule its previous decisions,[147] and therefore it should rarely be the case that the Commission should decide to change its mind about its own decisions and remove charities from the register as a consequence.

Mistaken understanding of the law

An institution which is registered because of a mistaken understanding of the law will not be charitable and must be removed from the register because the Commission no longer considers it to be a charity.[148] There are three ways in which an institution could be registered under a mistaken understanding of the law.

First, the Commission could base registration on a mistaken analysis of the law. Where, for example, it registers an institution which has non-charitable purposes.[149]

Second, the Commission might be mistaken as to the true objects of an institution where the promoters do not intend to deceive the Commission but there is a doubt about the true objects.[150] In such circumstances the court has on occasion looked at substance over form.[151]

Third, the Commission could argue that a decision of the court, albeit one that the Commission previously relied on as a previous precedent, can be distinguished because it is not relevant due to the passage of time, a change in social circumstances, a material difference of facts or that another decision of the court justifies removal on an alternative ground. There is a distinction between distinguishing precedents and 'making law' although at times the distinction will be fine.[152]

[146] RR 1 a – *Recognising New Charitable Purposes* (2001).

[147] *Re Compton* [1945] Ch 123 *per* Lord Greene MR at 139.

[148] S. 3(4) Charities Act 1993.

[149] For example see *Scott Baden Commonwealth Ltd* [1967] Ch.Com.A.R. 48, App D, Pt 2. See pp. 53–54 of this chapter.

[150] See Chapter 2, pp. 29–30.

[151] See Chapter 9, pp. 198–9.

[152] Pp. 65–67 of this chapter.

Distinguishing decisions of the court

It is quite legitimate for the court to distinguish an earlier decision of the Court. The basis for distinguishing a decision could be on the facts or relevance which might be due to the passage of time or a change of social circumstances. As previously discussed,[153] the advantage of distinguishing precedents is that it allows the court to make a decision without necessarily disturbing the rights of existing donors and testators.[154]

An example of this is *Re Scowcroft*[155] and *Re Bushnell*.[156] In *Re Scowcroft* a gift for 'the furtherance of conservative principles and mental and moral improvement' was held to be charitable. Whereas in *Re Bushnell* the testator created a fund to be used, *inter alia*, to engage lecturers and publish information to demonstrate 'that the full advantage of Socialised Medicine can only be enjoyed in a Socialist State'. Unlike *Re Scowcroft* the court held that the dominant purpose of the objects was political rather than educational and that the testator was trying to promote his own theory through education.[157] A similar approach of distinguishing precedents could be adopted by the Commission although as the Commission is not a court and has no law making powers[158] it would need to be confident that the Court would support its decision otherwise it would be acting unlawfully.

Although not directly concerned with the removal of charities from the register, the decisions of the Commission in *City of London Rifle and Pistol Club and Burnley Rifle Club*[159] not to register these charities had implications for the many gun clubs already on the register. Following the publication of their *Statement of Reasons*[160] the Commission issued a press release in which the then Chief Commissioner said:

> We shall now have to examine the position of clubs already on the register of charities.[161]

153 See p. 59 of this chapter. 154 *Ibid.*

155 *Re Scowcroft* [1898] 2 Ch 638. See generally J. Warburton *Tudor on Charities*, 9th edn (London: Butterworths, 2003) pp. 186–189.

156 *Re Bushnell* [1975] 1 WLR 1596.

157 For the fine line between charitable and non-charitable objects see Chapter 2, pp. 32–34.

158 *Rule* v. *Charity Commission* (High Court, 10 December 1979); [1979] Ch.Com.A.R.12–16. The Commission only has the powers set out in the Charities Acts 1993 and 2006 and other enactments. See pp. 45–52 of this Chapter.

159 *Statement of Reasons for the Commissioners' Decision to Disallow Applications for Charity Registration from the City of London Rifle and Pistol Club and the Burnley Rifle Club* (1993).

160 *Ibid.*

161 *Charity Commission Press Release*, 1 February 1993. The majority of rifle clubs are still on the register and it is unclear what their present position is.

In reaching its decision[162] the Commission had to go back to an antiquated and, originally, irrelevant case, *Re Stephens*.[163]

The gun clubs which were investigated had objects to encourage skill in shooting by providing instruction and practice in the use of firearms to Her Majesty's subjects so that they would be better able to defend the realm through service in the armed forces. It had previously been thought, relying on *Re Stephens*,[164] that rifle clubs with such objects were charities. In *Re Stephens*[165] a testator made a gift in his will to the National Rifle Association to form a fund to be called the Stephens Prize Fund:

> to be expended by the Council for the teaching of shooting at moving objects in any manner that they may think fit, so as to prevent as far as possible a catastrophe similar to that at Majuba Hill.

The testator did not say that the gift should be restricted to soldiers and Kekewich J construed the gift as being for all Englishmen. It was mentioned in the judgment that it was a matter of English history that at Majuba Hill the English soldiers were defeated because their opponents were excellent rifle shots. The gift was held to be charitable because it promoted the security of the nation.

The Commission[166] pointed out two particular aspects of Kekewich J's judgment in *Re Stephens*[167] which in its opinion rendered it irrelevant as an authority in support of the clubs' application for registration:

(A) Kekewich J found that the object in the testator's mind was clear. He desired that Englishmen should be taught to shoot with these particular weapons which were used in war for the destruction of their enemies and their own protection; and
(B) Kekewich J found that what the testator meant was that accurate shooting was to be taught amongst Englishmen in general.

By contrast, the Commission found that the clubs' purposes were not to teach members of the public in general to shoot with those particular weapons which are used in times of war. It decided that modern warfare no longer depended on the expert shooting skills of soldiers in the way it had at the Battle of Majuba Hill. Modern warfare depended more on fully trained service personnel, familiar with the latest communications, equipment and technological weaponry than the competent single-start shooter. Furthermore, it thought that the social and organisational changes affecting the recruitment and training

[162] A search on Westlaw over the last three years failed to reveal any decisions by the Court purely on the issue of charitable status.
[163] *Re Stephens* (1892) 8 TLR 792. [164] *Ibid.* [165] *Ibid.*
[166] *Statement of Reasons for the Commissioners' Decision to Disallow Applications for Charity Registration from the City of London Rifle and Pistol Club and the Burnley Rifle Club* (1993).
[167] *Re Stephens* (1892) 8 TLR 792.

of the armed forces rendered the idea that rifle club members fulfilling the role of a semi-trained third line at times of war anachronistic.[168] The Commission decided that even if *Re Stephens*[169] was still good authority it doubted it extended beyond the individual circumstances surrounding the decision; namely the avoidance of another disaster along the lines of Majuba Hill. In any event, the Commission considered that there had been such a radical change in circumstances since that case that it was not bound to follow it.[170]

In doing so the Commission relied on the *dicta* of Lord Simonds in *National Anti-Vivisection Society* v. *IRC*[171] and *Gilmour* v. *Coats*.[172] These decisions are authority for the proposition that the court can review its previous decisions in the light of changes in social habits and needs of a radical nature. They are not authorities which support the case for the loss of charitable status or removal in such circumstances. On the contrary they are authorities which support the case for a *cy-pres*[173] application of the property. The Commission was not saying that *Re Stephens*[174] was incorrectly decided, it was simply contending that, on the facts, it was no longer relevant. If this is correct the proper course of action would be to make a *cy-pres* scheme to modernise the objects[175] rather than removal.[176] However, the gun clubs' decision does illustrate the potential for the Commission to distinguish precedents on the facts and use the ground for mistaken understanding of the law to remove a charity affected by the passage of time.

By analogy with the question of removal, and providing another example of the way in which the Commission distinguishes decisions of the court, is its decision to register a charity with objects for the promotion of race relations, despite the apparent decision of the court to the contrary in *Re Strakosch*.[177] In *Re Strakosch*[178] it was decided that a trust to strengthen the bonds of unity between the Union of South Africa and the Mother Country which would incidentally be conducive to the appeasement of racial feeling between the Dutch and English-speaking sections of South Africa was not charitable. Such objects were both too vague and too political to be charitable in law.[179] Further, such an object was not 'within the spirit and intendment' of the Preamble to the

[168] Note that there was some evidence to the contrary: see Ch. Com. Dec. Vol. 1 (1993) p. 7. For a criticism of the Commission's reasoning see Clarke, P.'The Charitable Status of Rifle Clubs: the Explosion Occurs' 2 CL & PR, 1993/94, 2, 98–101.

[169] *Re Stephens* (1892) 8 TLR 792.

[170] See *ante* for a discussion on the *Decision of the Charity Commissioners for England and Wales; made 2 April 2001 relating to the Application for Registration as a Charity by the General Medical Council*, decision of the Commission in which it outlined the circumstances where it considers itself entitled to disregard decisions of the court.

[171] *National Anti-Vivisection Society* v. *IRC* [1948] AC 31 at 74.

[172] *Gilmour* v. *Coats* [1949] AC 426 at 443.

[173] S. 13(1)(e)(ii) Charities Act 1993. See Chapter 5, pp. 108–12.

[174] *Re Stephens* (1892) 8 TLR 792. [175] S. 13(1)(e)(ii) Charities Act 1993.

[176] S. 3(4) Charities Act 1993. [177] *Re Strakosch* [1949] 1 Ch 529. [178] *Ibid.*

[179] *Ibid.* at 536 and 538.

Statute of Elizabeth.[180] This decision was taken to be an obstacle to accepting as charitable objects for 'the promotion of racial harmony'. However, in the light of the Race Relations Act 1968, which promoted harmonious community relations among citizens of all races, beliefs and cultures,[181] and also a White Paper on racial disadvantage,[182] which placed emphasis on equality and the avoidance of discrimination based on race, the Commission decided to revisit *Re Strakosch*.[183]

The Commission noted that the objection to an object for the promotion of racial harmony in *Re Strakosch*[184] was that it was a political object and that the court had no means of judging whether a proposed change in the law would be for the public benefit. However, the Commission decided that this decision was no longer relevant.[185] As it observed, Parliament had already decided that the promotion of racial harmony was for the public benefit and as a result the objects had ceased to be political.[186] The Commission cited subsequent decisions of the court which could be said to be analogous to the promotion of race relations.[187]

The Commission was on quite safe ground as it was disregarding a precedent where it had statutory authority for doing so. Departing from a decision of the court will be less controversial where, as in this case, the Commission is extending the boundaries of charitable status in a way that is socially relevant[188] rather than contracting the boundaries and adversely affecting acquired legal rights based on the previously accepted position.[189]

More recently, the Commission considered whether it was bound by a decision of the court when looking at an application for registration (the decision is equally applicable in the context of removal) as a charity by The General Medical Council.[190] The Court of Appeal had decided in 1928 in *General Medical Council* v. *IRC*[191] that the GMC was not charitable because it operated primarily for the benefit of members of the medical profession rather than the public as a whole.[192] The Court of Appeal's decision was subsequently approved by the House of Lords in 1959 in *General Nursing Council for*

180 *Ibid.* at 538. 181 S. 25(3) Race Relations Act 1968.
182 Racial Disadvantage Cm 8476 (1982). 183 *Re Strakosch* [1949] 1 Ch 529.
184 *Ibid.* 185 [1983] Ch. Com. A.R paras. 15–20. 186 *Ibid.* para. 18.
187 *Ibid.* para. 19 (the preservation of public order and the prevention of breaches of the peace – *IRC* v. *City of Glasgow Police Athletic Association* [1953] AC 380; the mental and moral improvement of man on the basis that discrimination on the grounds of colour is immoral – *Re Hood* [1931] 1 Ch 240; *Re Price* [1943] Ch 422 and *Re South Place Ethical Society* [1980] 1 WLR 1565; and the promotion of equality of women with men – *Halpin* v. *Seear* [1977] Ch. Com.AR paras. 34–36.
188 For another example of the Commission extending the boundaries of charitable status in a way that is socially relevant see CC, *The Promotion of Human Rights* (2002) for the Commission's acceptance of objects for the promotion of human rights as a charitable object.
189 *Re Compton* [1945] Ch 123 *per* Lord Greene MR at 139.
190 *Decision of the Charity Commissioners for England and Wales; made 2 April 2001 relating to the Application for Registration as a Charity by the General Medical Council.*
191 *General Medical Council* v. *IRC* [1928] All ER 252. 192 *Ibid.*

England and Wales v. *St Marylebone Borough Council*.[193] The Commission decided that, notwithstanding legal precedent to the contrary, it would be able to reconsider the charitable status of an institution where:

(A) *There had been changes in the relevant legal framework*
In this particular case the Commission concluded that there had been no major changes in the law since *General Medical Council* v. *IRC*.[194] However, the Commission looked at the decision of the Court of Appeal of New Zealand in *Commissioners of Inland Revenue* v. *Medical Council of New Zealand*[195] which held that the Medical Council of New Zealand (a body with functions similar to the GMC) was established for a charitable purpose beneficial to the community by ensuring high standards in medical practice and surgery and the protection of the public. Although the decision is of only persuasive value in English law, the Commission considered that the case suggested that they could examine the cases of *General Medical Council* v. *IRC*[196] and *General Nursing Council for England and Wales* v. *St Marylebone Borough Council*[197] to determine their application to purposes and activities of the GMC in modern times.

(B) *Changes in the constitution and activities of the GMC*
The next ground that the Commission considered entitled it to disregard a decision of the court is where there are changes to the constitution and activities of a charity. The Commission noted constitutional changes to the GMC's constitution which were affected by Acts of Parliament, and concluded that the GMC had changed significantly since it was constituted under the Medical Act 1958.

(C) *Changes in social and economic circumstances and the general environment within which the body operates or in which its purposes may be carried out*
As in the case of the gun clubs,[198] the Commission considered that it could distinguish a decision of the court, rather than attempt to overrule a decision, where there had been a change in social and economic circumstances.[199]

In the context of the GMC the Commission noted the introduction of the National Health Service in 1948, which had transformed the environment in

[193] *General Nursing Council for England and Wales* v. *St Marylebone Borough Council* [1959] AC 540.

[194] *General Medical Council* v. *IRC* [1928] All ER 252.

[195] *Commissioners of Inland Revenue* v. *Medical Council of New Zealand* [1997] 2 NZLR 297.

[196] *General Medical Council* v. *IRC* [1928] All ER 252.

[197] *General Nursing Council for England and Wales* v. *St Marylebone Borough Council* [1959] AC 540.

[198] *Statement of Reasons for the Commissioners' Decision to Disallow Applications for Charity Registration from the City of London Rifle and Pistol Club and the Burnley Rifle Club* (1993).

[199] The Commission relied on *National Anti-Vivisection Society* v. *IRC* [1948] AC 31.

which medical services were provided and the increased regulatory activity within society generally. The Commission also noted the general recognition that regulation of public and quasi-public functions is necessary and in the public interest.

Despite decisions of the court[200] the Commission decided to register the GMC as a charity. Although the GMC[201] decision indicates that the Commission will not consider itself necessarily bound by a particular decision of the court, which is not on all fours with the facts of that decision, it does illustrate that the Commission recognises the need to justify departure from a decision of the court. This suggests that the Commission will be cautious and conservative in its approach to distinguishing specific decisions of the court to provide a basis for removal on the ground of mistaken understanding of the law. This might lead the Commission to remove an institution from the register on a different ground, which is now discussed.

Removal on a different ground

Another way of distinguishing previous decisions of the court is to select an alternative reason why an institution is not charitable.[202] For example, the court could distinguish a precedent by deciding that the institution was never a charity because it never had sufficient public benefit.[203]

It will be shown in Chapter 9 that there is scope to look at the substance of an institution rather than its form[204] and that very often there is a fine line between charitable and non-charitable objects.[205] Therefore, there will often be scope for the Court to decide that institutions are not charitable on a different basis due, for example, to a lack of public benefit[206] or because their real objects are non-charitable.[207] This would be on the basis that the institutions were never charitable.[208]

Making law

Applying the principles of the Court when distinguishing precedents is one thing, but 'making law' to attempt to widen the boundaries of charitable status is

200 *General Medical Council* v. *IRC* [1928] All ER 252; *General Nursing Council for England and Wales* v. *St Marylebone Borough Council* [1959] AC 540.

201 *Statement of Reasons for the Commissioners' Decision to Disallow Applications for Charity Registration from the City of London Rifle and Pistol Club and the Burnley Rifle Club* (1993).

202 For the Commission selecting alternative grounds for deciding questions of charitable status see *North Tawton Rugby Union Football Club* Ch. Com. Dec, Vol. 5 (1997) p. 7. See pp. 65–67 of this chapter.

203 For example the House of Lords decided that the Royal College of Surgeons was charitable in *Royal College of Surgeons of England* v. *National Provincial Bank Ltd* [1952] 1 All ER 984 and in doing so distinguished the court of Appeal decision in *General Medical Council* v. *IRC* [1928] All ER 252.

204 Chapter 9, pp. 198–9. 205 Chapter 2, pp. 32–34.

206 *National Anti-Vivisection Society* v. *IRC* [1948] AC 31 *per* Lord Simonds at 74.

207 *AG* v. *Ross* [1986] 1 WLR 252 *per* Scott J at 264. 208 *Ibid.* at 263.

another. An example of the Commission 'making law' is North Tawton Rugby Union Football Club.[209] Briefly, this organisation made an application for registration as a charity with objects to promote the amateur game of Rugby Union Football for the benefit of the public. The application was encouraged by the Rugby Football Union. Leaving aside the particular facts of the application, the difficulty facing the Commission and the applicant was that there were clear decisions of the court which supported the proposition that the promotion of sport as an end in itself, rather than as a way of achieving some other purpose which was charitable, was not a charitable purpose at common law.[210]

In the light of strong judicial precedent declaring the promotion of mere sport as not being a charitable purpose, the Commission considered that there was no scope for them to take a contrary view. It said:

> To do so would involve a radical departure from long established principles, of a kind which would have considerable implications for the breadth of the concept of charity law at common law, and which could only be taken by the Court.[211]

In the Commission's concluding remarks it said:

> Whilst we came to the conclusion that we could not accept the club's application for registration, we felt that the position at common law arising from the decision in the Re Nottage would benefit from reconsideration by the Court in the light of the role of sport in modern social conditions. Two factors in particular seemed to us to be of relevance in that connection: the decrease in the emphasis on, and the amount of, sport in schools and other educational institutions, which has led to children and young people increasingly taking part in sport outside such institutions; and the increased acceptance of the value from a health point of view of people of all ages taking part in healthy exercise. We could accordingly see much to be said for the view that it should be charitable to promote sport as a means to the promotion of physical health and fitness. Such an approach would in our view be a logical basis for the development of the law (foreshadowed by the approach taken by the majority of the Court of

[209] *North Tawton Rugby Union Football Club* Ch. Com. Dec. Vol. 5 (1997) p. 7.

[210] *Re Nottage* [1895] 2 Ch 649 which, as the Commission pointed out, has been recognised in several *dicta* of the House of Lords in other cases including those of Lord Wright in *National Anti-Vivisection Society* v. *IRC* [1948] AC 31 at pp. 41–42, Lord Normand and Lord Morton in *IRC* v. *City of Glasgow Police Athletic Association* [1953] AC 380 at pp. 394 and 399–400 respectively, Lord Reid in *IRC* v. *Baddely* [1955] AC 572 at pp. 596–7 and Lord Hailsham in *IRC* v. *McMullen* [1981] AC 1 at p. 15.

[211] Ch. Com. Dec. Vol. 5 (1997) p. 9. The Commission, in addition to considering whether the Club was charitable for the promotion of sport, also considered whether the Club could be charitable under the Recreational Charities Act 1958 but concluded that it was not. See Ch. Com. Dec. Vol. 5 (1997) pp. 9–12. The Commission also rejected the application on the basis that it was a self-regarding body and lacked the necessary public benefit: see Ch. Com. Dec. Vol. 5 (1997) pp. 12–13.

> Appeal in IRC v. McMullen [1981] AC 1) whilst at the same time leaving intact the basic principle that the promotion of sport pursued merely for its own sake is not a charitable purpose.[212]

Subsequently, the Commission issued a Discussion Document on *The Promotion of Sport*[213] which discussed and consulted on, *inter alia*, the conclusions reached by the Commission in *North Tawton Rugby Union Football Club* but concluded that:

> Since we are bound to work within the existing law, the paper does not consider how the law might be changed.[214]

In the event, the Commission issued RR 11–*Charitable Status and Sport*[215] which recognised two new charitable objects which do not directly promote particular sports but do allow sports to be used as a means to promote other previously recognised charitable objects. As a result, the promotion of community participation in healthy recreation by the provision of facilities for playing particular sports and the advancement of physical education of young people not undergoing formal education were both considered by the Commission to be charitable. The advancement of amateur sport is now contained in the Charities Act 2006 in its list of charitable purposes.[216] Sport is defined by section 2(3)(d) Charities Act 2006 as meaning sports or games which promote health and involve physical or mental skill or exertion. Although it is true that the Commission did not depart from the law (at that time) and recognise the promotion of sport as a charitable object in its own right, it is arguable that these two new objects effectively did just that.

Of course, the danger for charities on the register is that just as the Commission is forced into making decisions about charitable status it might subsequently change its mind and decide that charities no longer qualify under these new purposes. It is argued that, in those circumstances, the Commission will be removing a charity on the grounds of a mistaken understanding of the law on the basis that the Commission no longer considers it to be a charity.[217] However, even where an institution was never a charity it is arguable that its property could be rescued *cy-pres*.[218] This will now be explained.

Cy-pres application of property where the institution was never a charity

Where the court decides to overrule its previous decision and the Commission then removes a charity from the register because it was never charitable it is argued[219] that the Commission could have recourse to its power under section 14

[212] *North Tawton Rugby Union Football Club* Ch. Com. Dec.Vol. 5 (1997) p. 13.

[213] *Review of the Register Discussion Document: Promotion of Sport Consultation Document* (2001) p. 2.

[214] *Ibid.* [215] RR 11 – *Charitable Status and Sport* (Version 2003).

[216] S. 2(2)(g) Charities Act 2006. [217] Pp. 59–65 of this chapter.

[218] S. 14 Charities Act 1993. [219] Chapter 5, pp. 105–8.

of the Charities Act 1993 to make a scheme in relation to charitable property where the property is given for specific charitable purposes which fail *ab initio*. Purposes are deemed to have failed where any difficulty in applying property for those purposes makes that property available to be returned to the donors, rather than applicable *cy-pres*.[220] Section 14 empowers the Commission to make a *cy-pres* scheme in relation to property given for charitable purposes which are, due to an initial failure, held for non-charitable purposes.

Section 14 Charities Act 1993 makes provision for donors to be located through advertisements and inquiries[221] and puts in place a procedure for donors who cannot be identified or found to make a claim within six months of the scheme being made. The section aims to provide a practical and fair way of protecting the interests of donors while allowing for unclaimed property to be applied *cy-pres*. It follows that, even when institutions are removed from the register because they were registered by mistake, the effect of removal will be minimal where a *cy-pres* scheme is made under section 14 Charities Act 1993.

However, the argument that section 14 Charities Act 1993 can rescue charitable property where an institution was never a charity is less tenable where it is the Commission rather than the court who have decided that its previous decision was wrong and that as a result it must remove an institution from the register. The application of section 14 presupposes that there were charitable purposes which failed. Section 14 Charities Act 1993 refers to 'specific charitable purposes' [222] which fail. 'Charitable purposes'[223] are defined as those purposes listed in section 2(2) Charities Act 2006 or existing charity law[224] or by virtue of section 1 Recreational Charities Act 1958[225] and any purposes reasonably analogous to, or within the spirit of, those purposes[226] and any purposes reasonably analogous to, or within the spirit of, any purposes recognised under charity law[227] to be analogous to those analogous purposes.[228] These purposes are therefore established by the common law or Parliament[229] and not by the Commission.[230] It is arguable that, where the Commission changes its mind about one of its decisions on charitable status, section 14 Charities Act 1993 will not apply if the institution in question never had 'specific charitable purposes'. If section 14 does not apply then an institution's general property will be held beneficially or on resulting trusts for the donors and not for charity.[231] It would be unfair if charity was prejudiced through reliance on decisions of the Commission in the absence of a precedent from the court.

[220] S. 14(7) Charities Act 1993. [221] S. 14(1)(a) Charities Act 1993.
[222] S. 14(1) Charities Act 1993. [223] S. 2(1) Charities Act 2006.
[224] S. 2(8) Charities Act 2006 defines 'existing charity law' as 'means charity law as in force immediately before the day on which this section comes into force'.
[225] S. 2(4)(a) Charities Act 2006. [226] S. 2(4)(b) Charities Act 2006.
[227] S. 2(8) Charities Act 2006 defines *'charity law'* as *'the law relating to charities in England and Wales.'*
[228] S. 2(4)(c) Charities Act 2006. [229] See Chapter 2, pp. 23–26.
[230] See pp. 45–52 of this chapter. [231] Chapter 5, pp. 105–8.

Special trusts

Where an institution is removed from the register because it was never charitable and property is held on special charitable trusts,[232] these special trusts will not be removed from the register and will usually have a new trustee appointed by scheme of the Commission.[233] Special trusts are defined as:

> property which is held and administered by or on behalf of a charity for any special purposes of the charity, and is so held and administered on separate trusts relating only to that property[234]

The position of special trusts provides a further illustration of how the effect of removal might be limited.

Rectification

The time when the presumption of charitable status is lost, depends on whether an institution is removed because it was never a charity or was a charity but has ceased to be so.

Section 4(1) Charities Act 1993 reads:

> An institution shall for all purposes other than rectification of the register be conclusively presumed to be or have been a charity at any time when it is or was on the register of charities.

It is not clear what the grounds are for rectification of the register because they are not set out in section 4(1). The natural construction of rectification is that an institution has been mistakenly registered. Where an institution is removed from the register because the Commission no longer considers the institution to be a charity[235] on the grounds that it was never a charity[236] then it will lose the presumption of charitable status from its inception. In such a case HM Revenue and Customs would examine the institution's historical right to receive and continue to receive tax reliefs. If HM Revenue and Customs agreed with the Commission that the institution was never a charity then tax could be reclaimed in relation to the period the institution was awarded tax reliefs.[237]

[232] S. 97(1) Charities Act 1993. See Chapter 2, pp. 14–18. [233] S. 16(1)(b) Charities Act 1993.
[234] *Ibid.* [235] S. 3(4) Charities Act 1993. [236] See pp. 53–65 of this chapter.
[237] An institution ceasing to be charitable could be liable for capital gains tax and inheritance tax charges. Section 256(2)(a) Taxation of Chargeable Gains Act 1992 provides that, if property held on charitable trusts ceases to be held on charitable trusts, the trustees are to be treated as having disposed of the property for a consideration equal to its market value, with any gain on the disposal being treated as not accruing to the charity. Furthermore, section 256(2)(b) Taxation of Chargeable Gains Act 1992 provides that if and so far as any of that property represents, directly or indirectly, the consideration for the disposal of assets by the trustees, any gain accruing on that disposal shall be treated as not accruing to a charity. Under section 70 of the Inheritance Tax Act 1984, where settled property has been held 'for charitable purposes' only until the end of a period (whether defined by date or in some other way), there is to be an

On the other hand, if a charity is removed from the register under Section 3(4) Charities Act 1993 on the basis that it has 'ceased to exist' or 'does not operate' then the time when the presumption of charitable status is lost is when the institution is removed from the register. This is because an institution is presumed to be a charity 'at any time when it is or was on the register of charities'.[238] An exception to an institution enjoying the benefit of the presumption of charitable status until the date of removal is where the Commission no longer considers the institution to be a charity[239] due to 'any change in its trusts' in which case the date that the loss of charitable status takes place is the date at which the change takes place and not the date of removal. This is because section 3(5) Charities Act 1993 says:

> If the removal of an institution under subsection (4)(a) above is due to any change in its trusts, the removal shall take effect from the date of that change.

'Trusts' are defined as:

> the provisions establishing it as a charity and regulating its purposes and administration, whether those provisions take effect by way of trust or not, and in relation to other institutions has a corresponding meaning.[240]

It is submitted that removal from the register due to a change in 'trusts' could only be due to a loss of one or more of the essential indicia of charitable status which were outlined in Chapter 2.[241]

This interpretation of section 4(1) is supported by Hansard. During debates on section 4(3) Charities Act 1960[242] which was the predecessor to sections 3(4) and 3(5) Charities Act 1993, the Solicitor General said:

> the Commissioners cannot take a charity from the register retrospectively except in the solitary case of a change of purposes which is dealt with by Clause 4 (3).[243]

inheritance tax charge when the property ceases to be held for charitable purposes. For further reference see C McCall QC and G Newey QC 'Charities that Charge: The Impact of the Strategy Unit Report and the Charities Bill 2004' (Maitland Chambers, 6 July 2004). For a review of the tax reliefs available to charities see J Kessler QC *The Taxation of Charities*, 5th edn (London: Key Haven, 2005). The position of each charity will vary but for an assessment of the implications of the loss of charitable status for Nuffield Hospitals see *Joint Committee on the Draft Charities Bill Minutes of Evidence Supplementary Memorandum from Nuffield Hospitals (DCH 333)* www.parliament.the-stationary-office.co.uk/pa/jt200304/jtselect/jtchar/167/406. In practice HM Revenue & Customs may consider concessonary treatment where an institution has been mistakenly registered through no fault of the promoters, as in the case of the *School Fee Planning Charities* [1996] Ch.Com.A.R. paras. 187–191.

238 S. 4(1) Charities Act 1993. 239 S. 3(4)(a) Charities Act 1993.

240 S. 97(1) Charities Act 1993. 241 See Chapter 2, pp. 12–18.

242 S. 4(3) Charities Act 1960 refers to 'any change in its purposes or trusts.'

243 Hansard, Commons 1959–60 Vol. 626, 21 July 1960 p. 874.

Note that the Solicitor General was talking about a 'charity' being removed rather than an 'institution' which was never a charity. It is submitted that he did not refer to this situation because it would have been taken as read that for an institution to have been registered it must have originally been a charity. It is also submitted that when he referred to 'a change of purposes' it would have been more accurate to refer to the removal of one or more of the essential indicia[244] of charitable status.

To conclude, in respect of rectification under section 4(1) Charities Act 1993 it is only where an institution was never a charity that the loss of the presumption of charitable status dates back to its inception. Where under section 3(5) Charities Act 1993 the removal is due to 'any change in its trusts' the date of the loss of the presumption of charitable status is the date at which the change takes place and not the date of removal. In all other cases the presumption of charitable status will be retained by institutions along with charity tax reliefs until the date of removal. The retention of tax reliefs until the date of removal will limit the effect of removal for many institutions.

This analysis may have harsh consequences for charities whose trustees have not deliberately misled the Commission when applying for registration. There is a need for the law to be clarified to protect innocent charities and their donors from being unfairly treated.[245]

An institution was a charity but is no longer charitable

Introduction

Where an institution was a charity but is no longer so there are two reasons why the Commission's powers of removal are limited. First, where the institution's objects have ceased to be charitable due to the passage of time or a change in social circumstances its property can be rescued by a *cy-pres* scheme.[246] Second, even where a charity amends its objects from charitable to non-charitable purposes its original property will be held for charitable purposes.[247]

Cy-pres where the institution was a charity but is no longer charitable

Section 13(1) Charities Act 1993 provides:

> Subject to subsection (2) below,[248] the circumstances in which the original purposes of a charitable gift can be altered to allow the property given or part of it to be applied cy-pres shall be as follows…

[244] See Chapter 2, pp. 12–18.
[245] See Chapter 7, pp. 137–140 for arguments under the Human Rights Act 1998 and Chapter 2, pp. 69–71 for the need for clarification.
[246] Section 13(1)(e)(ii) Charities Act 1993. See also *National Anti-Vivisection Society* v. *IRC* [1948] AC 31 *per* Lord Simonds at 74.
[247] Pp. 73–75 of this Chapter.
[248] S. 13(2) Charities Act 1993 reads as follows: 'Subsection (1) above shall not affect the conditions which must be satisfied in order that property given for charitable purposes may

Section 13(1)(e)(ii) Charities Act 1993 provides one of the circumstances for a *cy-pres* application:

> Where the original purposes, in whole or in part, have, since they were laid down … ceased, as being useless or harmful to the community or for other reasons, to be in law charitable

The common law basis for this statutory provision is the House of Lords decision *National Anti-Vivisection Society* v. *IRC*.[249] In that case Lord Simonds looked, *obiter*, at the question of whether a charity which was once regarded as charitable could ever cease to be regarded as such. He contrasted this with an institution which, although mistakenly held by the court to be so, was never charitable. Lord Simonds said:[250]

> A bequest in the will of a testator dying in 1700 might be held valid on the evidence then before the Court but on different evidence held invalid if he died in 1900. So, too, I conceive that an anti-vivisection society might at different times be differently regarded. But this is not to say that a charitable trust, when it has once been established can ever fail. If by a change in social habits and needs, or, it may be, by a change in the law the purpose of an established charity becomes superfluous or even illegal, or if, with increasing knowledge it appears that a purpose once thought beneficial is truly detrimental to the community, it is the duty of trustees of an established charity to apply to the Court or in suitable cases to the Charity Commissioners or in educational charities to the Minister of Education and ask that a cy-pres scheme may be established.[251] And I conceive that there might be cases in which the Attorney General would think it his duty to intervene to that end. A charity once established does not die, though its nature may be changed. But it is wholly consistent with this that in a later age the Court should decline to regard as charitable a purpose, to which in an earlier age that quality would have been ascribed, with the result that (unless a general purpose would fail unless charitable intention could be found) a gift for that purpose would fail. I cannot share the apprehension of the Master of the Rolls that great confusion will be caused if the Court declines to be bound by the beliefs and knowledge of a past age in considering whether a particular purpose is today for the benefit of the community. But if it is so, then I say that it is the lesser of two evils.

In a later judgment[252] Lord Simonds added:

> I do not seek to qualify what I recently said in National Anti-Vivisection Society v. IRC that there may be circumstances in which the Court will in a later age hold an object not to be charitable which has in earlier ages been

be applied *cy-pres* except in so far as those conditions require a failure of the original purposes.'

249 *National Anti-Vivisection Society* v. *IRC* [1948] AC 31. 250 *Ibid.* at 74.

251 Now section 13(1)(e)(ii) Charities Act 1993 which provides for a *cy-pres* application where the objects of a charity 'have ceased to be in law to be charitable'.

252 *Gilmour* v. *Coats* [1949] AC 426 at 443.

> held to possess that virtue. And the converse case may be possible. That degree of uncertainty in the law must be admitted. But I would ask your Lordships to say that it is only a radical change of circumstances, established by sufficient evidence, that should compel the Court to accept a new view of this matter.

These passages indicate that once a charity has been established it cannot cease to be charitable because its objects have become dated and that it must be a 'radical change of circumstances' which causes the court to think in terms of *cy-pres*[253] application of a charity's property.

The Commission have questioned whether the property of a charitable company will be held for charitable purposes where, due to a change in social circumstances, its objects cease to be charitable.[254] This is because a charitable company does not hold its general property on charitable trusts[255] and therefore it could be argued that it would continue to hold its property beneficially for its objects which would be non-charitable.

It is argued in Chapter 5[256] that the better view is that the Court would treat a charitable company's property as being dedicated for charitable purposes,[257] so that the result would be the same as if the property were held on charitable trusts: namely, that the directors would be under an obligation to apply for a *cy-pres*[258] scheme.

The obligation to apply property *cy-pres* where an institution was originally charitable but has ceased to be so due to the passage of time or a change in social circumstances will limit the Commission's power of removal because the property will be applied for charitable purposes.

'Any change in its trusts'

An institution can be removed from the register which the Commission 'no longer considers is a charity'[259] when there is 'any change in its trusts'.[260] What is meant by '*trusts*'?

'Trusts' in relation to a charity are defined in Section 97(1) Charities Act 1993 as:

> the provisions establishing it as a charity and regulating its purposes and administration, whether those provisions take effect by way of trust or not, and in relation to other institutions has corresponding meaning.

253 S. 13(1)(e)(ii) Charities Act 1993.

254 RR 6 *Maintenance of an Accurate Register of Charities* (2000) Annex E. See also Dutton, J., 'Charitable Companies Ceasing to be Charitable' 7 CL & PR, 1, 2001, p. 31.

255 *Liverpool and District Hospital for Diseases of the Heart* v. *AG* [1981] 1 Ch 193 *per* Slade J at 214.

256 Chapter 5, pp. 108–12. 257 *Re Vernon's Will Trusts* [1972] Ch 300.

258 S. 13(1)(e)(ii) Charities Act 1993.

259 S. 3(4) Charities Act 1993. 260 S. 3(5) Charities Act 1993.

Removal from the register due to a change in 'trusts' could only be due to a loss of one or more of the essential indicia of charitable status which were outlined in Chapter 2.[261]

The position is straightforward for unincorporated charities. A change of charitable purposes to non-charitable purposes by an unincorporated charity will result in the charity ceasing to be charitable.[262] This will rarely happen in practice for two reasons. First, where a charity has a gross income in its last financial year of not more than £10,000,[263] does not hold 'designated land'[264] and is not a company or other body corporate,[265] then although the charity trustees may resolve[266] to amend the purposes of a charity they can only replace purposes with purposes which are charitable purposes.[267] Furthermore, the Commission's consent is required before the resolution is effective.[268] Second, the Commission insists, at the registration stage, that powers of amendment in the governing instrument are expressed to be subject to the prior consent of the Commission. Therefore, in practice, non-charitable objects could only be adopted as a result of a mistake by the Commission when giving prior approval to the adoption of new objects.[269]

The purported exercise of a power to amend the objects of a charitable company will not be effective, irrespective of what is contained in the Memorandum and Articles of Association, without the prior written consent of the Commission.[270] Again non-charitable objects could only be adopted as a result of a mistake by the Commission when giving prior written approval to the adoption of new objects.

Removal of a charity where there has been 'any change in its trusts'[271] is not an additional ground for removal. It is merely a reason why the Commission

[261] See Chapter 2, pp. 12–18.

[262] See Chapter 2, pp. 20–22. For the position of property see Chapter 5, pp. 108–12.

[263] S. 74C(1)(a) Charities Act 1993.

[264] S. 74C(1)(b) Charities Act 1993. 'Designated Land' is defined in section 74C(1) Charities Act 1993 as 'land held on trusts which stipulate that it is to be used that it is to be used for the purposes, or any particular purposes, of the charity'.

[265] S. 74C(1)(c) Charities Act 1993. [266] S. 74C(2) Charities Act 1993.

[267] S. 74C(3) Charities Act 1993. [268] S. 74C(9) & 74A(1)(a) Charities Act 1993.

[269] For an example of the Commission mistakenly approving non-charitable objects as charitable objects see *Scott Baden Commonwealth Ltd* [1967] Ch.Com.A.R. 48, App D, Pt 2.

[270] S. 64(2)(2A)(a) Charities Act 1993. Note that a charitable company can convert to a Community Interest Company but any property acquired under any disposition or agreement previously made otherwise than for full consideration in money or money's worth, or any property representing property so acquired, any property representing income which has previously accrued, or income from any such property will remain held for charitable purposes. See section 39(3)(a)-(c) Companies (Audit, Investigations and Community Enterprise) Act 2004. In such circumstances the CIC would become the trustee of the charitable property which would continue to be registered on the Charities Register if it met the registration thresholds: see Chapter 1, pp. 12–13. For this reason it is unlikely that many charitable companies will apply to become CICs.

[271] S. 3(5) Charities Act 1993.

might no longer consider an institution to be a charity.[272] It will be shown in Chapter 5[273] even where charities amend their purposes from charitable to non-charitable their original property prior to the amendment will be held on trust for charitable purposes irrespective of whether the governing instrument is removed.

'Ceased to exist'

The Commission has the power to remove charities which have ceased to *'exist'*.[274] In order to analyse what is meant by *'ceased to exist'* there is a need to distinguish between the governing instrument as machinery for holding property and administering a charity[275] and the abstract concept of charity distinct from its governing instrument.[276] For example, an incorporated or an unincorporated charity's governing instrument will cease to exist when it is dissolved[277] but so long as there is property available for charitable purposes albeit with a new governing instrument, for example, where it has been transferred to another charity[278] then charity in its broader sense, as distinct from its original governing instrument, will survive.[279] In turn, this will limit the Commission's powers of removal to a certain extent.

Therefore, a charity's governing instrument might be removed from the register but its property continue to be applied for charitable purposes. A charity cannot cease to exist simply because its purposes have become outdated.[280] Where a charity's property has been applied *cy-pres* by way of a scheme[281] of the Commission, either by providing the governing instrument with updated charitable purposes, or by transferring the property to another charity with different charitable purposes, the charity's governing instrument will change in form but its property will continue to be held for charity. How a charity's governing instrument or property ceases to exist will differ according to whether it is unincorporated, such as a trust or an unincorporated association, or incorporated, such as a charitable company limited by guarantee.

Even when a charity has ceased to exist, the Commission's power of removal will be limited because there will be occasions when the charity's governing instrument and its property can survive. For example, in the case of a charitable company it could be restored to the register,[282] a charitable company's property having been deemed *bona vacantia* could be applied *cy-pres* by

[272] S. 3(4) Charities Act 1993. [273] Chapter 5, pp. 108–12. [274] S. 3(4) Charities Act 1993.
[275] *Re Vernon's Will Trusts* [1972] Ch 300 at 304. See Chapter 5, pp. 105–8.
[276] *Ibid. per* Buckley J at 304. [277] *Re Roberts* [1963] 1 WLR 406.
[278] See sections 13, 16, 26, 18(2)(ii) or 74 Charities Act 1993 for the Commission's powers to assist in the transfer of charitable property.
[279] *Re Vernon's Will Trusts* [1972] Ch 300 *per* Buckley J at 304.
[280] S. 13 Charities Act 1993. See *National Anti-Vivisection Society* v. *IRC* [1948] AC 31. Under section 13(5) charity trustees have a duty to apply for a *cy-pres* scheme.
[281] S. 13 Charities Act 1993. [282] S. 63(3) Charities Act 1993.

the Crown.[283] For all charities with special trusts, those trusts will survive even if a charity ceases to exist and will fall to be transferred by way of a scheme to be held by new trustees.[284]

The position will now be analysed according to whether a charity is a trust without permanent endowment, a trust with permanent endowment, an unincorporated association or a corporate charity.

Trusts

The position differs according to whether a charitable trust has permanent endowment.[285]

Trusts without permanent endowment

A charitable trust without permanent endowment can be terminated in a number of ways. A trust can be terminated by its trustees exercising a power of termination.[286] A trust can be terminated by its trustees exhausting its assets in furtherance of its charitable purposes.[287] The same principle[288] would apply where a trust has no funds because its liabilities exceed its assets. A trust can be terminated by its trustees transferring assets to another charity under a power in the trust deed or by order of the Commission.[289] Alternatively, the trustees of an unincorporated charity[290] with a gross income in its last financial year of less than £10,000[291] which does not hold *'designated land'*[292] can resolve, where it is expedient in the interests of the transferor charity,[293] and the purposes of the receiving charity are substantially similar,[294] with the consent[295] of the Commission, to transfer the property of the charity to another charity. A charitable trust can cease to exist because it is established for a limited period of time[296] or where the property reverts.[297] A charitable trust can cease to exist where its objects are dependent on a particular institution which closes or premises which cease to be available.[298] Property can also be applied *cy-pres*

[283] *Re Slevin* [1891] 2 Ch 326. [284] S. 16(1)(b) Charities Act 1993.

[285] S. 96(3) Charities Act 1993 defines 'permanent endowment' as follows: 'A charity shall be deemed for the purposes of the Act to have a permanent endowment unless all property held for the purposes of the charity may be expended for those purposes without distinction between capital and income, and in this Act 'permanent endowment' means, in relation to any charity, property held subject to a restriction on its being expended for the purposes of the charity.'

[286] *Re Roberts* [1963] 1 WLR 406. [287] *Re Withall* [1932] 2 Ch 236. [288] *Ibid.*

[289] Where there is no such power in the trust deed then an application can be made to the Commission for authority under section 26 Charities Act 1993.

[290] S. 74(1)(c) Charities Act 1993. [291] S. 74(1)(b) Charities Act 1993.

[292] S. 74(1)(a) Charities Act 1993. Section 74(1) Charities Act 1993 defines 'designated land' as 'land held on trusts which stipulate that it is to be used for the purposes, or any particular purposes, of the charity'.

[293] S. 74(4)(a) Charities Act 1993. [294] S. 74(4)(b) Charities Act 1993.

[295] S. 74A(2) Charities Act 1993. [296] *Re J W Laing Trust* [1984] Ch 143.

[297] See the Reverter of Sites Act 1987.

[298] *Re Rymer* [1895] 1 Ch. 19; *Re Slatter's Will Trust* [1972] Ch 286.

for the objects of another charity[299] leaving the governing instrument to be removed from the register. The Commission could make a scheme for the administration of a charity which could then replace the trust deed.[300] The Commission could also use its protective power to make a scheme for the administration of a charity which could replace the existing trust deed.[301]

It is arguable, where the Commission makes a scheme which transfers property to another charity, that a charitable trust will survive.[302] The rationale for this argument is that the Commission does not have the power to destroy charity by way of a scheme,[303] although there might be several reasons why this might not be so in the case of a charitable trust without permanent endowment.

First, the authority for this proposition is *Re Faraker*,[304] which concerned a trust with permanent endowment. Second, the decision is inconsistent with the principle that a charitable trust without permanent endowment will terminate when its assets have been exhausted.[305] Logic dictates that a transfer by way of a scheme of the Commission has a similar effect. Third, the scheme transferring property from a charitable trust would not directly destroy the trust. It would be the consequential effect of transferring the property that would have this effect.

Even where a trust without permanent endowment transfers its property, as described above, to another charity, although the trust will terminate (arguably where the transfer is by way of a scheme of the Commission)[306] because it will have exhausted its assets[307] its property will continue to be applied by another charity for charitable purposes. Furthermore, even where a charity ceases to exist its special trust property will survive and will be transferred by the Commission to new trustees.[308] In these instances the effect of removal will be limited as only the governing instrument will be removed.

Trusts with permanent endowment

The permanent endowment of a charitable trust cannot, without authority,[309] be expended as income and capital. Section 96(3) Charities Act 1993 defines 'permanent endowment' as follows:

> A charity shall be deemed for the purposes of the Act to have a permanent endowment unless all property held for the purposes of the charity may be expended for those purposes without distinction between capital and income, and in this Act 'permanent endowment' means, in relation to any charity, property held subject to a restriction on its being expended for the purposes of the charity.

[299] S. 13 Charities Act 1993. [300] S. 16(1)(a) Charities Act 1993.
[301] S. 18(2)(ii) Charities Act 1993. [302] *Re Faraker* [1912] 2 Ch 488.
[303] *Ibid. per* Farwell LJ at 495. [304] *Re Faraker* [1912] 2 Ch. 488.
[305] *Re Withall* [1932] 2 Ch 236. [306] *Ante.* [307] *Re Withall* [1932] 2 Ch 236.
[308] S. 16(1)(b) Charities Act 1993. [309] S. 75, 75A & 75B Charities Act 1993.

A trust with only permanent endowment will continue indefinitely except in four instances where it no longer has permanent endowment.[310]

First, a charitable trust can cease to exist because it is established for a limited period of time[311] or where the property reverts.[312]

Second, a charity will be brought to an end if its objects are dependent on a particular institution or premises and the institution closes or the premises are no longer available.[313]

Third, trustees of an unincorporated charity with permanent endowment and an income can resolve, with the consent of the Commission, to spend the permanent endowment if, *inter alia*, it is satisfied that the purposes set out in the trusts could be carried out more effectively and in that way terminate the trust.[314] There are extra requirements where the capital of the fund is given by a particular individual,[315] a particular institution[316] or by two or more individuals or institutions in the pursuit of a common purpose,[317] and the relevant charity's gross income exceeds £1,000 in its last financial year, and the market value of the permanent endowment exceeds £10,000. Here the Commission might direct the charity trustees to give public notice[318] and take into account representations.[319] Before concurring with the resolution to spend permanent endowment the Commission must take into account any evidence available to it as to the wishes of the donor or donors,[320] and any changes in circumstances relating to the charity, such as the making of the gift or gifts including, in particular, its financial position, the needs of its beneficiaries, and the social, economic and legal environment in which it operates.[321] The Commission must not concur with the resolution unless it is satisfied that freeing the fund from its restrictions would be within the spirit of the gift[322] and that the charity trustees have complied with the obligations imposed by them under section 75A Charities Act 1993. Section 75B Charities Act 1993 allows for the expenditure of permanent endowment which is held on special trusts[323] on the same terms as described above.

Fourth, the trustees of an unincorporated charity with a gross income in its last financial year of less than £10,000 which does not hold designated land can resolve, in the circumstances described in the previous paragraph[324] and, with the consent of the Commission, to transfer the property of a charity to another charity.[325]

[310] *Re Withall* [1932] 2 Ch 236. [311] *Re J W Laing Trust* [1984] Ch 143.
[312] See the Reverter of Sites Act 1987.
[313] *Re Rymer* [1895] 1 Ch 19; *Re Slatter's Will Trust* [1972] Ch. 286.
[314] S. 75 Charities Act 1993. [315] S. 75A(1)(a)(i) Charities Act 1993.
[316] S. 75A(1)(a)(ii) Charities Act 1993. [317] S. 75A(1)(a)(iii) Charities Act 1993.
[318] S. 75A(6)(a) Charities Act 1993. [319] S. 75A(6)(b) Charities Act 1993.
[320] S. 75A(8)(a) Charities Act 1993. [321] S. 75A(8)(b) Charities Act 1993.
[322] S. 75A(9)(a) Charities Act 1993.
[323] As a result of a direction under section 96(5) Charities Act 1993.
[324] Pp. 76–77 of this chapter. [325] S. 74, 74A & 74B Charities Act 1993.

Where the Commission transfers permanent endowment by way of a scheme[326] it is arguable that the charitable trust will survive because it does not have the power to destroy charity by way of a scheme.[327] *Re Faraker*[328] shows that the argument is stronger than in the case of a charitable trust without permanent endowment because that case concerned a charitable trust with permanent endowment. On the other hand, where permanent endowment has been transferred, this should lead to the termination of the trust if it has no other assets in the same way that it would terminate if its assets are exhausted.[329] It would not be the scheme which would directly destroy the trust, but the transfer of property that would have this effect.

Other than section 75, 75A and 75B Charities Act 1993 the only way in which the trustees could expend all the permanent endowment of the charity would be if the court gave authorisation. There are no recorded precedents of the court providing itself or the Commission with a general power to expend permanent endowment with a view to terminating a charitable trust. The authorities relate to particular circumstances and cannot be said to illustrate a general power by the court or the Commission to authorise the expenditure of permanent endowment without recoupment.

In *Andrews* v. *M'Guffog*[330] the trustees spent some capital as income in order to build a school in accordance with the testator's wishes which proved to be more costly than the funds provided for this purpose. The House of Lords distinguished between the charity intended to be created and the means by which this purpose was directed to be achieved. The question as to whether recoupment would be required was remitted back to the Court of Session. In *Re Willenhall Chapel Estates*[331] the court allowed part of a permanent endowment fund set aside to maintain an incumbent to be used to repair the chapel at which he officiated and which formed part of the charity's property. The court distinguished between charities with numerous beneficiaries where recoupment would be the usual course of action, and this case where the incumbent was the sole beneficiary of the income, and was willing to give that income up. Finally, in *AG* v. *Day*[332] the court ordered that costs be met out of a permanent endowment fund where an order to pay out of accumulated income would prejudice the persons entitled to costs. All three cases show that it will only be in exceptional cases that the court will authorise the expenditure of permanent endowment without recoupment.

The Commission has no general power to vary the terms of permanent endowment. Its only statutory powers in relation to the expenditure or transfer of permanent endowment are contained in sections 74 to 75 Charities Act 1993. Section 26 Charities Act 1993 prohibits the authorisation of an act 'expressly

[326] S. 16(1)(a) Charities Act 1993. [327] *Re Faraker* [1912] 2 Ch 488 *per* Farwell LJ at 495.
[328] *Ibid.* [329] *Re Withall* [1932] 2 Ch 236. [330] *Andrews* v. *M'Guffog* [1886] 11 AC 313.
[331] *Re Willenhall Chapel Estates* [1865] 2 Dr & Sm 467.
[332] *AG* v. *Day* [1900] 1 Ch 31.

prohibited by Act of Parliament … or by the trusts of the charity.' Arguably, the authorisation of the expenditure of permanent endowment is generally forbidden by the Charities Act 1993[333] (except where provided by section 75, 75A and 75B) and also forbidden by the trusts of the charity.[334] That argument is even stronger where the authorisation is given with a view to terminating the charity. One of the Commission's general objectives is to promote the effective use of charitable resources[335] and not to destroy charities.[336]

The presence of permanent endowment will therefore limit the Commission's scope for removing charities on the basis of them ceasing to 'exist'. Even where a charity with permanent endowment has 'ceased to exist' its special trust property will survive and be transferred by the Commission to new trustees.[337]

Unincorporated associations

As an unincorporated association tends to be construed by the court as holding its property on trust for the purposes of the association[338] the principles[339] in relation to trusts and the limits on the Commission's powers of removal will govern the termination of unincorporated associations.

Companies limited by guarantee

Even where a company ceases to exist, there are a number of ways in which the charity can survive. The company could be restored to the register,[340] its property having been deemed *bona vacantia* could be applied *cy-pres* by the Crown,[341] or where special trusts are transferred by way of a scheme to new trustees.[342] In such instances the effect of removal will be limited.

Before examining the ways in which a charity can survive in more detail, it is necessary to examine how a company can cease to exist and as a result be removed from the register of charities.[343] A company will cease to exist when it is struck off the register of companies, where it is not carrying on business, or is not in operation.[344] It will also cease to exist where it is voluntarily wound-up by the members or compulsorily by the court.[345]

333 S. 96(3) Charities Act 1993.
334 For a discussion of the expenditure of permanent endowment in the context of total return see Hill, J. and Smith, J. 'Permanent Endowment and Total Return' 7, CL & PR, 2, 2001, pp. 125–130 and Dutton, J. 'Endowed Charities: A Total Return Approach to Investment?' 7 CL & PR, 2, 2001, pp. 131–135.
335 S. 1B(3)4. Charities Act 1993.
336 *Re Faraker* [1912] 2 Ch 488 *per* Farwell J at 495.
337 S. 16(1)(b) Charities Act 1993.
338 *Neville Estates Ltd* v. *Madden* [1962] Ch 832.
339 See pp. 76–77 of this chapter.
340 S. 63(3) Charities Act 1993.
341 *Re Slevin* [1891] 2 Ch. 326.
342 S. 16(1)(b) Charities Act 1993.
343 Under section 3(4) Charities Act 1993.
344 S. 1000 Companies Act 2006.
345 These procedures are provided for by the Insolvency Act 1986 as amended by the Enterprise Act 2002.

Striking off

A company is dissolved without any winding-up when the company is struck off the register of companies by the Registrar of Companies if he has reasonable cause to believe that a company is not carrying on business, or is not in operation after sending a letter to the company inquiring whether that is the case.[346] Once a statutory procedure has been followed, the Registrar may strike the company off the register of companies and the company will be dissolved.[347]

In addition section 1003 Companies Act 2006 allows the directors of a company which has not, in the previous three months, *inter alia*,[348] traded or otherwise carried on business to apply to the Registrar of Companies to have the company struck off the register and dissolved.[349]

Petitions to wind up a company

In addition to a winding-up petition being presented by persons such as members and creditors, the Attorney General has the power to present a petition.[350] He may decide to do so, for example, where a charitable company is inactive, has failed to file annual returns over a long period of time and difficulties have arisen over dealings with property.[351]

The Commission also has the power to present a winding-up petition.[352] It can only do so after it has instituted an inquiry[353] and is satisfied that there is or has been misconduct or mismanagement in the administration of the charity or that it is necessary or desirable to act for the purpose of protecting the property of the charity.[354]

The survival of charity following dissolution

Even where the charitable company has been dissolved there are a number of ways in which charity can survive either in terms of its governing instrument or its general or special trust property. First, where the company is restored to the register.[355] Second, where the Crown applies the property deemed *bona vacantia cy-pres* for charitable purposes.[356] Third, where the company holds special trusts which are then transferred by scheme to new trustees.[357] In these instances removal will be limited.

[346] S. 1000 Companies Act 2006. [347] *Ibid.* [348] See section 1003(1) Companies Act 2006.

[349] An email to the author from Companies House dated 5 April 2006 confirmed that there were no statistics available for the reasons why applications were made under section 652 Companies Act 1985, the predecessor to section 1000 Companies Act 2006.

[350] S. 63(1) Charities Act 1993.

[351] See *Liverpool & District Hospital for Diseases of the Heart* v. *AG* [1981] 1 Ch 193 at 200.

[352] S. 63(2) Charities Act 1993. [353] Under section 8 Charities Act 1993.

[354] The conditions laid down by section 18(1)(a) & (b) Charities Act 1993.

[355] S. 63(4) Charities Act 1993. [356] See p. 82 of this Chapter.

[357] S. 16(1)(b) Charities Act 1993.

Restoration to the register

A charitable company which has been dissolved may have its dissolution declared void[358] on application to the Registrar[359] by a former director or member, or on application to the court[360] by an interested party[361] including the Commission[362] with the same effect.[363] Furthermore, the Commission can apply to have a company restored to the register of companies where it has been struck off under section 1000 Companies Act 2006.[364] This power may, typically, be exercised by the court where the assets of a charitable company are in the hands of third parties who were not included in the winding-up. Therefore, the court may make the order to restore the company to the register of companies to allow proceedings to be taken to recover those assets.[365] Where the restoration of a charitable company to the register of companies in turn leads to its restoration onto the register of charities the effect of removal will be limited.

Bona vacantia property applied *cy-pres* by the Crown

The general property of a charitable company is not held on trust but is held subject to a legally binding obligation to apply the property for charitable purposes.[366] The position is analogous to a trust but strictly speaking the property is not held on trust.[367] On dissolution, any remaining general property will be deemed to be *bona vacantia*.[368] However, the Crown will as a matter of custom apply the property to charitable purposes through the exercise of its *cy-pres* prerogative.[369] Where the property of a charity is applied *cy-pres* for charitable purposes, this will limit the effect of removal.

358 S. 1028(1) Companies Act 2006. 359 S. 1024(1) Companies Act 2006.
360 S. 1029(1) Companies Act 2006. 361 S. 1029(2) Companies Act 2006.
362 S. 63(3) Charities Act 1993. 363 S. 1032(1) Companies Act 2006.
364 S. 63(4) Charities Act 1993.
365 See J. Warburton, *Tudor on Charities*, 9th edn (London: Butterworths, 2003) pp. 510–511, paras. 13–14. The court has refused to make an order for restoration to allow a company to take a legacy under a will of a testator who died after the date of dissolution. The court decided this on the basis that to do so would dispossess other persons who obtained a vested interest in the property under a title not derived from the company: see *Re Servers of The Blind League* [1960] 1 WLR 564 at 565.
366 *Liverpool and District Hospital for Diseases of the Heart* v. *AG* [1981] 1 Ch 193 *per* Slade J at 214. Note that Companies cannot hold their general property as permanent endowment, which is not held on trust, because under section (2) and (2A) Charities Act 2006 the members of a company can amend the provisions of the memorandum and articles of association including any restriction on property being expended as capital or income.
367 *Liverpool and District Hospital for Diseases of the Heart* v. *AG* [1981] 1 Ch 193 *per* Slade J at 214; *Re Vernon's Will Trusts* [1972] Ch 300.
368 S. 1012(1) Companies Act 2006. 369 *Re Slevin* [1891] 2 Ch. 326.

Special trusts

Where a charitable company holds special trust property as a trustee[370] this property will not form part of the general property of the company and will survive dissolution.[371] In such cases the court or the Commission will need to appoint a new trustee.[372] The survival of special trust property will limit the effect of removal.

The survival of charity following dissolution – Conclusion

Even where the charitable company has been dissolved there are a number of ways in which charity can survive either in terms of its governing instrument or its general or special trust property.[373]

'Does not operate'

For the reasons explained earlier in this chapter[374] a charity 'does not operate' where it does not qualify for registration[375] because it does not have a gross income of £5,000 or £100,000 in the case of an excepted charity[376] and yet legally exists.

It is arguable that the Commission can use this power to remove charities which are not carrying out charitable activities. However, this interpretation is not supported in this book.[377] The interpretation of the power to remove charities which do not 'operate' supported in this book would limit the Commission's power of removal.

Ominously, the Commission's Annual Report 2000–2001 makes reference to 'inactive charities'.[378] The Commission set up a special project in 1999 to investigate why charities which had not updated their details for four years had failed to do so. At the end of March 2001, of the 18,800 charities originally identified as being inactive, just over 700 were still being investigated by the Commission. The remainder had either been removed from the register or were confirmed as still being active. No further details were given about the criteria for being inactive or, indeed, the value of the charities' assets. The Commission has indicated that it intends to continue to identify inactive charities.[379]

It is disturbing to note that the then Chief Commissioner, when questioned by the Public Accounts Committee on the criteria for removal of inactive

[370] *Liverpool and District Hospital for Diseases of the Heart* v. *AG* [1981] 1 Ch 193 at 214.

[371] S. 1012(1) Companies Act 2006 exempts property held by a company on trust from being deemed *bona vacantia*.

[372] S. 16(1)(b) Charities Act 1993.

[373] As shown by pp. 75–83 of this Chapter.

[374] P. 8 of this chapter.

[375] S. 3A(2)(d) Charities Act 1993.

[376] S. 3A(2)(b) & (c) Charities Act 1993.

[377] See pp. 50–52 of this chapter.

[378] [2000/1] Ch. Com. A. R. p. 15, para. 5.3.

[379] See *Briefing Paper For The Joint Committee on The Draft Charities Bill Charity Commission – The Future* (September 2004).

charities, was unable to give an overall valuation for the assets held by the charities which had been removed.[380] Furthermore, it will be shown in Chapter 6[381] that the Commission is describing charities that are removed because they have governance problems as not operating which suggests that it might have introduced an activities test for continuation on the register.

Conclusion

To conclude, the Commission's powers of removal under section 3(4) Charities Act 1993 ('no longer considers is a charity', 'ceased to exist' or 'does not operate') are limited. Institutions removed as a result of rectification[382] of the register will retain their tax reliefs until the date of removal, except where they were never charitable or where they are removed because they have amended their trusts.[383] It is argued that this interpretation of section 4(1) Charities Act 1993 further limits the effect of removal.

The overall conclusion of this chapter is that the Commission's powers of removal are limited.

380 Public Accounts Committee, 28 November 2000, reported in *Charity Finance*, December 2001.
381 Chapter 6, pp. 121–3. 382 S. 4(1) Charities Act 1993. 383 S. 3(5) Charities Act 1993.

4

Limits on the Commission's powers to remove controversial charities from the register

Introduction

This chapter seeks to illustrate three of the basic propositions of this book[1] through an examination of three types of controversial charity.

The first basic proposition is that the Commission's powers of removal are limited.[2] The second basic proposition is that there is a fundamental problem of legality with the Commission deciding whether an institution does not have charitable objects, and should therefore be removed from the register because the Commission does not have law making powers.[3] The third basic proposition is that there is a need for greater clarity about the Commission's powers of removal.[4] A related question is the legal uncertainty surrounding charitable status.[5]

This chapter examines examples of controversial charities through case studies. These are charities connected to the state either through funding agreements or trusteeship,[6] schools which charge fees[7] and new religious movement charities.[8] Each of the case studies illustrates the three basic propositions described above.

The methodology employed in this chapter is first to describe each of the types of charity and explain why they are controversial; second, to set out the possible grounds for removal based on indications given by the Commission; third, to make a critical analysis of those possible grounds for removal; and fourth, to demonstrate how that critical analysis illustrates the basic propositions.

Charities connected to the state

The first category of controversial charities to be explored in this chapter is charities connected to the state.

[1] Chapter 1, pp. 1–4. [2] See Chapter 3, pp. 45–52. [3] *Ibid.*
[4] Chapter 2, pp. 12–18. [5] *Ibid.* [6] Pp. 85–89 of this chapter. [7] Pp. 89–93 of this chapter.
[8] P. 94 of this chapter. See *Review of the Register General Key Messages, Questions and Answers* (2001) where the Commission answers what is presumed to be the most popular questions about the future status of schools and religious charities.

Why are charities connected to the state controversial?

An example of a charity connected to the state would be a charity with recreational objects which then enters into a contract with a local authority to provide leisure services and facilities to the general public.[9] This type of charity has become controversial because charities are increasingly becoming involved in the delivery of public services, there is a debate about the extent to which charities should provide public services,[10] and charities have experienced difficulties when contracting with the state to provide public services.[11]

Possible grounds for removal

In RR 7 – *The Independence of Charities from the State*,[12] the Commission gives its views on the extent to which charities are required by law to be independent from the state. It indicates that the Commission might seek to remove charities from the register on the basis that their relationship with government bodies affects their independence. Given the large number of charities on the register that have funding arrangements with government bodies, RR 7 makes disturbing reading.

The Commission accept that the state can lawfully set up charities.[13] However, it indicates that it might seek to remove charities from the register if their independence is compromised. For example, the Commission says that a local authority could not expect to convert its leisure department into a charity if its purpose was to carry out the local authority's leisure policies, as the charity could not be said to be independent.[14]

The Commission give two possible grounds for a loss of charitable status. First, an institution may be created with a stated purpose that is charitable but with an unstated purpose that is concerned with giving effect to the wishes and policies of a governmental authority. If this is the case, then the Commission

[9] This type of charity was the subject of the Commission's decision in *Applications for Registration of (1) Trafford Community Leisure Trust and (2) Wigan Leisure and Cultural Trust* 21 April 2004.

[10] See *The Future Role of the Third Sector in Social and Economic Regeneration: Final Report*, July 2007, Cm 7189. See also 'Blair to Assign NHS Role to the Voluntary Sector' *Third Sector* 21 June 2006 and Allsop, I. 'A Growth in Spending' *Charity Finance* pp. 18–20.

[11] See Plummer, J. 'Compact Table of Shame' *Third Sector* 14 February 2007 and Little, M. 'Sector is Losing Out to Private Bids' *Third Sector* 31 January 2007.

[12] RR 7 – *The Independence of Charities from the State* (Version February 2001). Note that under the Charities and Trustee Investment (Scotland) Act 2005 an institution will not meet the 'charity test' if its constitution expressly permits the Scottish Ministers or a Minister of the Crown to direct or otherwise control its activities: see section 7(4)(b) the Charities and Trustee Investment (Scotland) Act 2005. See also 'Drawing a Line' *Third Sector* 8 February 2006.

[13] RR 7 – *The Independence of Charities from the State* (Version February 2001). For a critique of RR 7 see Garton J. 'Charities and the State' *Tru. LI* 2000 14 (2) 93–102.

[14] *Op. cit.* RR 7, para. 3.

regards the institution as non-charitable.[15] The following factors are cited as evidence that an institution is not really a charity:

(A) It is necessarily dependent on a government authority for funding;
(B) It receives that funding on terms that enable the government authority to make decisions about what services are to be provided and who is to benefit from those services; and
(C) In making those decisions, the government authority is able to pursue its own wishes and policies without having a duty to act solely in the interests of the institution.

Second, the Commission state that if the charity's governing instrument authorises trustees to take part in decisions in which they have a conflict of interest then, although the Commission concedes this will usually amount to a problem of governance,[16] it also considers this may be a factor pointing to a non-charitable purpose.[17]

Critical analysis of the possible grounds for removal

Starting with the assertion that an institution may be created with a stated purpose that is charitable but an unstated purpose that is concerned with giving effect to the wishes and policies of a governmental body, it was shown in Chapter 2[18] that the court has, on occasion, looked at the real objects of an institution, where there is a doubt about whether they are charitable, to determine whether it is a charity. The difficulty with this approach is that even if the real objects demonstrate a lack of independence because they are directed at implementing the policies of a government authority it is nevertheless argued that this will not affect charitable status.[19]

Even a very high level of involvement by the state will not necessarily prove fatal to charitable status. In *Construction Industry Training Board* v. *Attorney General*,[20] the board was created by statutory instrument made under the Industrial Training Act 1964 to make provision for the training of persons employed, or to be employed, in the construction industry, and to research into matters relating to training. Under the Act, grants to the board, investments of any money made by it, proposals for the exercise of its functions and the appointment of its members, were under the control of the Minister of Labour

[15] In *Applications for Registration of (1) Trafford Community Leisure Trust and (2) Wigan Leisure and Cultural Trust* 21 April 2004, the Commission upheld its stance in RR 7 that a lack of independence from the state can adversely affect charitable status where the purpose is to further the non-charitable purposes of securing and implementing the policies of a government authority.

[16] Note that it is permissible for conflicts of interest to be authorised by the governing instrument: see *Bray* v. *Ford* [1896] AC 44.

[17] RR 7-*The Independence of Charities from the State* (Version February 2001) para. 10.

[18] Chapter 2, pp. 27–31. [19] Chapter 2, p. 43.

[20] Construction Industry Training Board v. Attorney General [1973] 1 Ch. 173.

who was empowered to amend or revoke any order to wind up training boards, and to make provision for the application of surplus moneys. Despite the minister's substantial and far reaching powers over the charity, the Court of Appeal held by majority that the jurisdiction of the court had not been ousted by the minister and that the board was in fact a charity. Buckley LJ remarked[21] that the fact that the Act conferred on the minister the right to control the board in certain specified respects such as investment, and that the court could not properly interfere with any of his decisions, did not result in the board being beyond the jurisdiction of the court. Ploughman LJ commented that, if it was accepted, as Russell LJ suggested in his dissenting judgment (which Ploughman LJ agreed with on this point of law), that where an institution is established in terms which 'substantially oust the jurisdiction of the Court'[22] then the institution could not be a charity.

This decision suggests that even a very high level of involvement or control by the state will not be fatal to charitable status. Indeed it is difficult to imagine a higher degree of involvement by the state than in this case. It follows that if the Commission did look through a charity's objects and determined the real objects displayed a lack of independence from the state, then it would not be open to the Commission to remove a charity from the register on the basis that it had non-charitable objects.

The second assertion made by the Commission in RR 7 is that if a charity's governing instrument authorises trustees to take part in discussions in which they have a conflict of interest then, although the Commission concedes that this will usually amount to a problem of governance, the Commission also considers that it may also be a factor pointing towards a non-charitable purpose.[23] If the Commission has difficulty with the level of involvement from the state, then it is submitted that it is far more likely to be on the basis that the state is putting its interests before that of the charity. If this is the case then, it is argued that the state could be held accountable as a charity trustee on the basis that it was one of 'the persons having the control and management of the administration' of the charity,[24] and that it had been acting in conflict of interest.[25] In such circumstances the appropriate course of action would be for the Commission to use its powers under the Charities Act 1993 to act for the protection of the charity[26] and not to remove the charity from the register.[27]

In overall conclusion to both assertions made by the Commission, although it is accepted that the Commission does, on occasion, have the power[28] to examine the real objects of an institution and, if they are non-charitable, remove it from the register, it is submitted that in RR 7 the Commission simply came to the wrong conclusion that independence is a component of the essential indicia

21 *Ibid.* at 188. 22 *Ibid.*
23 RR 7 – *The Independence of Charities from the State* (Version February 2001) para 10.
24 S. 97(1) Charities Act 1993. 25 *Bray* v. *Ford* [1896] AC 44.
26 Ss. 18 & 19 Charities Act 1993. 27 S. 3(4) Charities Act 1993. 28 See Chapter 2, pp. 27–31.

of charitable status.[29] It follows that the Commission will encounter objections if it should try to remove charities from the register because they are connected to the state through funding agreements or trusteeship.

How the critical analysis supports the basic propositions

The example of charities connected to the State illustrates three of the basic propositions of this book.[30] First, the Commission's powers of removal are limited[31] because, as argued in this book,[32] a lack of independence from the state does not mean that an institution is non-charitable and it would not therefore be open to the Commission to remove such a charity from the register. Second, the Commission has a problem of legality because it has no power to decide whether purposes are charitable in law.[33] It is argued in this book that if the Commission removes a charity from the register because of a lack of independence from the State this will exceed the scope of its powers because a lack of independence from the State does not equate to a non-charitable purpose.[34] Third, the Commission's powers of removal require clarification because due to the Commission's assertions[35] it is not certain whether a lack of independence from the State leads to a charity's purposes being non-charitable.[36]

Charitable schools which charge fees

The second category of controversial charities is fee-charging charitable schools, although it should be noted that the principles discussed in this part of the book are equally applicable to fee-charging hospitals and fee-charging charities generally.

Why charitable schools which charge fees are controversial

The charitable status of fee-paying schools is an old chestnut which is periodically discussed.[37] Opponents tend to argue that it is wrong for such schools to be awarded the tax reliefs which accompany charitable status when, although, in theory, such schools are open to anyone, in reality, only the wealthy can afford the fees.[38] Those in favour tend to argue that a broad cross section of the community send their pupils to such schools through a combination of financial planning and financial sacrifice.

[29] Chapter 2, p. 43. [30] Chapter 1, pp. 1–4. [31] *Ibid.* [32] *Ibid.*

[33] Chapter 1, pp. 1–4 and Chapter 3, pp. 45–52. [34] Chapter 2, p. 43.

[35] RR 7 – *The Independence of Charities from the State* (Version February 2001).

[36] Chapter 2, p. 43.

[37] For a recent discussion see House of Commons Hansard Debates 25 October 2006; col. 1595. For a review of the debate see Morris, D. *Schools – An Education in Charity Law*, 1st edn (Aldershot: Dartmouth, 1996) pp. 24–29. See also pp. 89–93 of this chapter and chapter 7, pp. 152–7.

[38] 'Poor Little Rich Schools' *Guardian Education*, 23 April 2002.

Possible grounds for removal

The Commission has given mixed messages about the removal of schools which charge fees. In RR 8 – *The Public Character of Charity*,[39] the Commission asserted that a requirement to pay for a charity's services could reduce the availability of benefits to those who are less well-off which, if taken to its extreme conclusion, would be incompatible with public benefit which is essential for charitable status.[40] RR 8 is vague about the issue but certainly removal from the register is not ruled out.

The Strategy Unit Report recommended that the Commission should run an ongoing programme to check the level of charges.[41] Although it is contemplated that underperforming charities would be encouraged to develop their provision of facilities rather than lose their charitable status[42] it is clear from the report that charities which did not co-operate could face removal from the register.[43]

During the passage of the Charities Bill, the Commission was criticised by the Joint Committee that its equivocal stance would render the proposed removal of the presumption of public benefit meaningless. The Commission[44] subsequently submitted a supplementary memorandum[45] confirming that it would be carrying out public benefit checks on schools which charge fees. When examining the question of charging fees, the Commission said that it would apply the broad principles set out in *Re Resch's Will Trusts*,[46] namely that both direct and indirect benefits could be taken into account when assessing the benefit to the public; that charging fees for services did not prevent the institution from benefiting the public; but that any institution which wholly excluded the poor could not be a charity.

Subsequently, in the lead up to the enactment of the Charities Act 2006 and the abolition of the presumption of public benefit[47] the Commission have been issuing mixed messages. Andrew Hind, chief executive of the Commission, was quoted as saying that there is a worrying lack of clarity in the underlying case law governing public benefit.[48] This appears to suggest a cautious approach. However, Dame Suzi Leather, the new chair of the Commission was also quoted

[39] Version February 2001, paras. 19–20 and Annex D. [40] *Ibid.* para. 19.

[41] The Strategy Unit Report, *Private Action, Public Benefit A Review of Charities and the Wider Not-for-Profit Sector*, paras. 4.26–4.30.

[42] *Private Action, Public Benefit* para. 4.30. Presumably this could include the making of a *cy-pres* under section 13 Charities Act 1993 to allow for more scholarships and bursaries where, for example, a school's reserves and fees are high.

[43] *Private Action, Public Benefit*, para. 7.75.

[44] Uncorrected transcript of oral evidence HC 660 ix.

[45] *Public Benefit and the Effect of the Proposed Legislation* (7 June 2004).

[46] *Re Resch's Will Trusts* [1969] 1 AC 514. [47] S. 3(2) Charities Act 2006.

[48] House of Commons Standing Committee A [Lords] 25 October 2006; col. 1585 *per* John Grogan.

as saying that she will apply the test of public benefit robustly, and talked about holding seminars where there will be a discussion of social mores and the way in which public benefit might be defined in the modern day.[49] Removal of charities from the register was not therefore ruled out.[50]

Following the enactment of the Charities Act 2006 the Commission has issued guidance [51] which looks at the issue of charities charging fees. It has reiterated that charities must not charge fees at a level which totally exclude[52] the poor, unless there are other reasonable ways available for those persons to benefit.[53] However, the Commission now appears to be more inclined to use its powers to appoint new trustees[54] or give directions[55] where charities do not co-operate by increasing the level of public benefit.[56]

Critical analysis of the possible grounds for removal

As pointed out in the previous paragraph, an area where the Commission will be scrutinising charitable schools' public benefit is over the question of charging fees.[57] Yet the legal authorities suggest that there will be limited grounds for the Commission to challenge charities which charge fees and have a limited beneficiary class, even though a significant section of the public is excluded. Certainly, an institution, which excluded the poor from the outset would not be charitable. As Lindley LJ said in *Re Macduff*:[58]

> I am quite aware that a trust may be charitable though not confined to the poor. But I doubt very much whether a trust would be declared to be charitable which excluded the poor.

The leading case on the subject is *Re Resch's Will Trusts*.[59] This was an appeal to the Privy Council involving consideration, *inter alia*, of the extent to which a charitable hospital could charge fees without any profit motive on the part of the trustees, and at approximately cost price. In this case, a testator bequeathed two thirds of the net income of his residuary estate to the Sisters of Charity for the general purposes of St Vincent's Private Hospital. The hospital had eighty-two beds and was close to a public hospital with 500 beds which was also run by the

[49] *Ibid.*

[50] The government has given a commitment to review the operation of the Charities Act 2006 with particular reference to public benefit and charitable status in three years' time. See House of Commons Debates 25 October 2006; col. 1618 *per* Hilary Armstrong.

[51] *Charities and Public Benefit The Charity Commission's General Guidance on Public Benefit* (January 2008).

[52] *Ibid.* F 11. Principle 2 C: People in poverty must not be excluded from the opportunity to benefit.

[53] *Ibid.* F 10. Restrictions based on ability to pay any fees charged.

[54] S. 18(1)(ii) Charities Act 1993.

[55] S. 19 A & B Charities Act 1993.

[56] *Ibid.* J 6. Working with Charities which are not meeting the Public Benefit.

[57] See *Review of the Register General Key Messages, Questions and Answers* (2001). For a decision of the Commission on the question of charging fees see *Charity Commission Review Decision made on the application for registration of Odstock Private Care Limited* 25 September 2007.

[58] *Re Macduff* [1896] 2 Ch 451 at 464.

[59] *Re Resch's Will Trusts* [1969] 1 AC 514.

Sisters of Charity. It was argued by the next of kin that a gift which, in effect, excluded the poor was not charitable because it was not available to the whole community. Nevertheless, the gift was held to be charitable because the essential element of public benefit was present. Lord Wilberforce remarked that, in this particular case, charges were not low, but on the evidence it could not be said that the poor were excluded.[60] Only those who had not contributed sufficiently to a medical benefit scheme, needed to stay in hospital longer than their benefit would cover or could not get a reduction of or exemption from the charges could claim to be excluded. Lord Wilberforce considered the general benefit to the community to include the relief to the beds and hospital staff of the public hospital, the benefit of having a type of nursing and treatment which supplemented that provided by the funded hospital and the benefit of the standard of care in the publicly funded hospital which arose from the juxtaposition of the two.[61]

Under the present law there is no requirement for charitable schools to provide bursaries or scholarships, or to share facilities with state schools.[62] Politically it may be advisable, but it is not required by charity law. It should also be noted that a key factor in *Re Resch's Will Trusts*[63] was that the charges made were comparable with those made at similar institutions. Weight was given to what the market dictated was affordable. One can readily see that charitable schools could use a similar argument where they are filled with fee-paying pupils. *Re Resch's Will Trusts*[64] provides a very liberal test of public benefit in respect of charities which charge fees for their services.

The evidence to the Joint Committee from the Independent Schools Council[65] was that first 31.5 per cent of children at ISC schools receive help with their fees: 23% of them from the school itself. ISC was making the point that entry to its schools was not restricted to a privileged few. Second, as to the quality of the education provided, ISC cited the OECD programme for International Student Assessment (PISA) report in 2001 which compared combined reading literacy scores in 27 countries. UK independent schools achieved the best results by a wide margin.[66] Third, some ISC schools provide for pupils with special educational needs. ISC estimate that 12 per cent of children in ISC schools have special education needs[67] including dyslexia , dyspraxia, and

[60] *Ibid.* at 544. [61] *Ibid.* at 544.

[62] Although note that the Commission regards bursaries as a way of demonstrating public benefit. See *Charities and Public Benefit The Charity Commission's General Guidance on Public Benefit F 10. Restrictions based on ability to pay any fees charged.*

[63] *Ibid.* at 539. [64] *Re Resch's Will Trusts* [1969] 1 AC 514.

[65] *Memorandum from the Independent Schools Council* (DCH 9) *to the Joint Committee on the Draft Charities Bill – Minutes of Evidence* www.publications.parliament.uk. In their evidence ISC say that it represents 508,000 children in 1,278 schools. 83 per cent of ISC schools are charities (1,061 in total).

[66] *Knowledge and Skills for Life: First Results from PISA 2000*, Table 7.13, OECD 2001.

[67] *ISC Survey of Member Schools*, January 1999.

special needs as gifted children. Fourth, ISC claim to engage in a range of partnership activities with maintained schools to extend benefits to them. Fifth, ISC claim that their schools give £2.30 back to charity for each £1 gained through charitable status.

It will not therefore be difficult for charities to meet the test of public benefit set by *Re Resch's Will Trusts*.[68] As Lord Phillips of Sudbury said when criticising this case in the Committee Stage of the House of Lords[69] when the Charities Bill was being debated:

> It seems clear to me that if these tests were applied to an independent school, which made little or no concession to the poor by way of bursaries or the like – not making its facilities available more widely – it too could claim that it met a need of the same sort; namely, a type of education and schooling which provided smaller classes, better facilities, exclusion of difficult pupils and so on.

It is difficult to see what type of school will fail the public benefit test because it was recognised during the passage of the Charities Bill that even where a school is unable to increase its public benefit because, for example, it is situated in a rural location with no state schools nearby[70] or where a charitable school is for disabled children or those with learning difficulties it will face different pressures to show public benefit and that the Commission will need to take this into account.[71]

How the critical analysis supports the basic propositions

The example of charitable schools which charge fees illustrates three of the basic propositions of this book.[72] First, it shows that the Commission's powers are limited, because case law indicates that it will only be in extreme cases that it will be able to remove charities that fail the public benefit test where fees are too high, even though a significant section of the public are excluded.[73] Second, there would be a problem of legality if in the future the Commission tried to reinterpret the law and remove charitable schools from the register where fees were too high and the Commission was of the view that too many people were being excluded. Third, there is a need for the law of public benefit to be clarified by Parliament or the court, in the light of modern conditions, to explain to what extent charitable schools can charge fees, and how much access they need to give to those pupils who cannot afford those fees.

68 *Re Resch's Will Trusts* [1969] 1 AC 514.
69 Charities Bill [HL] (Committee Stage) col. GC 112, 9 February 2005.
70 Charities Bill [HL] Report Stage, 12 October 2005; col. 317 and House of Commons Hansard Debates, 25 October 2006; col. 1610–1611.
71 House of Commons Hansard Debates, 25 October 2006; col. 1610–1611.
72 Chapter 1, pp. 2–3.
73 See *Re Macduff* [1896] 2 Ch 451 at 464; *Re Resch's Will Trusts* [1969] 1 AC 514.

New religious movement charities

The third example of a controversial charity is new religious movement charities.[74]

Why new religious movement charities are controversial

These charities are controversial because primarily they are new rather than established and tend to attract public and judicial concern.[75] Allegations are often made that some new religious movements are involved in activities which are illegal or immoral, such as brainwashing or activities which lead to the breakdown of the family.[76]

Possible grounds for removal

There are two possible grounds for removal. First, failure on the part of an institution to demonstrate public benefit and second, a failure on the part of an institution to further a 'religion'[77] for the purpose of charity law.

Failure to demonstrate public benefit

The Commission's decision to reject the Church of Scientology's application for charitable status[78] was the first recorded decision of the Commission where it was publicly stated that new religious movement charities would have to demonstrate public benefit when the presumption of public benefit was rebutted by such factors (in this particular case) as differing from established religions, being the subject of public concern or judicial concern. Following the Charities Act 2006,[79] which abolishes the presumption of public benefit, it might reasonably be expected that the Commission will now take a closer look at registered new religious movement charities which fall within these categories.

Although some new religious movement charities are controversial, historically the Commission have not sought to remove them from the register on the ground that they have failed the public benefit test. This is probably a result of the Commission being less rigorous in the past[80] when registering charities because of a reliance on the presumption of public benefit.[81]

74 See King, J. 'Watch Out There's A Charity About', *The Spectator*, 28 October 2000 30–31.

75 For example, The Church of Scientology: see *Decision of the Charity Commissioners for England & Wales made on 17 November 1999.*

76 See the website of Centre for Studies on New Religions: www.cesnur.org.

77 S. 2(2)(c) Charities Act 2006. It is arguable that the common law requirement for worship for the purpose of public benefit survives the Charities Act 2006. See pp. 95–97 of this chapter.

78 *The Church of Scientology Decision of the Charity Commissioners for England and Wales 17 November 1999.*

79 S. 3(2) Charities Act 2006.

80 Nathan *The Charities Act 1960*, 1st edn (London: Butterworths, 1962) pp. 44–45.

81 *National Anti-Vivisection Society* v. *IRC* [1948] AC 31 *per* Lord Simonds at 66–67.

When the register was established in 1961 by the Charities Act 1960 charities were registered on the basis of their objects without the need to complete a detailed questionnaire.[82] The Commission has, until recently, been passive about the registration of new religious movement charities. Evidence of this approach may be found in the Commission's Annual Report in 1976.[83] When commenting on the increasing concern about the activities of 'less well known religions and religious sects' it said:

> In registering an organisation as a charity we are concerned only with the question whether it is established for purposes which are exclusively charitable according to the law of England and Wales. Registration is not an indication that we are satisfied about the integrity of the methods by which it pursues its objects, provided these are lawful

This suggests that there are some charities on the register which have been mistakenly presumed to satisfy the requirement of public benefit. In particular, there has never been a systematic review of the application of the public benefit test for charities on the register. As explained previously,[84] the Strategy Unit[85] proposed that the Commission carry out such a review, which could lead to the removals.

Not promoting a religion for the purposes of charity law

The second possible ground for removal is a failure on the part of an institution to further a 'religion' for the purpose of charity law.[86] The Commission looked at the question of what constitutes 'religion' for the purpose of charity law in the application for charitable status by the Church of Scientology.[87] In deciding whether the Church of Scientology should be registered as a charity, the Commission concluded that the Church was not advancing a religion for the purposes of charity law. At that time 'religion' for the purposes of charity law was defined exclusively by the common law as faith in a god and worship of that

[82] Today applicants for charitable status need to complete a form App. 1 which can be accessed on www.charity-commission.gov.uk.

[83] Paras. 103–108. For further evidence, see a press notice concerning an inquiry into the doctrines and practices of the Exclusive Brethren [1976] Ch. Com. A.R. pp. 34–36 and the two Unification Church charities, The Holy Spirit Association for the Unification of World Christianity and Sun Myung Moon Foundation [1981] Ch. Com. A.R. pp. 25–27, paras. 71–73; [1982] Ch. Com. A.R. p. 14, paras. 36–38 and 46–48 App. C.

[84] Pp. 90–91 of this chapter.

[85] Cabinet Office, Strategy Unit Report, *Private Action, Public Benefit A Review of Charities and the Wider Not-for-Profit Sector* (2002) paras 4.26–4.30. To date the Commission have issued the following guidance: *Public Benefit – the Charity Commission's Approach* (January 2005), *Public Benefit – The Charity Commission's Position on how Public Benefit is Treated in the Charities Bill* (July 2005) and *Charities and Public Benefit The Charity Commission's general guidance on public benefit* (January 2008).

[86] S. 2(2)(c) Charities Act 2006.

[87] *The Church of Scientology Decision of the Charity Commissioners for England & Wales 17 November 1999.*

god.[88] Although the Commission accepted that Scientology recognised a supreme being, it did not accept that the core practices of Scientology, being auditing and training, constituted 'worship' for the purposes of charity law, as these practices did not display the essential characteristics of reverence and veneration for a supreme being.

It concluded that worship should have the essential characteristic of 'reverence',[89] submission to the object worshiped, veneration of that object, praise, thanksgiving, prayer or intersession.[90] They also noted Picarda QC's opinion that religion involves not merely a faith of a particular kind, but also worship. In turn, Picarda referred to the definition of 'religion' in *Webster's New International Dictionary* as 'service and adoration of God or god as expressed in the form of worship'.[91] The Commission noted that it would not be possible to worship with reverence a mere ethical or philosophical idea.[92] The Commission then considered whether Scientology contained 'worship' within its practices.

It considered that the core religious practices were auditing and training. Auditing was described by the Church of Scientology as a unique form of personal counselling which helps an individual look at his own existence and improves his own ability to confront what and where he is, and is conducted at auditing sessions during which an individual is audited.[93] Training in Scientology involves the study of the works of the founder of Scientology, L. Ron Hubbard. Courses are supervised and the end of each course is marked by the award of a certificate.[94]

The Commission decided that auditing appeared to be a form of counselling and concluded that training appeared to be more like an educational activity. The Commission concluded that it could not find in auditing and training, whether taken separately or together, the reverence and veneration for a supreme being which it considered necessary to constitute worship in English charity law.[95] The Commission therefore concluded that Scientology was not a religion for the purpose of charity law.

Following The Church of Scientology[96] decision, the Commission might decide to look at registered new religious movement charities to see whether

[88] Applying *Re South Place Ethical Society* [1980] 1 WLR 1565 *per* Dillon J at 1572. However, the common law is not entirely clear: see Chapter 7, pp. 145–51.

[89] *R* v. *Registrar General ex parte Segerdal* [1970] 2 QB 697 *per* Winn LJ.

[90] *Ibid. per* Buckley LJ at 709 F-G.

[91] Picarda, H. *The Law and Practice Relating to Charities*, 3rd edn (London: Sweet and Maxwell, 1999) p. 74.

[92] *R* v. *Registrar General ex parte Segerdal* [1970] 2 QB 697 *per* Dillon J at p. 1573 A.

[93] *The Church of Scientology Decision of the Charity Commissioners for England & Wales 17 November 1999.*

[94] *Ibid.* [95] Which was at the time defined by the common law. See pp. 95–96 *ante*.

[96] *The Church of Scientology Decision of the Charity Commissioners for England & Wales 17 November 1999.*

they are furthering a 'religion' for the purpose of charity law and in particular whether the element of 'worship' is present.

Critical analysis of the possible grounds for removal

As outlined in the previous paragraph, the two potential grounds for removal of a new religious movement charity are a lack of public benefit and a failure to further a 'religion' for the purpose of charity law.

Failure to demonstrate public benefit

The old common law presumption[97] of public benefit of charities with objects to advance religion had three aspects. Charities will now need to demonstrate[98] these from a charity's inception.[99]

The first aspect is that the law, 'assumes that it is good for man to have and to practise a religion.'[100] This is presumably on the basis that the advancement of religion is beneficial to mankind because it provides a moral code and therefore encourages good behaviour.[101] The problem is that many of the religions that are controversial are remarkably similar to established religions in terms of doctrine. It follows that it will be quite easy for them to satisfy this element of the public benefit test. For example, in *Founding Church of Scientology* v. *United States*,[102] the court concluded that Scientology had many of the characteristics of other recognised religions. Furthermore, the court also concluded that the theories of Scientology relating to auditing[103] and the claimed curative powers for the process were not properly subject to courtroom evaluation as to truth or falsehood. The court noted that many established religions claimed for their practices the power to treat or prevent disease or to include accounts of miraculous cures.

In *Church of the New Faith* v. *Commissioners for Payroll Tax*,[104] the Australian Court decided in favour of the Church of Scientology being classified as a 'religious institution' and therefore exempt from payroll tax. Certain criteria alleged to negate religion and relied on by the Supreme Court of Victoria were rejected by Murphy J[105] as unacceptable. These included:

(A) The absence of a belief in a personal god or supreme being;
(B) The presence of contradictions in the accepted writings and beliefs;
(C) The fact that the organisation in question has revised its beliefs;
(E) The absence of a 'complete or absolute moral code';

[97] *National Anti-Vivisection Society* v. *IRC* [1948] AC 31 *per* Lord Simonds at 66–67.
[98] Following the abolition of the presumption of public benefit: see section 3(2) Charities Act 2006.
[99] See Chapter 2, pp. 34–35. [100] *Gilmour* v. *Coats* [1949] AC 426 *per* Lord Reid at 459.
[101] See the Opinion of Quint F commissioned by the Charity Law Association, 'The Draft Charities Bill Public Benefit and the Advancement of Religion', 9 July 2004. www.charitylawassociation.org.
[102] *Founding Church of Scientology* v. *United States* 409 F2d 1146 (1969).
[103] For an explanation of auditing see pp. 95–96 of this chapter.
[104] *Church of the New Faith* v. *Commissioners for the Payroll Tax* (1983) 154 CLR 120.
[105] *Ibid*. at paras. 1–48.

(F) The adoption or adaptation of teachings, symbols, rituals and other practices from other religions;
(G) The absence of elements of propitiation and propagation;
(H) The absence of public acceptance;
(I) The absence of any claim to be the true faith; and
(J) The presence of commercialisation.

Murphy J then gave examples of established religions which would not satisfy such criteria and commented[106] that:

> Christianity claims to have begun with a founder and twelve adherents. It had no written constitution, and no permanent meeting place. It borrowed heavily from the teachings of the Jewish religion, but had no complete and absolute moral code. Its founder exhorted people to love one another and taught by example. Outsiders regarded his teachings, especially about the nature of divinity, as ambiguous, obscure and contradictory, as well as blasphemous and illegal. On the criteria used in this case by the Supreme Court of Victoria, early Christianity would not have been considered religious.

The reluctance of the Court to decide that a charity advancing religion does not satisfy the first requirement of public benefit that it is good for man to have and practice a religion is further illustrated by *Holmes* v. *AG*.[107] Here the court decided that neither the practices of the Exclusive Brethren nor its doctrines suggested that the religion was contrary to the public interest.

The second aspect of public benefit is that activities which are permitted to be carried out by a religious charity's governing instrument must be beneficial and not non-beneficial[108] or harmful to the public.[109] Those activities might include those which are illegal or immoral or involve the break up of the family all of which are contrary to public policy.[110] The problem with the second requirement is that, as explained in Chapter 2,[111] the court has not given sufficient guidance on what constitutes 'harm' or 'benefit'. There will be cases where it is obvious what is harmful and what is beneficial, but between these two opposites the position is unclear. To illustrate the point, allegations of harmful undue influence might equally be made about mainstream established charities which are generally accepted as beneficial. Ian Williams makes this point succinctly:

> Cults split up families and take children away from their parents – in the Roman Catholic Church they call it vocation. Irrational beliefs, such as that

[106] *Ibid.* at para. 46. [107] *Holmes* v. *AG*, *The Times*, 11 February 1981.

[108] *Coats* v. *Gilmour* [1948] 1 All ER 521 *per* Lord Greene MR at 524. Note that in *Re Watson* [1973] 1 WLR 1472 Ploughman J said that if there was evidence that the purpose was subversive to all mankind, then the presumption of public benefit would be rebutted. The analysis of Lord Greene MR in the Court of Appeal carries greater weight.

[109] See Chapter 2, pp. 37–38.

[110] See Picarda, H. 'New Religious and Ethical Movements as Charities' 131 *NLJ* 436 1981.

[111] Chapter 2, pp. 37–38.

> God spoke in Korean – was that less plausible than his being monolingual in Hebrew, Latin or Arabic? And would any dispassionate observer accept, without faith, the doctrines of resurrection, or the Athanasian Creed?[112]

Perhaps for this reason, there is a dearth of modern cases deciding the issue of whether a religious institution, or any institution, is not charitable because its doctrine and / or objects are harmful to the public or illegal.[113]

There is a third aspect of public benefit concerned with worship. For worship to be for the benefit of the public it must allow for public access from members of the church living in the wider community.[114] It was argued in Chapter 2[115] that actual attendance by a sufficient section of the community is not required so long as there is public access to worship. It follows that so long as public access is offered it does not matter that the number of worshipers is small.[116] Charities will not therefore have difficulty proving public benefit in such circumstances.

To conclude, it will be difficult for the Commission to remove charities from the register on the basis that the requirement of public benefit has not been satisfied.[117] Many new religious movements are similar to established religions and therefore difficult to distinguish in terms of public benefit.[118] In addition, there is a lack of guidance from the Court on what constitutes *'harm'* or *'benefit'*.[119] Finally, the apparent absence of a requirement for actual attendance at public services of worship means that even a very small number of worshipers will be sufficient to satisfy the public benefit requirement. All of these factors will make it difficult for the Commission to remove charities from the register on the basis that the requirement of public benefit has not been satisfied.[120]

Not promoting a 'Religion' for the purpose of charity law

The statutory definition of 'religion,' as contained in the Charities Act 2006, reads as follows:

[112] See Williams, I. *The Alms Trade: Charities Past, Present and Future,* 1st edn (London: Harper Collins, 1989) p. 124.

[113] Two cases were cited in Lord Simonds' judgment in *National Anti-Vivisection Society* v. *IRC* [1948] AC 31 at 64. Both cases involved bequests to religions which at the time were regarded as illegal. The first, *De Costa* v. *De Pas* (1753) Amb 228 involved a bequest for instructing people in the Jewish religion which was applied for the benefit of the Foundling Hospital. The second, *Carry* v. *Abbot* (1803) 7 Ves 490, 496 involved the residue of an estate which was bequeathed for the instruction in the Catholic faith. In both cases the Court ruled that the bequest should be applied as the King by sign manual should direct. The Roman Catholic Relief Act 1832 and the Jewish Relief Act 1846 validated charitable trusts for the purposes of these religions.

[114] *Neville Estates* v. *Madden* [1962] Ch 832. [115] Chapter 2, p. 36.

[116] *Neville Estates* v. *Madden* [1962] Ch 832. Note that the court accepted that there was sufficient public benefit in *Holmes* v. *AG* The Times, 11 February 1981 because outsiders were allowed to attend meetings of the Brethren other than the celebration of the Eucharist and business meetings and the Brethren or some of them attempt to proselytise by conducting public campaigns.

[117] See Chapter 2, p. 36. [118] See earlier in this paragraph.

[119] Chapter 2, pp. 37–38. [120] See Chapter 2, p. 36.

'religion' includes –

(i) a religion which involves belief in more than one god, and
(ii) a religion which does not involve belief in a god[121]

This definition does not say whether there is still a common law requirement to 'worship'[122] and, if so, what form that 'worship' should take. Arguably the common law requirement to worship still applies, at least for the purpose of public benefit, and therefore an alternative ground for removal would be that new religious movement charities are not promoting a 'religion' for the purpose of charity law, because the common law requirement to 'worship' is not satisfied.[123] This was the Commission's approach in the Church of Scientology decision[124] but there are difficulties with using this argument to argue that an institution is not a charity.

First, it is unclear what is the common-law requirement to 'worship'. The only decision of the English Court which fully considers the nature of religious worship is *R* v. *Registrar General ex parte Segerdal.*[125] In that case religious 'worship' was defined as meaning 'reverence or veneration of God or of a Supreme Being'[126] characterised by 'submission to the object worshipped, veneration of that object, praise, thanksgiving, prayer or intersession'.[127] However, even this decision is of only persuasive value because it was dealing with the question whether a Church of Scientology chapel was a 'meeting place for religious worship' for the purpose of the Places of Religious Worship Act 1855, and not whether the Church satisfied the common law requirement to 'worship' for the purpose of charity law. There are no English common-law decisions directly on the point. An examination of decisions of the court in other jurisdictions looking at whether the Church of Scientology conducts religious 'worship', in contexts other than charity law,[128] demonstrates how there is a fine distinction between religious and non-religious 'worship'. For example in *Church of the New Faith* v. *Commissioners for Payroll Tax*[129] the High Court of Australia looked at whether the Church of Scientology was a religion for the purpose of payroll tax. Although not using the word 'worship' the court recognised that there was a requirement for there to be an acceptance of canons of conduct in order to give effect to that belief. The High Court decided that the Church of Scientology satisfied this requirement.

In *Founding Church of Scientology* v. *United States*,[130] the United States Court of Appeals in the District of Columbia found that the Church of Scientology

[121] S. 2(3)(a) Charities Act 2006. [122] See pp. 95–97 of this chapter. [123] *Ibid.*

[124] The Church of Scientology *Decision of the Charity Commissioners for England & Wales 17th November 1999.* See pp. 95–97 of this chapter.

[125] *R* v. *Registrar General ex parte Segerdal* [1970] 2 QB 697.

[126] *Ibid. per* Lord Denning MR at 707. [127] *Ibid. per* Buckley LJ at 709.

[128] There are no decisions of the court in other jurisdictions on what constitutes 'worship' for the purpose of charity law.

[129] *Church of the New Faith* v. *Commissioners for the Payroll Tax* (1983) 154 CLR 120.

[130] *Founding Church of Scientology* v. *United States* 409 F2d 1146 (1969).

was a *bona fide* religion for the purpose of the 'free exercise clause' and that 'auditing' was a practice of the Church of Scientology and integrated into its doctrines. Again, although the court did not use the term 'worship' it is nevertheless submitted that this is what it meant. Yet the opposite conclusion was reached in *Missouri Church of Scientology* v. *State Tax Commission of Missouri*[131] where it was held that the Church of Scientology did not qualify for tax relief in respect of its property because it was not used 'exclusively for religious worship'. In defining 'religious worship' as 'Generally ... expressed by prayers, reverence, homage and adoration paid to a deity for divine guidance', the court concluded that the Church of Scientology did not conduct 'religious worship'. This was because it found that it was in reality an applied philosophy rather than a religion devoted to 'religious worship'.

The differing conclusions of the court in other jurisdictions when looking at the question of religious 'worship' in relation to the Church of Scientology shows that, more generally, the Commission could not be confident of its power to remove a new religious movement institution from the register, which it did not consider was furthering a 'religion' because it was not conducting 'worship' for the purpose of charity law.

Second, even if in the Church of Scientology[132] decision the Commission correctly analysed 'worship' as requiring 'reverence',[133] it is arguable that the Commission incorrectly concluded, on the facts, that auditing was akin to personal counselling, rather than being a *bona fide* religious practice involving reverential 'worship'. It is unclear whether religious practices such as auditing are any different to any other type of spiritual direction or service of reconciliation on a one-to-one basis.[134] The distinction between religious and non-religious 'worship' appears fine, and it is submitted that the Commission could be open to challenge if it removed a new religious movement charity from the register for a similar reason.[135]

Third, it is unclear whether the common-law requirement to 'worship'[136] survives the new definition of 'religion'[137] under the Charities Act 2006 which includes polytheistic[138] and non-theistic beliefs,[139] but does not require religious charities to conduct 'worship'. Arguably there is still a requirement for 'worship' at least for the purpose of public benefit,[140] but the position is not clear. If there is no requirement to 'worship', then it would be more difficult to remove new

[131] *Missouri Church of Scientology* v. *State Tax Commission of Missouri* 560 SW 837 (1977).

[132] *The Church of Scientology Decision of the Charity Commissioners for England & Wales 17 November 1999.*

[133] Pp. 95–97 of this Chapter.

[134] Such as the Roman Catholic sacrament of reconciliation. See Catechism of the Catholic Church www.vatican.va/archive/catechism/ccc_toc.htm.

[135] For Human Rights arguments see Chapter 7, pp. 146–9. [136] See pp. 95–97 of this chapter.

[137] S. 2(2)(c) Charities Act 2006. [138] S. 2(3)(a)(i) Charities Act 2006.

[139] S. 2(3)(a)(ii) Charities Act 2006. [140] Pp. 94–95 of this chapter.

religious movement charities like the Church of Scientology, which some consider to be more of an applied philosophy[141] than a religion, because the statutory definition of 'religion' now includes non-theistic beliefs.[142]

How the critical analysis supports the basic propositions

The example of new religious movement charities has illustrated three of the basic propositions of this book.[143] First, the Commission's powers of removal are limited because the Commission will have difficulty disproving public benefit in the case of a new religious movement charity, and disproving that a new religious movement is a 'religion' for the purpose of charity law. Second, if the Commission attempts to develop its own views on the law of public benefit or the scope of the definition of 'religion' for the purpose of charity law, then this will support the basic proposition that there is a problem of legality in that it has no power to make law. Third, the Commission's powers of removal need clarification because it is not clear what constitutes public benefit,[144] or what will qualify as a 'religion'[145] for the purpose of charity law.

Conclusion

This chapter has illustrated how the application of three of the basic propositions of this book[146] apply to the removal of three types of controversial charity from the register.

[141] See *Missouri Church of Scientology* v. *State Tax Commission of Missouri* 560 SW 837 (1977).
[142] S. 2(3)(a)(ii) Charities Act 2006. [143] Chapter 1, pp. 1–4.
[144] See pp. 94–95 of this chapter. [145] *Ibid.* [146] Chapter 1, pp. 1–4.

5

Property

Introduction

It is one of the basic propositions[1] of this book that a distinction needs to be made between the governing instrument of a charity and property held for charitable purposes. While a charity might be removed from the register it does not necessarily mean that its property will be lost to charity. It is argued in this chapter that it will rarely be the case that property will be lost to charity when the charity is removed from the register, where its property is applied *cy-pres*[2] for charitable purposes. Removal of the governing instrument of the charity where its property continues to be applied for charitable purposes means that the effect of removal will not be drastic. This is a further illustration of the overall thesis that the Commission's powers of removal are limited.

The Dormant Accounts Project being carried out by the Commission, which involves the use of its powers to make use of charitable property where it is left fallow, indicates that the Commission is as much interested in removing inactive charities from the register as it is in maximising the use of charitable property.[3]

Before exploring how the effect of removal might be minimal there is a need to examine the relevant objective of the Commission.[4]

The position of the Commission

The Commission has, *inter alia*, a charitable resources objective,[5] which is defined as meaning the promotion of the effective use of charitable resources.[6] Therefore, irrespective of the question of the removal of institutions from the register, the Commission must do all it can to save charitable property and ensure that it is effectively applied.

[1] Chapter 1, pp. 1–4. [2] Ss. 13 & 14 Charities Act 1993. See pp. 105–8 of this chapter.

[3] See *The Dormant Accounts Project* (last modified 22 May 2003) and *Briefing Paper For The Joint Committee on the Draft Charities Bill Charity Commission-The Future* (September 2004), para. 14.

[4] S. 1B(2)4 & 1B(3)4 Charities Act 1993. [5] S. 1B(2)4 Charities Act 1993.

[6] S. 1B(3)4 Charities Act 1993.

The general thrust of charity law and, in particular, the Charities Acts 1993 and 2006 is towards saving charitable property through the Commission's *cy-pres* scheme-making powers,[7] ensuring effective governance in respect of that property through its scheme-making powers,[8] and protecting charitable property which is at risk through the use of its powers to protect charitable property.[9]

Charity law even provides several instances where the Commission has the power to preserve property for charity where it is not held upon charitable trusts. For example, the Commission has the power to make schemes to alter the purposes of a charity to allow the property to be applied *cy-pres* for other charitable purposes, where property has been given for specific charitable purposes that fail *ab initio*,[10] where property has ceased to be held for charitable purposes under a reverter provision in a governing instrument,[11] and where the original purposes have ceased to be charitable in law, as being useless or harmful to the community or for other reasons.[12] There are other examples where charity law has been developed to preserve property for charity.[13]

In order to understand the distinction between a charity's governing instrument and its property, one needs to answer the question what is 'charity'?

What is 'charity'?

It was shown in Chapter 2[14] that there is no need for a charity to have a formal written governing instrument so long as there is a legal obligation to carry out charitable purposes. A charity may have an informal governing instrument where, for example, it is constituted by oral trusts.[15] It is therefore possible that a charity's governing instrument (formal or informal) might be removed from the register but its property preserved for charity. In this chapter it is argued that it is more important to look at the intention of the donor than the governing instrument to determine whether property is held for charitable purposes.

The court has never set great store by governing instruments. They have been described as a 'mechanism provided for the time being and from time to time for holding its property and managing its affairs'[16] and 'mere machinery for achieving the purposes'.[17] In *Re Vernon's Will Trusts*,[18] the fact that a charity had ceased to exist did not prevent the court from applying a legacy *cy-pres* where the purposes of the charity were carried on by another body. Buckley J said:

[7] Ss. 13 & 14 Charities Act 1993. [8] Ss. 16 & 18(2)(ii) Charities Act 1993.
[9] Ss. 18 & 19 Charities Act 1993. [10] S. 14 Charities Act 1993.
[11] See the Reverter of Sites Act 1987. [12] S. 13(1)(e)(ii) Charities Act 1993.
[13] For example see the Recreational Charities Act 1958 and the Charitable Trusts (Validation) Act 1954.
[14] Chapter 2, pp. 12–18. [15] *Ibid.* [16] *Re Vernon's Will Trusts* [1972] Ch 300 at 304.
[17] *Re Finger's Will Trusts* [1972] Ch 286. [18] *Re Vernon's Will Trusts* [1972] Ch 300.

> In such cases the law regards the charity, an abstract conception distinct from the institutional mechanism provided for holding and administering the fund of the charity ...[19]

It should also be noted that the *cy-pres* power contained in section 13 Charities Act 1993 confers a power on the Commission to alter 'the original purposes of the charitable gift'.[20] It is not necessarily a power to amend the purposes as set out in the governing instrument of the charity. It could involve a scheme with new charitable objects and administrative provisions[21] or it could involve transferring the property to another charity.[22] The emphasis in section 13 Charities Act 1993 is on the intention of the donor and the effective application of property for charity.

It is also an established legal principle that the purposes and administrative provisions of a charity's governing instrument may change, but the charity remains in being and can receive legacies left to it in a will prior to the date when the changes were made.[23] In this context, the provisions of a governing instrument are regarded as the means to the charitable end:

> and so long as the charitable end is well established the means are only machinery, and no alteration of the machinery can destroy the charitable trust for the benefit of which the machinery is provided.[24]

It is important, therefore, not to over-emphasise the effect of a charity's removal from the register where its property continues to be available for charitable purposes. To do so would be to place greater importance on the governing instrument of a charity than the court does.[25]

There is now a need to examine whether property will ever be lost to charity when removed from the register. The circumstances where this question arises involves institutions which where never charitable and institutions which have ceased to be charitable.

The institution was never a charity

It is far from clear what the position is where the institution was never a charity. The House of Lords in *National Anti-Vivisection Society* v. *IRC*[26] did not address the status of an institution's property where the institution was never a charity. There is a crucial distinction to be made between a court deciding that its earlier decision was wrong, and a court deciding that its earlier decision was

[19] *Ibid.* at 304. [20] S. 13(1) Charities Act 1993. [21] Ss. 13 & 16(1)(a) Charities Act 1993.
[22] Ss. 13 & 14B(2)(b) Charities Act 1993.
[23] *Re Lucas* [1948] Ch 424 *per* Lord Greene MR at 426–427.
[24] *Re Faraker* [1912] 2 Ch 488 *per* Farwell LJ at 495.
[25] Note that although the name of the charity is a valuable asset, a charity can have a name without a formal governing instrument. See [1991] Ch.Com.A.R. para. 107.
[26] *National Anti-Vivisection Society* v. *IRC* [1948] AC 31.

correct at the time, but due to the passage of time purposes are no longer regarded as charitable. The more difficult analysis in relation to the ownership of charitable property is where the court rules that its earlier decision was wrong.[27] In that case, the Commission would have registered an institution as a charity following an erroneous decision of the court even though the institution was never a charity.

Arguably, in such situations, section 4(1) Charities Act 1993 confers a conclusive presumption that an institution whilst on the register was charitable and as a result, if it was discovered that the institution was never a charity, the conclusive presumption would operate so as to deem the institution to be a charity and allow for its property to be applied *cy-pres*.[28] This would be on the basis that the Court decided that it had made a mistake. It has to be said that this is a rather strained construction of section 4(1) Charities Act 1993. Importantly, the presumption of charitable status does not apply where the institution is removed as a result of rectification.[29] Where an institution is registered by mistake, it should follow that it ought not to enjoy the benefit of charitable status, in which case the property should not be automatically available for the institution where there is evidence that donors intended to give to the institution because it had charitable status. This conclusion is supported by the House of Lords in *Kleinwort Benson Ltd* v. *Lincoln City Council*.[30] In this case, the House of Lords decided that, as a general rule of law, where payments are made under a settled understanding of the law, which is subsequently ruled by the court to be wrong, the payer (in this case the donor) is entitled to be refunded.[31]

The Commission supports this analysis in RR 6 – *Maintenance of an Accurate Register of Charities*.[32] In that document, the Commission does not make a distinction between where it has made a mistake (for whatever reason) and where the law has been corrected.[33] In either case, the Commission takes the view that as the property was never held for charitable purposes it would not be regarded as charitable property.

The Commission does make the point that, although the institution is not charitable, some of its assets might be held on separate charitable trusts for particular charitable purposes.[34] It rightly says that it is the intention of the donor that is important when deciding the terms of those special charitable trusts. The objects of the institution are irrelevant to this process.[35]

[27] Chapter 3, pp. 52–65.

[28] See J Warburton J *Tudor on Charities*, 9th edn (London: Butterworths, 2003) para. 11–048. See Chapter 3, pp. 69–71.

[29] S. 4(1) Charities Act 1993.

[30] *Kleinwort Benson Ltd* v. *Lincoln City Council* [1999] 2 AC 349.

[31] For a discussion of this decision of the House of Lords, see McMeel, G. *The Modern Law of Restitution*, 1st edn (2000) Chapter 3 and Roger, A. 'Administration of Justice: A Time for Everything Under the Law: Some Reflections on Retrospectivity' LQR 2005, 121 (Jan), 57–79.

[32] (2000), paras. 15–20. [33] *Ibid.* para. 15. [34] *Ibid.* para. 18. [35] *Ibid.* para. 20.

The argument that it is the donor's intention which is paramount when determining whether property is charitable, rather than the objects of the institution might, in addition to property held on special charitable trusts, also be used in respect of an institution's general property. Section 14 Charities Act 1993 empowers the Commission to make a *cy-pres* scheme in relation to property given for charitable purposes which is, due to an initial failure, held for non-charitable purposes. Purposes are deemed to have failed where any difficulty in applying property to those purposes makes that property available to be returned to the donors rather than applicable *cy-pres*.[36] Section 14 could be used to save property for charity irrespective of whether it was governed by a trust, a constitution or a memorandum and articles of association. The section provides another example of charity law stepping in to save non-charitable property for charity.[37]

Section 14 is based on the decision of the Court of Appeal in *Re Ulverston and District New Hospital Building Trusts*,[38] which decided that where a charitable appeal failed, *ab initio*, the funds from identifiable sources could be presumed to have been given for the particular charitable purpose, and would therefore be held on resulting trusts for the donors, but funds from anonymous sources would be presumed to have been made by donors with a general intention in favour of charity.

Section 14 enables funds to be applied *cy-pres* when either donors have not made a 'relevant declaration'[39] to the effect that, in the event of the specific charitable purposes failing, they wish the trustees holding the property to give them the opportunity to request the return of the property, or the donors have had the benefit of prescribed advertisements and inquiries cannot be found,[40] or donors have executed a disclaimer.[41] In addition the section provides a conclusive presumption (without advertisement or inquiry) that property will belong to donors who cannot be identified where it consists:

(A) of the proceeds of cash collections made by means of collecting boxes or by other means not adapted for distinguishing one gift from another;[42] or
(B) of the proceeds of any lottery, competition, entertainment, sale or similar money-raising activity, after allowing for property given to provide prizes or articles for sale, or otherwise to enable the activity to be undertaken.[43]

Subsections 14(4)(a) and (b) allow the court and the Commission to direct that property not falling into the above categories shall nevertheless be treated as property belonging to donors who cannot be identified where it would appear to them:

[36] *Re Koeppler's Will Trusts* [1985] 2 All ER 869.
[37] See pp. 105–8 of this chapter.
[38] *Re Ulverston and District New Hospital Building Trusts* [1956] Ch 622.
[39] S. 14(3)A Charities Act 1993.
[40] S. 14(1)(a) Charities Act 1993.
[41] S. 14(1)(b) Charities Act 1993.
[42] S. 14(3)(a) Charities Act 1993.
[43] S. 14(3)(b) Charities Act 1993.

(A) unreasonable, having regard to the amounts likely to be returned to the donors, to incur expense with a view to returning the property; or
(B) that it would be unreasonable, having regard to the nature, circumstances and amounts of the gifts, and the lapse of time since the gifts were made, for the donors to expect the property to be returned.

It is important to note that, under section 14 Charities Act 1993, it does not have to be shown that the donors have a general charitable intention. The purpose of the section is to save property for charity which would otherwise have been paid into court to await claims by donors.

The reasons why the Commission might have mistakenly registered an institution which was never a charity were discussed in Chapter 3.[44] There seems to be no reason why section 14 cannot be used to save property for charity in these circumstances. However, before section 14 could be used, although a general charitable intention need not be demonstrated, it would have to be shown that the donors intended to give to purposes which were charitable. This might be evidenced by large numbers of donors electing to use the Gift Aid scheme, which depends upon the recipient being charitable.

For section 14 to apply, it must be shown that property was given for 'specific charitable purposes'.[45] The section was originally intended to avoid the problem of appeals failing,[46] however, it is not expressly restricted to charitable appeals and could therefore be used more generally where charities have failed *ab initio*. In this context it would not be unreasonable to interpret 'specific charitable purposes' as the opposite of 'general charitable purposes'. This would cover a wide range of charities as most tend to have specific objectives.

The section provides a practical and fair way of balancing the interests of donors, who deserve some effort being made to contact them, and situations where funds could not realistically be expected to be returned to donors and can be sensibly applied for *cy-pres* purposes.

If it cannot be argued that property is held on separate charitable trusts or that property can be applied *cy-pres* by way of a section 14 scheme, then the property of an institution which was never a charity will, depending on the intention of the donors, be held by the institution beneficially or on resulting trusts for the donors and not for charity.

The institution was a charity but has ceased to have charitable purposes

There is a general principle that charitable objects cannot cease to be charitable because they have become outdated or impractical.[47] The appropriate course of

[44] Chapter 3, pp. 53–65. [45] S. 14(1) Charities Act 1993.
[46] See *Re Ulverston and District New Hospital Building Trusts* [1956] Ch 622.
[47] See Chapter 3, pp. 71–73.

action in such circumstances is for the trustees to apply for a *cy-pres* scheme to modernise the purposes.[48] The most relevant *cy-pres* occasion is set out in sub-section 13(1)(e)(ii) Charities Act 1993 where the original objects have:

> ceased, as being useless or harmful to the community or for other reasons, to be in law charitable

This subsection is crucial in the context of removal. It is a statutory enactment of the dicta of Lord Simonds in *National Anti-Vivisection Society* v. *IRC*,[49] where he said that once a charity had been created it could not fail, and that the appropriate course of action would be to make a *cy-pres* scheme to reform the objects and to allow the property to be applied for contemporary *cy-pres* purposes.

The Commission does not have the power to make law.[50] Because it has so few modern precedents to follow it is pressed into making law when looking at questions of charitable status.[51] In doing so it runs the risk of coming to the wrong conclusion. In respect of charities already on the register the Commission has a legitimate way of modernising outdated objects through the use of its *cy-pres* powers, rather than deciding that an institution is not charitable due to the passage of time and then removing it from the register.[52]

Traditionally the Commission has adopted a cautious approach to modernising outdated objects through the use of its *cy-pres* powers.[53] However, there are two reasons why the Commission might adopt a more radical approach in future.

First, in recent years it has come under pressure to apply the doctrine of *cy-pres* more flexibly. Although in its review of *cy-pres*[54] the Commission confirmed the main principle: that regard needs to be had to the original trusts, it also emphasised that it would apply *cy-pres* flexibly and without applying artificial barriers.[55] This would include considering widening objects under one head of charity to include objects under another head of charity.

More recently, the Strategy Unit,[56] in the context of facilitating charity mergers, has recommended a further review of *cy-pres* by the Commission with a view to making *cy-pres* more flexible either by amending section 13 Charities Act 1993, or, in the case of mergers, by a more extensive use of section 13(1)(c) Charities Act 1993, which allows for the *cy-pres* application of property with similar purposes, which can be more effectively used in conjunction to common purposes. Section 15 Charities Act 2006 [57] inserted a new

[48] See section 13 Charities Act 1993.

[49] *National Anti-Vivisection Society* v. *IRC* [1948] AC 31 at 74.

[50] See Chapter 1, pp. 1–4 . [51] Chapter 3, pp. 45–52.

[52] S. 13 Charities Act 1993. See Chapter 3, pp. 71–73 for further discussion.

[53] [1988] Ch.Com.A.R., paras. 50–55. [54] *Ibid.* [55] *Ibid.* paras. 72–77.

[56] Cabinet Office, Strategy Unit Report, *Private Action, Public Benefit: A Review of Charities and the Wider Not-for-Profit Sector* (2002) paras. 4.57–4.62.

[57] In respect of sections 13(1)(c), 13(1)(d) and 13(1)(e)(iii) Charities Act 1993.

consideration in relation to *cy-pres*.[58] In addition to considering the spirit of the gift, the Commission will need to consider 'the social and economic circumstances' prevailing at the time of the proposed alteration of the original purposes. This should encourage a more frequent and radical application of *cy-pres* schemes.

Second, if the Review of the Register[59] results in radical new purposes being accepted as charitable by the Commission then this might eventually impact on the way in which the Commission applies *cy-pres*. A radical development of charitable status might lead to the Commission concluding that many charities on the register have purposes which have ceased to be charitable in law and require *cy-pres* modernisation.

The limitation of *cy-pres* is that it only allows for property to be applied for another charitable purpose recognised by the court or Parliament. It does not allow the Commission to create new charitable purposes[60] and apply the property for those purposes. No matter how radical the Commission are when applying *cy-pres*, they can never legitimately apply property *cy-pres* for novel charitable purposes.

Cy-pres may be used to prevent two types of charity being removed from the register. These are inactive charities and charities with the same or similar purposes which, if they did not merge, would probably fail due to market pressures.

Many inactive charities may have become inactive because their objects are no longer relevant. The Commission's Annual Report 2000–2001 suggests removing inactive charities from the register and it has subsequently indicated that this remains an objective.[61] No doubt many of these charities could equally be candidates for a *cy-pres* scheme. Given the Commission's objective of promoting the effective use of charitable resources,[62] if it has a choice between removing an inactive charity, and applying its property *cy-pres*, one would expect the Commission to take the later course.

Consolidating and merging charities is a major issue for the charity sector. A report[63] has highlighted that the general public think that there are too many charities and that charities with similar purposes should be merged. As the Commission does not have the power to remove charities solely on the basis that they have duplicate purposes, it may well increasingly look to its power to make *cy-pres* schemes under section 13(1)(c). This is used where property available for similar charitable purposes can be merged, leaving the decanted

[58] S. 13(1A)(b) Charities Act 1993. [59] See Chapter 3, pp. 65–67.

[60] The Commission does not have law-making powers. See Chapter 3, pp. 45–52.

[61] [2000/1] Ch.Com.A.R. para. 4.7 and see also *Briefing Paper For The Joint Committee on the Draft Charities Bill Charity Commission-The Future* (September 2004), para. 14.

[62] S. 1B(2)4 Charities Act 1993.

[63] See D. Morris, 'Legal Issues in Charity Mergers' (Liverpool University Charity Law Unit, 2001). See www.liv.ac.uk/law/units/clu.htm.

charity to be removed on the basis that it does not operate.[64] The Charities Act 2006[65] may well facilitate this development through the provision of more flexible grounds for *cy-pres* with the need to have regard to the social and economic circumstances[66] in addition to the spirit of the gift.[67]

It is unnecessary, for the purposes of this book, to go into too much detail about the doctrine of *cy-pres*. The important point to make is that a charity cannot be removed from the register simply because its objects have dated or have ceased to be charitable in law.

In the context of charities which cease to be charitable, the position of charitable companies merits special attention. The Commission has questioned whether the property of a charitable company will be held for charitable purposes where, due to a change in social circumstances, its objects cease to be charitable.[68] This is because a charitable company does not hold its general property on charitable trusts,[69] and therefore it could be argued that it would continue to hold its property beneficially for its objects which would be non-charitable following the company's removal from the register.

It is submitted that the better view is that the court would treat its property as being dedicated for charitable purposes,[70] so that the result would be the same as if the property were held on charitable trusts; namely, that the directors would be under an obligation to apply for a *cy-pres* scheme.[71]

Even though a charitable company does not hold its property on trust it does, in common with all charities, hold its assets subject to a legal obligation to apply the property for its charitable purposes.[72] Indeed, it would be strange if the court treated a charitable company any differently than other charities in terms of applying its property *cy-pres*.

Where objects are changed from charitable to non-charitable, sections 3(4) Charities Act 1993 provides a ground for removal where the Commission no longer considers an institution to be a charity due to 'any change in its trusts'.[73] There is no reason why charity trustees could not exercise a power of amendment in this way where it is contained in the charity's governing instrument.[74] However, there is a distinction between amending the governing instrument from a charitable form to a non-charitable one and the property of a charity being converted from charitable to non-charitable.

64 S. 3(4) Charities Act 1993. But note that the Commission has gone on record saying that it will not force charities to merge. See *RS4 a – Collaborative Working and Mergers: Summary* (March 2003).

65 S. 15(2) Charities Act 2006 introduces a new consideration of the '*social and economic circumstances*' into sections 13(1)(c), 13(1)(d) and 13(1)(e)(iii) Charities Act 1993.

66 S. 13(1A)(b) Charities Act 1993.

67 S. 13(1A)(a) Charities Act 1993.

68 RR 6 – *Maintenance of an Accurate Register of Charities* (2000) Annex E. See also Dutton J *Charitable Companies Ceasing to be Charitable* 7 *CL & PR*, 1, 2001 p. 31.

69 *Liverpool and District Hospital for Diseases of the Heart* v. *AG* [1981] 1 Ch 193.

70 *Re Vernon's Will Trusts* [1972] Ch 300.

71 S. 13(5) Charities Act 1993.

72 *Liverpool and District Hospital for Diseases of the Heart* v. *AG* [1981] 1 Ch 193 at 214.

73 S. 3(5) Charities Act 1993. See Chapter 3, pp. 73–75.

74 See Chapter 2, pp. 20–22.

In the case of unincorporated charities their property is held on charitable trust.[75] In *Baldry* v. *Feintuck*[76] it was held that, even though the governing instrument contained an express power of amendment, it was not open to the trustees to amend the original trusts over the property from charitable to non-charitable. It follows that if the trustees of an unincorporated charity amend the trusts from charitable to non-charitable then it would only be property acquired after the amendment that would be held for non-charitable purposes. In practice, the Commission insist that powers of amendment included in governing instruments cannot be exercised without its consent.[77]

In the case of an incorporated charity, the general property is not held on trust.[78] Nevertheless, if the trustees amended an incorporated charity's purposes from charitable to non-charitable, it is argued in this book that the court would impose a trust over the original property because it treats its property as being dedicated to charitable purposes[79] and would be unaffected by such an amendment.[80] This would be unlikely in the case of charitable companies because there is a statutory restriction preventing them from changing their objects without the prior written permission of the Commission.[81] Any attempt to amend the objects without the prior written consent of the Commission would be invalid.[82]

Where one of the other essential indicia[83] has been lost, the position for charitable property would appear to be the same. For example, where trustees amend a governing instrument to oust the jurisdiction of the court, then the original property will continue to be held for charitable purposes.

For time charities, at the end of the set period of time, the property will cease to be charitable.[84] For charitable property which reverts, the property will cease to be held on charitable trusts.[85] Where nobody can be identified to receive the property, it will be applied *cy-pres*.[86]

To conclude, it is only property acquired after a charity loses one or more of the essential indicia of charitable status that would be available for non-charitable purposes.

What happens to the property of a charity which is removed from the register?

Finally, where an institution is removed from the register when, in fact, it is a charity, the institution will continue to hold its property for charitable purposes.

75 Chapter 2, pp. 12–18.
76 *Baldry* v. *Feintuck* [1972] 1 WLR 552 *per* Brightman J at 557. 77 Chapter 2, pp. 20–22.
78 *Liverpool and District Hospital for Diseases of the Heart* v. *AG* [1981] 1 Ch 193 at 214.
79 *Re Vernon's Will Trusts* [1972] Ch 300. 80 S. 64(1)(a) & (b) Charities Act 1993.
81 S. 64(2)(a) & (b) & (2A)(a) Charities Act 1993. 82 S. 64(2)(a) & (b) Charities Act 1993.
83 See Chapter 2, p. 12. 84 *Re Rymer* [1895] 1 Ch 19.
85 See for example section 2 School Sites Act 1841 and *Fraser* v. *Canterbury Diocesan Board of Finance* [2006] 1 AC 377.
86 See the Reverter of Sites Act 1987.

As shown in Chapter 1,[87] registration does not determine charitable status, it provides a conclusive presumption for all purposes that an institution is a charity while it is on the register, unless rectification applies.[88]

Conclusion

There is a distinction between the governing instrument of a charity and its property. It will rarely be the case that charitable property will be lost to charity when a charity's governing instrument is removed from the register.[89]

[87] Chapter 1, pp. 12–13.
[88] S. 4(1) Charities Act 1993. See pp. 5–10 *ante*.
[89] Pp. 105–8 of this chapter.

6

The Commission's powers of investigation and the use of those powers to remove charities from the register

Introduction

In this chapter the Commission's powers of investigation will be examined to explore the extent to which investigations lead to the removal of charities from the register under section 3(4) Charities Act 1993.

The chapter looks specifically at the use of the Commission's powers to protect charity property under sections 18 and 19 Charities Act 1993 to see whether there is a consequential removal of governing instruments from the register. This is a natural line of inquiry flowing from Chapter 5 which pointed out the distinction between the governing instrument of a charity and its property.[1]

The chapter illustrates, through documentary analysis of the Commission's published inquiry reports over a two-year period, one of the basic propositions[2] of this book that the Commission's powers of removal are limited and charities will only rarely be removed from the register. This chapter also illustrates through documentary analysis that the Commission's own interpretation of its powers of removal is unclear and inconsistent where following inquiry it removes charities which have ceased to exist or operate.[3] This supports another of the basic propositions[4] that the Commission's powers of removal require clarification.

Powers of investigation and protection

This part of the chapter looks in more detail at how the Commission uses its powers in such a way that there is a consequential removal of charities from the register. The starting point for the launch of the Commission's powers of protection is the commencement of a Commission investigation (referred to in the Charities Act 1993 as an inquiry).[5] The investigation can either be in relation to a particular charity or a class of charities.

[1] Chapter 5, pp. 104–5. [2] Chapter 1, pp. 2–3. [3] Pp. 121–3 of this chapter. [4] *Ibid.*
[5] S. 8 Charities Act 1993. Except in the case of section 19B Charities Act 1993. See pp. 120–1 of this Chapter.

The Commission has the power[6] to publish its findings but this is at its discretion. Recently the Commission has published the findings of its inquiries on its website and the inquiries covered in this chapter were all sourced from there.[7]

Following the institution of an inquiry, the Commission can use its powers to act for the protection of charity property. Before it does so it must be satisfied,[8]

(A) that there is evidence of misconduct or mismanagement in the administration of the charity or (but in the case of section 18(2) 'and' (see below);
(B) that it is necessary or desirable to act for the purpose of protecting the property of the charity or securing a proper application for the purposes of the charity of that property or of property coming to the charity;
(C) except in the case of the Commission's power to direct the application of charity property.[9] In this case, the Commission must instead be satisfied that a person or persons in possession or control of any property held by or on trust for a charity is or are unwilling to apply it properly for the purposes of the charity, and that it is necessary or desirable to make an order to secure the proper application of that property for the purposes of the charity.

These powers do not expressly include the removal of an institution from the register. They are ultimately concerned with the preservation of charitable property for charitable purposes. It will be helpful to summarise the Commission's powers under sections 18 and 19 Charities Act 1993 before looking at how they are exercised in practice. The powers may be paraphrased as follows.

Sections 18(1) and 19 protective powers

These are intended as temporary powers by order to:

(A) suspend[10] any trustee, charity trustee, officer, agent or employee of the charity from the exercise of his office or employment pending consideration being given to his removal (under section 18(ii) suspensions cannot be for more than twelve months) and where such persons are also members of the charity suspend[11] their membership of the charity;
(B) appoint[12] such number of additional charity trustees as they consider necessary for the proper administration of the charity;
(C) vest[13] charity property in the Official Custodian, or require the persons in whom any such property is vested to transfer it to him, or appoint a person to transfer any such property to him;

[6] S. 8(6) Charities Act 1993.
[7] www.charity-commission.gov.uk/investigations/inquiryreports/afrad.asp.
[8] S. 18(1)(a) & (b) Charities Act 1993.
[9] S.19B Charities Act 1993. Pp. 120–1 of this chapter.
[10] S. 18(1)(i) Charities Act 1993.
[11] S. 18A(2) Charities Act 1993.
[12] S. 18(1)(ii) Charities Act 1993.
[13] S. 18(1)(iii) Charities Act 1993.

(D) order[14] any person holding property on behalf of the charity, or any trustee for it, not to part with the property without the approval of the Commission;
(E) order[15] any debtor of the charity not to make any payment in or towards the discharge of his liability to the charity without the approval of the Commission;
(F) restrict[16] (notwithstanding anything in the trusts of the charity) the transactions which may be entered into, or the nature or amount of the payments which may be made without the approval of the Commission (e.g. fundraising contracts);
(G) appoint[17] (in accordance with section 19 Charities Act 1993) an Interim Manager in respect of the property and affairs of the charity;
(H) direct[18] the charity trustees, any trustee for the charity, any officer or employee of the charity, or (if a body corporate) the charity itself, to take any action specified in the order which the Commission considers expedient in the interests of the charity; and / or
(I) direct[19] a person or persons in control of charitable property who is, or are, unwilling to apply it properly for the purposes of the charity where the Commission is satisfied that it is necessary or desirable to secure the proper application of that property for the purposes of the charity.

Section 18(2) protective powers

These powers are intended as more permanent action by the Commission. They include:

(A) removal[20] of a trustee, employee, agent or employee who has been responsible for or privy to the misconduct or mismanagement, or has, by his conduct, contributed to it, or facilitated it; and / or
(B) power by order[21] to establish a scheme for the administration of the charity.

Each of these powers should be examined to see how they lead to the removal of charities from the register.

Appointment of additional trustees

The Commission has been known to use its power under section 18 Charities Act 1993 to appoint additional trustees to form a majority. This can indirectly lead to the removal of charities from the register.

[14] S. 18(1)(iv) Charities Act 1993. [15] S. 18(1)(v) Charities Act 1993.
[16] S. 18(1)(vi) Charities Act 1993. [17] S. 18(1)(vii) Charities Act 1993.
[18] S. 19A Charities Act 1993. [19] S. 19B Charities Act 1993.
[20] S. 18(2)(i) Charities Act 1993. [21] S. 18(2)(ii) Charities Act 1993.

For example, in *The Alzheimer's Foundation for Research into Alzheimer's Disease* inquiry[22] the Commission used this power to appoint four additional trustees to act for a charity which had three existing trustees. The additional trustees formed a majority and could out vote the existing trustees. Following the conclusion of the inquiry, the Alzheimer's Foundation for Research into Alzheimer's Disease was wound up.

If the Commission appoints additional trustees to form a majority of the trustees, particularly where those trustees are representatives, or even former representatives, of a rival charity, then this could lead to the transfer of property from the failing charity to another more successful existing charity including the rival charity.

Appointment of an interim manager

Similarly the Commission can use its power to appoint an interim manager[23] and as in the case of the appointment of additional trustees this can lead to the transfer of a charity's property and the removal of its governing instrument from the register.

For example, in the *Tracheotomy Patients Aid Fund Inquiry*[24] the charity had objects to help tracheotomy patients and to promote research into the prevention of the condition giving rise to tracheotomies. Of the four trustees reported as acting when the inquiry began one had died, one could not be traced, one had not attended any meetings but had been asked to sign minutes which recorded his attendance. That left the remaining trustee who was the wife of the founder trustee.

The Commission's main conclusion was that there was no effective independent trustee body and that the running of the charity had been left to the chief executive. The founder had resigned his position as a trustee in order to take on a paid position as chief executive. He was accountable for the remuneration received.[25] The founder's wife had acted as a trustee even though there was a conflict of interests. Furthermore, the level of fundraising costs and the level of expenses were high and insufficient steps had been taken to apply the income of the charity.

In the absence of an effective and independent trustee body, the accounts of the charity were frozen, the chief executive suspended from employment, the assets of the charity were vested in the Official Custodian, and a receiver and manager was appointed. The receiver and manager concluded that, in the

[22] See *Third Sector* 18th August 2004. There is no record of this charity, on the register of charities, nor a record of it being removed from the register.

[23] The term Receiver and Manager has now been replaced by interim manager. See section 112 Charities Act 2006.

[24] See www.Charity-Commission.gov.uk/investigations/inquiryreports/afrad/asp.

[25] Under the general equitable principle that a trustee must not acquire remuneration or benefits by virtue of his position *per* Cohen J in *Re Macadam* [1946] Ch 73 at 82.

absence of a sound administrative base, and in the absence of a long-standing name and reputation for its charitable work, the charity's assets should be distributed to established charities with similar objects. Before the charity could be wound up, a settlement was reached with the chief executive in respect of a claim by the charity for unlawful remuneration and by the chief executive for loss of earnings and expenses. The charity was then removed from the register on the ground that it had ceased to exist.

The appointment of an interim manager can therefore lead to the removal of a charity from the register without the need for the Commission to have immediate recourse to its power of removal under section 3(4) Charities Act 1993.

Making schemes

There are several reported investigation cases where the Commission has used its scheme making powers to either dissolve a charity and pass its assets to a newly formed charity or to amalgamate charities into a newly formed charity. Either of these courses of action involve removal from the register.

In the case of *Iran Aid*,[26] the charity was investigated by the Commission because there were allegations that the charity was being used as a terrorist organisation, the Mujaheddin el khalq (MKO), to raise funds. Under the Terrorism Act 2001 the MKO is a proscribed organisation.

The Commission froze the charity's bank account and appointed a receiver and manager to take on the management of the charity and report back to the Commission on the running of the charity. The Commission came to the following conclusions:

(A) *Fund-raising*
The Commission found that some donors were misled into believing that they were personally sponsoring individual children when this was not in fact the case. The Commission also found evidence of misleading promotional literature and complaints by donors about high-pressure 'selling' techniques.

(B) *The Charity's Records*
The Commission found that the trustees had not met their obligation to maintain proper accounting records as required by the charity's governing instrument, the common law and statute. The Commission and the receiver and manager failed to gain access to the charity's records because according to the Commission the trustees failed to co-operate and occupied the charity's premises with the expressed intention of denying access to the records.[27] The occupation ended with the destruction of all records

[26] See www.Charity-Commission.gov.uk/investigations/inquiry reports/afrad/asp.

[27] Provided he is acting within the powers set out in the order the receiver is entitled to possession of all the property and to exercise all the powers previously exercised by the trustees. See *Rezafard* v. *Runacres* unreported, 4 November 1998, Ferris J.

which might have been expected to show how the charity distributed its funds.

(C) *Transmission of funds to Iran and their Application*
Neither the Commission nor the receiver and manager found any evidence to show how the charity spent its funds in Iran. The Commission concluded that, at least, there had been mismanagement in the affairs of the charity.

A remedial scheme was established, directing the receiver and manager to dissolve the charity and pass its assets to a new independent charity – the Iran Aid Foundation. Following dissolution the charity was removed from the register. Removal was therefore achieved indirectly as a consequence of the Commission using its powers to protect charitable property.[28]

Another example of the Commission using its power to make a scheme to dissolve a charity is *The Royal Masonic Hospital Association* inquiry.[29] The Receiver and Manager applied for a scheme of the Commission under section 16 of the Charities Act 1993 to acquire the power to dissolve the charity and pass its assets to other Masonic charities whose objects provided for the relief of the sick or the infirm, as he thought fit. This followed the closure of the Royal Masonic Hospital which was the subject of a separate inquiry.[30] Once the assets had been distributed and the charity dissolved it was removed from the register.

Removal of trustees

When the Commission has removed trustees it has led to several high profile appeals.[31] One such appeal *Jones* v. *AG*[32] demonstrates the primary concern of the Court to protect property. In that case the court removed the trustee and appointed the NSPCC in his place.

The removal of a trustee can indirectly lead to removal. For example, in the *Charitable Assets and Activities of Mr and Mrs Dove in connection with Reading Medical and Rescue Unit* inquiry[33] Mr and Mrs Dove were removed as trustees of the charity because they were found to have supplied misleading information and failed to act properly in their capacity as trustees of charitable

[28] For criticism of this inquiry see Lords Hansard 7 June 2005; col. 813 *per* Lord Swinfen.

[29] Registered charity number 265152.

[30] [1994] Ch.Com.A.R. p. 16. The hospital was sold by the appointed receiver and manager because this charity was in financial crisis and the Commission made a scheme to provide for the proceeds of sale.

[31] When the Commission removes trustees there is no need for the charity or any of its trustees to obtain a certificate of leave to appeal from the Commission or a High Court judge. See section 18(9)(b) Charities Act 1993.

[32] *Jones* v. *AG* [1974] Ch 148. See also *Weth* v. *AG* [1999] 1 WLR 686 (CA) and *Scargill* v. *AG* unreported 4 September 1998, Neuberger J; [1998] Ch.Com.A.R. p. 22. These decisions are reviewed in Phillips, A. 'Retirement and Removal of Trustees' *Trusts & Estates Law Journal*, July / August 1999.

[33] Registered charity number 1039826.

funds. The remaining trustees then decided to wind up the charity, and it was removed from the register.

The institution of the inquiry leads the trustees to conclude that they should dissolve the charity

Sometimes trustees conclude that they no longer wish to continue the work of the charity. This could be because of a variety of reasons, ranging from other charities carrying out similar work, through to the trustees realising that they find the duties and responsibilities of being a charity trustee too much.

In the *46115 (Scots Guardsman) Steam Locomotive Trust Limited* Inquiry[34] the issues involved an internal dispute between the trustees about the validity of trustee appointments. Due to a lack of funding, there was an overall disagreement between the trustees about the locomotive's future. The Commission indicated that, although not a finding of the inquiry, winding up the charity might not only be the most pragmatic solution to the constitutional problems but would also probably be the most effective way to achieve restoration of the locomotive. The trustees accepted the Commission's advice, transferred the locomotive to another charity with similar objects, wound up the charity and the Commission duly removed it from the register.

New powers under the Charities Act 2006

A couple of the new powers to protect charity, which have been conferred on the Commission by the Charities Act 2006, could, when exercised, lead indirectly to removal from the register.

First, the Commission has a new power to give specific directions for the protection of charity[35] which the Commission considers to be expedient in the interests of the charity. The purpose of this power is to allow the Commission to have access to intermediate powers, short of using its powers to suspend or remove persons from their positions in a charity. Although it would be open to the Commission to direct the trustees to transfer the property to another charity, or expend it until it is exhausted and then apply for the charity to be removed, it is submitted that this will rarely happen because the intention behind the section was to provide intermediate powers concerned with correcting poor governance.[36]

Second, the Commission has a new power[37] to direct the application of charity property where it is satisfied that it is necessary or desirable to make an order for the purpose of securing the proper application of that property for the purposes of the charity. Theoretically, this power could be used to transfer property from one charity to another leaving the decanted charity to be removed

[34] Registered charity number 107794. [35] S. 19A Charities Act 1993.

[36] Charities Bill [Lords] Standing Committee A 11 July 2006; col. 192 *per* Edward Miliband.

[37] S. 19B Charities Act 1993.

from the register, but this is unlikely as the Commission has gone on record as saying it will not force charities to merge.[38]

Although the Commission's position has been strengthened by these new powers, the rights of charities have also been improved by a combination of the Commission's general duty[39] to have regard to the principles of best regulatory practice (being proportionate, accountable, consistent, transparent and targeted only at cases in which action is needed) and the right of charities to appeal to the Charity Tribunal.[40] It is too early to say how these powers will be exercised but they are not likely to disturb the findings in this chapter that indirect removals are rare.[41]

Documentary analysis

Documentary analysis has been conducted on 513 reported inquiries between 2003 and 2004. The purpose of this research is to give an objective analysis of how many charities were removed by the Commission as a result of an inquiry and on what grounds.

In many cases it was the trustees who decided to dissolve the charity and apply for it to be removed from the register rather than the Commission. The result was the same but the decision was the trustees' rather than the Commission's. In these cases, of the 513 reported inquiries, in forty-nine cases the trustees decided themselves to dissolve and apply for removal or, in percentage terms, 9.5 per cent.

Of the 513 reported inquiries, the Commission removed thirty-one charities from the register (fewer than the number of trustees deciding to apply for removal). Of the charities removed by the Commission, twenty were removed on the ground that they did not operate, nine because they had ceased to exist, one because of a change in purposes or trusts, and one because the Commission no longer regarded the institution as charitable. The grounds for removal merit further attention.

Does not operate

Of the thirty-one charities removed from the register by the Commission, twenty were removed because they did not operate.[42] Expressed in percentage terms, 64.5 per cent of the charities removed were removed on this ground. Of the 513 reported inquiries the percentage of charities removed because they did not operate was 3.9 per cent.

[38] See RS4 a – *Collaborative Working and Mergers: Summary* (March 2003). See Chapter 9, pp. 196–7.

[39] S. 1D(2)4 Charities Act 1993.

[40] Schedule 4 3(1) & (2) Charities Act 2006. See Chapter 8, pp. 174–7.

[41] Pp. 12–13 of this chapter.

[42] The meaning of 'does not operate' was analysed in Chapter 3, pp. 83–84.

The theme of the inquiry reports was that there had been a failure of governance, either through mismanagement or misconduct or because there were no trustees or no trustees that can be found, leading to a cessation in charitable activities.[43]

Some of the reports involve no charitable activity[44] others indicate that not only was there no charitable activity but there was non-charitable activity.[45] In cases where there were breaches of trust the Commission decided not to seek restitution on behalf of the charities. In one case this was because of the amount involved and because the charity was no longer operating[46] and in another case this was because there would be no advantage to the charity.[47] There was no explanation why these decisions were taken.[48]

As a general comment, there is no consistent guidance arising from the inquiry reports as to when a charity does not operate. There is even some confusion in the reports about whether a charity was removed because it did not operate or had ceased to exist.[49]

In some inquiry reports, non-charitable activity was equated with the charity not operating and the charity was removed from the register. For example, in *Yes! Positive Thinking Foundation*[50] the Commission described a charity which had the hallmarks of being '*captive*' because its professional fundraisers were related to, or close business associates of the trustees. The professional fundraisers did not have contracts as required by the Charities Act 1992. Staff were appointed without open and fair recruitment and salaries being paid in cash to evade tax. There was no evidence of the charity applying funds in furtherance of its objects. The Commission reported its findings to the police, the Benefits Agency and HM Revenue and Customs and removed the charity from the register on the basis that it did not operate and did not seek restitution for the charity.

[43] For examples see *Signpost Phab*, registered charity number 292023 (no current trustees and no charitable activity) and *Ebony Housing Project*, registered charity number 1062349 (unauthorised benefits and conflicts of interest and no charitable activity).

[44] For example, *International Redevelopment Foundation*, registered charity number 1052950.

[45] For example, see *Life Builders International Network*, registered number 1061941.

[46] *Ebony Housing Project, ibid.* [47] *Tower Hill Community Trust*, date of inquiry 7 March 2003.

[48] The Commission must take a proportionate approach to regulation when performing its general function of investigating charities under section 1C(2)3 Charities Act 1993. Under section 1D(2)4. Charities Act 1993 the Commission, when performing its general functions, has a general duty to *'be proportionate ... and targeted only at cases in which action is needed'.*

[49] See *R. W. Bailey Memorial Trust*, registered charity number 1046422, where the inquiry report says it was removed because it did not operate, and the registered charity details say it was removed because it had ceased to exist. The same occurs in *Signpost Phab*, *ibid*. In *Phab Harwich*, registered number 1041823, the inquiry report says that this charity was removed because it had ceased to operate and had ceased to exist.

[50] Registered charity number 1092021.

Ceased to exist

Of the 513 reported inquiries, nine were removed because they had ceased to exist.[51] This is 29 per cent of the total number of institutions removed and 1.94 per cent of the total number of inquiry reports.

Of the charities removed on this ground, five were removed after eighty-four charities were investigated because they failed to submit annual returns and accounts. These charities were listed in three inquiry reports called *Enforcing Submission of Annual Return and Accounts Reports*.[52] No specific details were given in the inquiry reports, but a search of the central register details revealed that five were removed on this ground.

Of the remaining four charities, two were removed because they had been struck off the companies register.[53] In *Hands of Hope Children's Cancer Fund*[54] there was £10,000 left in a bank account. Rather than go to the expense of restoring the company to the register the Commission, with the consent of the Treasury Solicitor, made a scheme transferring the funds to another charity, Sargent Cancer Care for Children.[55] Following that transfer the charity was removed from the register. A general procedure was agreed for similar cases.

The Royal Masonic Hospital Association[56] had objects to further the work of the Royal Masonic Hospital.[57] Following the Hospital's closure the trustees sought to use its funds to reinstate the Hospital. A receiver and manager was appointed who recommended that a scheme be made giving him the power to dissolve the charity and apply the remaining funds for charitable purposes. Once this had happened the charity was removed from the register on the ground that it had ceased to exist.

The Martin Foundation Trust[58] was removed because, as the Commission said in its report, it had ceased to operate in May 2000 and had effectively ceased to exist at that date.

Change in trusts

Only one charity was removed on this ground. This represents 3.25 per cent of the total charities removed from the register. Of the total 513 inquiries, 0.19 per cent were removed for this reason. In *Heavitree Social Centre*[59] a social centre and grounds organisation had amended its constitution to become a charity but had continued to carry out non-charitable activities. Its real property had

[51] The meaning of 'ceased to exist' was analysed in Chapter 3, pp. 75–83.

[52] www.charity-commission.gov.uk/investigations/inquiryreports/afrad.asp.

[53] See *Hands of Hope Children's Cancer Fund*, registered charity number 1054815, and *The Sulis Trust* 1010428.

[54] *Ibid.* [55] Registered charity number 1085616.

[56] Registered charity number 265152. [57] Registered charity number 205793.

[58] *The Martin Foundation Trust*, registered charity number, 1067149.

[59] Registered charity number 300829.

originally been conveyed for non-charitable social club purposes. The Commission concluded that the solution was for the charity to amend its objects so that it ceased to be a charity because in reality it was a social club. Funds acquired following its conversion to being a charity would continue to be held for charitable purposes, although its real property would be held for the new non-charitable purposes.

No longer considers is a charity

Only one charity was removed on this ground representing 3.25 per cent of the total number of charities removed from the register. Of the total 513 reported inquiries only 0.19 per cent were removed for this reason.

In *Christian Corps International*[60] the charity had objects to advance the Christian faith particularly in the business world. The Commission found that the charity's four trustees owned a wholesale jewellery company and that company owned a jewellery manufacturing company based in Thailand. All the trustees and members of the charity worked for the wholesale company. Although this company covenanted 70 per cent of its profits to the charity, the Commission considered that the contribution by the charity, through its trustees and members, and its supporters amounted to non-charitable expenditure. In so far as the trustees and members benefited, this could not be regarded as incidental.

The charity published a newsletter and carried out a small amount of broadcasting in furtherance of its objects. These activities also promoted the products of the wholesale company. The charity's property included a chapel and a library but members of the public were not encouraged to use these facilities. The Commission concluded that there was very little charitable activity and that the institution was neither established for exclusively charitable purposes nor was it established for the benefit of the public. The Commission therefore removed the institution from the register of charities.

It should be noted that two of the charities[61] which were removed because they did not operate could arguably have been removed because they were sham charities.[62] In conclusion, the Commission is presently reluctant to remove charities from the register on the basis that they no longer appear to be charitable.

Conclusion

The Commission's powers of protection under sections 18 and 19 Charities Act 1993 are designed as their statutory heading indicates for the 'protection of charity', and not for a way of indirectly bringing about the removal of charities.

[60] Registered charity number 327193.

[61] *Yes! Positive Thinking Foundation* and *Bright Sparks Theatre School*. See pp. 121–2 of this Chapter.

[62] See Chapter 3, pp. 54–56.

The powers of removal under section 3(4) Charities Act 1993 are not designed to punish trustees failing to carry out the trusts of a charity.[63]

The documentary analysis supports this conclusion about the Commission's powers of protection. Of the 513 inquiry reports examined from 2003 to 2004, the Commission only decided to remove thirty-one from the register. This shows that the Commission generally recognises that its powers of protection are to protect charitable property, and not indirectly to bring about the removal of charities.

The Commission's powers of protection, and the approach taken by the Commission in investigation cases, corroborates the basic proposition[64] of this book, that the Commission's powers of removal are limited and that it will only be in rare cases that a charity can be removed from the register. When this happens, it is more likely to be on the grounds that the charity has ceased to exist or does not operate, than the Commission considering that an institution is no longer a charity.[65]

It was also shown that the Commission often gives inconsistent reasons in its inquiry reports as to why a charity has been removed when it is removed because it does not operate or has ceased to exist.[66] This supports the basic proposition that the Commission's powers of removal need to be clarified.[67]

One potential problem might be that the Commission starts to equate breaches of trust with grounds for removal on the basis that a charity does not operate. The Commission is under a general duty to undertake proportionate regulation,[68] and therefore where funds are insignificant it would be open to the Commission not to seek restitution and to remove a charity from the register. The difficulty is that it is not clear what would amount to proportionate regulation and there is therefore a need for the Commission to clarify its position. This further supports the basic proposition of the book that the Commission's powers of removal need clarification.

[63] See Nathan, *The Charities Act 1960*, 1st edn (London: Butterworths, 1962) p. 52, where the architect of the original powers of protection commented on the intention of Parliament.

[64] Chapter 1, pp. 1–4. [65] S. 3(4) Charities Act 1993.

[66] See pp. 121–3 of this chapter. [67] Chapter 1, pp. 1–4.

[68] Under section 1D(2)4 Charities Act 1993, the Commission, when performing its general functions, has a general duty to 'be proportionate … and targeted only at cases in which action is needed'.

7

How the Commission's powers to remove charities from the register may be affected by changes to the law of charitable status

Introduction

This chapter examines the effect of the Human Rights Act 1998 and the Charities Act 2006 on the Commission's powers to remove charities from the register.

The Human Rights Act 1998 could restrict the ability of the Commission to remove institutions. As public authorities,[1] both the court and the Commission have a duty to exercise their powers in conformity with the Human Rights Act 1998. It is a basic proposition[2] of this book that there is a problem of legality with the Commission deciding that an institution is not a charity and removing it from the register. It has been shown that there are so few decisions of the court determining what is charitable in law that the Commission is forced into becoming a *de facto* lawmaker.[3] It has already been shown that,[4] in practice, the Commission often has to second-guess what the court would decide if faced with the same facts. Following the Human Rights Act 1998, if the Commission does second-guess the court, it will need to take into account that the court would interpret charity law in accordance with Convention rights.[5]

When exercising its power of removal, under section 3(4) Charities Act 1993, to remove an institution on the ground that the Commission no longer considers it to be a charity the Commission will need to consider Convention rights which are potentially relevant to all charities, namely Article 1, Protocol 1: Right to Property and Article 14: Freedom from Discrimination in Respect of Convention Rights; and specific Convention rights, namely Article 9: Freedom of Thought, Conscience and Religion; Article 2, Protocol 1: Right to Education, and Article 10: Freedom of Expression, which are potentially relevant to particular categories of charity. These general and particular Convention rights could restrict the Commission's powers of removal by widening the application of the law of charitable status. Each of these Convention rights will be explored in this chapter.

[1] S. 6(3) Human Rights Act 1998. [2] Chapter 1, pp. 1–4. [3] Chapter 3, pp. 45–52.
[4] See Chapter 3, pp. 65–67. [5] S. 1 Human Rights Act 1998.

The Human Rights Act 1998 has already had an effect on the way the Commission interprets charity law and exercises its powers. The most obvious example of this influence on the Commission is the recognition of the promotion of human rights as a charitable purpose.[6] It had been assumed following *McGovern* v. *AG*[7] that the promotion of human rights was not charitable.[8] The Commission has also adopted a more flexible approach to the application of the *Compton* test[9] which is discussed in this chapter. In addition, the Commission has issued operational guidance on the implications of the Human Rights Act 1998 on its work and has concluded that it has implications for the exercise of its powers to remove charities from the register.[10]

Even prior to the Human Rights Act 1998 coming into force,[11] the Commission started to take into account Convention rights when determining applications for charitable status.[12] This indicates that the Commission will actively consider whether the law of charitable status and the exercise of its powers have been affected by the Human Rights Act 1998 and, in turn, whether its powers to remove charities from the register have consequently been restricted. If the Commission is to take into account the Human Rights Act 1998 when interpreting the law of charitable status then it will need to do so on a correct analysis of the law. This chapter aims to show that the Human Rights Act 1998 might cause the Commission to take a broader view of the law of charitable status than it has to date. This will further limit its power to remove charities from the register.[13]

The impact of the Human Rights Act 1998 can also be seen in the Charities Act 2006, which amends[14] the Recreational Charities Act 1958 to remove the restriction of a beneficiary class restricted solely to women.[15] The Charities Act 2006 also widens the definition of 'religion' for the purposes of charity law from being solely monotheistic to being polytheistic and non-theistic.[16] Furthermore, the Charities Act 2006 abolishes the common law presumption of public benefit for the first three heads of charity,[17] so that all charities need to demonstrate public benefit.[18] As a result, the likelihood of a breach of Article 14, on the basis that some charities enjoy the presumption while others do not, will disappear. For example, previously, religious charities enjoyed the presumption and

[6] RR 12 – *The Promotion of Human Rights* (version January 2005).

[7] *McGovern* v. *AG* [1982] Ch 321. The court did not directly decide this point.

[8] Moffat, G. 'Charity, Politics and the Human Rights Act 1998: Chasing a Red Herring?' 4 *IJNL* 1.

[9] See p. 135 of this chapter.

[10] OG 71 *Human Rights Act 1998* B2-18 September 2000.

[11] The Human Rights Act 1998 came into force on 2 October 2000.

[12] See *Decision of the Charity Commissioners for England and Wales 17th November 1999 Application for registration as a charity by The Church of Scientology (England and Wales).*

[13] Chapter 1, pp. 1–4. [14] S. 5(2) Charities Act 2006.

[15] S. 1(2) Recreational Charities Act 1958. [16] S. 2(3)(a)(i)(ii) Charities Act 2006.

[17] See *National Anti-Vivisection Society* v. *IRC* [1948] AC 31 at 65 *per* Lord Simonds.

[18] S. 3(2) Charities Act 2006.

charities with objects for the promotion of the moral and spiritual welfare of the community did not.

Some of the provisions of the Charities Act 2006 have the effect of broadening the scope of charitable status making it harder for the Commission to remove charities from the register but some of the provisions restrict the scope of charitable status making removal easier. These are explained later in the chapter.[19]

The Human Rights Act 1998

The long title to the Human Rights Act 1998 states that it is an Act 'to give further effect to the rights and freedoms guaranteed under the European Convention on Human Rights'.[20] The effect of the Human Rights Act 1998 is to give direct access[21] to the European Convention on Human Rights. Before 1998, the Convention had a limited but important effect on the domestic law in creating rights and duties.[22]

Before the Human Rights Act 1998, the courts could:[23]

(A) Interpret ambiguous legislation consistently with the Convention.[24]

(B) Seek to apply the common law (where it was uncertain, unclear or incomplete) and exercise judicial discretion consistently with the Convention.[25]

(C) Take into account that, although public authorities when exercising their discretionary powers had no duty to exercise them consistently with the Convention,[26] the human rights context was relevant to whether it had acted reasonably and had had regard to all relevant considerations.[27]

(D) Where a dispute concerns directly effective European Union law, the courts could and still do take account of the Convention because European Union law includes the principles recognised by the Convention.[28]

[19] Pp. 167–9 of this chapter.

[20] European Convention for the Protection of Human Rights and Fundamental Freedoms (Rome 1950).

[21] The White Paper, *Rights Brought Home* (Cm 3782, 1997), para. 1.19 says that the aim of the legislation 'is a straightforward one. It is to make more directly accessible the rights which the British people already enjoy under the Convention. In other words, to bring those rights home.'

[22] Lester and Pannick, *Human Rights Law and Practice*, 2nd edn (London: LexisNexis UK, 2004) p. 24.

[23] *Ibid.*

[24] *R* v. *Secretary of State for the Home Department, ex p Brind* [1991] 1 AC 696, HL at 747–748 and at 760.

[25] *Derbyshire County Council* v. *Times Newspapers Ltd* [1992] QB 770, CA at 812 D-E, 822 D-E and 830 A-B.

[26] *R* v. *Secretary of State for the Home Department, ex p Brind* [1991] 1 AC 696, HL at 748 A-F.

[27] *R* v. *Ministry of Defence ex p Smith* [1996] QB 517 at 554 E-G.

[28] Article F(2) of the Maastricht Treaty.

Prior to the enactment[29] and coming into force[30] of the Human Rights Act 1998, the only reported decision of the Commission which took the Convention into account was the decision of the Commission not to register the Church of Scientology.[31] The potential impact of the Human Rights Act 1998 had not therefore been fully explored by the Commission prior to the Human Rights Act 1998 coming into force on the 2 October 2000.

Public authorities

The Human Rights Act 1998 imposes a duty on public authorities to act[32] in a manner compatible with Convention rights.[33]

Section 6(3) Human Rights Act 1998 defines a 'public authority' as including:

(A) court or tribunal; and
(B) any person certain of whom functions are functions of a public nature but does not include the Houses of Parliament, or a person exercising functions in connection with proceedings in Parliament.

The Commission's powers of removal under section 3(4) Charities Act 1993 are a function of a public nature and therefore the Commission is a 'public authority' for the purposes of removal. Section 6 of the Human Rights Act 1998 imposes a duty on public authorities to act in a manner compatible with Convention rights. When exercising its power of removal, the Commission must follow the general law including decisions of the Court interpreting Convention rights.[34] It has already been shown[35] that because there are so few decisions of the court, in practice, the Commission has to second-guess what it thinks the court would decide if faced with the same set of facts.

Of particular relevance is section 2 Human Rights Act 1998, which requires United Kingdom courts and tribunals to take account of the jurisdiction of the Strasbourg institutions, such as the European Court of Human Rights, where they are relevant to the determination of a question in relation to a Convention right. United Kingdom courts and tribunals are not bound to follow the jurisdiction of the Strasbourg institutions but they ought to where they are relevant.[36] The courts and tribunals may be assisted by the judgments of the domestic courts of other jurisdictions, whether in relation to provisions of the Convention

[29] 9 November 1998. [30] 2 October 2000.

[31] See *Decision of the Charity Commissioners for England and Wales 17th November 1999 Application for registration as a charity by The Church of Scientology (England and Wales).*

[32] S. 6(6) Human Rights Act 1998 defines an 'act' as including a failure to act. This will be relevant to the discussion on Article 14 later at pp. 140–5 of this chapter.

[33] S. 6 Human Rights Act 1998. [34] See Chapter 1, pp. 1–4. [35] Chapter 3, pp. 45–52.

[36] As explained by The Lord Chancellor, Lord Irvine of Lairg, explained at the Committee stage of the Bill in the House of Lords, 583, HL Official Report (5th Series); Cols. 514–515 (18 November 1997).

or in relation to other human rights institutions.[37] When deciding matters of charitable status, the court must look beyond traditional English charity law. It follows that when the Commission second-guesses the court, it too must take into account Strasbourg jurisdiction and decisions of courts from other jurisdictions. In the context of exercising its powers of removal, where the Commission examines the charitable status of institutions and their entitlement to remain on the register it will have to take into account Convention rights.

Section 2 Human Rights Act 1998 is reinforced by section 3 of that Act, which deals with the relationship between Convention rights and United Kingdom legislation. It requires primary and subordinate legislation to be interpreted and applied consistently with Convention rights, so far as it is possible. This means that the Commission, as a public authority, must interpret its powers of removal under section 3(4) Charities Act 1993 so far as possible, in a way in which is compatible with Convention rights. Section 3 Human Rights Act 1998 introduces a radical new way of interpreting legislation. As Lord Cooke of Thorndon said during the second reading debate in the House of Lords:[38]

> Section 3(1) will require a very different approach to interpretation from that to which the United Kingdom Courts are accustomed. Traditionally, the search has been for true meaning; now it will be for a possible meaning that would prevent the making of a declaration of incompatibility.[39]

Before exploring the Convention rights and their application to charitable status in more detail, it is necessary to examine whether the Human Rights Act 1998 applies to the removal of charities from the register.

Does the Human Rights Act 1998 apply to the removal of charities from the register?

It could be argued that the removal of charitable status would not affect the ability of an institution to carry out its purposes such as manifesting a religion (protected by Article 9), or expressing free speech (protected by Article 10). The removal of charitable status would allow institutions more freedom to carry out their purposes and apply their property as they wish as they would not be constrained by charity law and regulation by the Commission.[40] Alternatively, it could be argued that the removal of tax reliefs and the enhanced ability to fundraise[41] that charitable status provides could limit the purposes that institutions carry out. If the purposes of a charity are protected by a Convention right,

[37] *Reyes* v. *R* [2002] UKPC 11, [2002] 2 AC 235.

[38] 582 HL Official Report (5th Series) Col 1272 (3 November 1991).

[39] See section 4 Human Rights Act 1998.

[40] See Chapter 2, pp. 12–14 for the essential indicia of charitable status.

[41] Chapter 9, pp. 130–1.

then it could be argued that there has been a breach of that Convention right. It could also be argued that the removal of charities from the register must be on a non-discriminatory basis so that any difference in treatment can be justified as being both objective and reasonable.[42] Otherwise there might be a breach of Article 14: Prohibition against Discrimination.

It could be argued that charitable institutions themselves do not have rights under the Human Rights Act 1998. It was shown in Chapter 5[43] that the court has never placed great store by governing instruments and that its focus has always been on the application of property for the benefit of beneficiaries and charitable purposes. Rights such as they exist, belong not to institutions but to the donors. It could be argued that when donors give to a charity, which is subject to the existing law of public benefit,[44] the rule against political objects[45] and the restriction on political campaigning, then their human rights have not been violated if an institution is removed because the donors know that institutions do not have rights under the Human Rights Act 1998, that institutions are subject to existing charity law and that, knowing this, they still decided to donate. On the other hand, they could argue that because charity law has not yet fully accommodated Convention rights they were not offered a choice and that their choice should have been broadened following the Human Rights Act 1998.

Even if the Human Rights Act 1998 applies to the removal of charities from the register the various Convention rights are subject to limits and they may prevent the Human Rights Act 1998 applying. These limits will be discussed in relation to each Convention right reviewed.

In addition states are allowed a margin of appreciation in respect of social and economic policy[46] which would include the removal of charities from the register which do not qualify for charitable status. Balanced against the margin of appreciation is the special importance awarded by the court to particular Convention rights such as Freedom of Expression (Article 10)[47] and Freedom of Thought, Conscience and Religion (Article 9).[48]

These issues will be discussed further in this chapter but it should be noted at this stage that it is not clear whether the Human Rights Act 1998 applies to the removal of charities from the register. It is the element of doubt which may well influence the Commission to adopt a more cautious approach to the removal of charities from the register.

It is now necessary to examine the general principles and limitations before exploring the various relevant Convention rights in detail.

[42] *Belgium Linguistic case* (1968) (No. 2) 1 EHRR 252 paras. 9–10.
[43] See Chapter 5, pp. 104–5. [44] Chapter 2, pp. 34–42. [45] Pp. 157–60 of this chapter.
[46] *R* v. *DPP ex p Kebilene* [2000] 2 AC 326, HL at 381 C–D.
[47] *R* v. *DPP ex p Kebilene* [2000] 2 AC 326, HL.
[48] *Kokkinakis* v. *Greece* (1993) 17 EHRR 397, Ect HR, para. 31.

General principles

Convention rights are intended to guarantee 'not rights that are theoretical or illusory but rights that are practical and effective'.[49] A discussion of the Human Rights Act 1998 and its effect on the Commission's power of removal is not therefore theoretical.

An important principle behind Convention rights is that a fair balance should be struck between 'the demands of the general interest of the community and the requirements of the protection of the individuals' fundamental rights'.[50] Central to the principle of fair balance is the principle of proportionality.[51]

A restriction on a freedom guaranteed by a Convention right must be proportionate to the legitimate aim pursued.[52] A measure will only satisfy the proportionality test if three criteria[53] are satisfied:

(A) The legislative objective must be sufficiently important to justify limiting a fundamental right.
(B) The measures designed to meet the legislative objective must be rationally connected to that objective – they must not be arbitrary, unfair or based on irrational considerations.
(C) The means used to impair the Convention right must be no more than is necessary to accomplish the legitimate objective – the more severe the detrimental effects of the measure,[54] the more important the objectives must be if the measure is to be justified in a democratic society.

The application of these criteria will depend on a number of factors including the importance of a Convention right.

Finally, the doctrine of the margin of appreciation allows national authorities to evaluate local needs and conditions when applying Convention rights.[55] In doing so they will still be subject to European supervision.[56] There is a reluctance to interfere with a state's social and economic policy,[57] which would generally include charity law and regulation. On the other hand, the European Court of Human Rights has recognised particular Convention rights involving personal liberty such as Article 10: Freedom of Expression and

[49] *Airey* v. *Ireland* (1979) 2 EHRR.

[50] *Sporrong and Lonnroth* v. *Sweden* (1982) EHRR 35 at 52.

[51] Lester and Pannick *Human Rights Law and Practice*, 2nd edn (London: Lexis Nexis UK, 2004) p. 89.

[52] *Handyside* v. *United Kingdom* (1976) 1 EHRR 737 at 754.

[53] *De Freitas* v. *Permanent Secretary of Ministry of Agriculture, Fisheries, Lands and Housing* [1999] 1 AC 69, PC *per* Lord Clyde at 80.

[54] *R (Farrakam)* v. *Secretary of State for the Home Department* [2002] EWCA Civ 606, [2002] QB 1391 at 1418, para. 77.

[55] *Buckley* v. *United Kingdom* (1996) 23 EHRR 101 at 129, Ect HR para. 75.

[56] *Handyside* v. *United Kingdom* (1976) 1 EHRR 737 at 754.

[57] *R* v. *Kebilene* [2002] 2 AC 326, HL at 381.

Article 9: Freedom of Thought, Conscience and Religion as meriting strict scrutiny of a state's conduct.[58]

Limits on Convention rights

Some Convention rights contain specific limitations in similar terms to the general limitations discussed in the previous paragraph. In the case of Article 9: Freedom of Thought, Conscience and Religion, and Article 10: Freedom of Expression, the state must show that any restriction on the exercise of such rights is 'prescribed by law' and is 'necessary in a democratic society' for the protection of 'health or morals' for the advancement of specified objectives. Because the state may interfere with the exercise of rights where those conditions are satisfied, the rights themselves must be broadly interpreted.[59] Exceptions to the rights under the Convention must be narrowly interpreted.[60]

Prescribed by law

Where the Convention requires that states act in accordance with the law, the state's conduct must have some basis in domestic law.[61] The Commission's power of removal is contained in sections 3(4) Charities Act 1993. This fulfils the condition that removal from the register is 'prescribed by law'. However, the requirement also relates to the quality of the law so that any arbitrary interference with Convention rights is protected.[62] To avoid arbitrary laws, there are two fundamental requirements. First, the law must be adequately accessible. Second, the law must be formulated with sufficient precision to enable a citizen to regulate his conduct.[63] In general terms it has been argued[64] in this book that there are ambiguities in the law relating to the removal of charities from the register. For example, there is scope for argument that non-charitable activities are relevant to the question of charitable status rather than being indicative of a breach of trust.[65] Such distinctions are at times difficult to make and, to the extent that they have never been adequately clarified,[66] it could be argued that the Commission is prevented from applying the limitations on Convention rights in the context of removing charities from the register.

Furthermore, the exercise of the Commission's power of removal is based on the law of charitable status. It was shown in Chapter 2 that areas of that body of law are arguably arbitrary particularly within the area of public benefit, which

[58] *Ibid.* [59] *Niemietz* v. *Germany* (1992) 16 EHRR 97 at 112.
[60] *Sunday Times* v. *United Kingdom* (1979) 2 EHRR 245 at 281.
[61] *Sunday Times* v. *United Kingdom* (1979) 2 EHRR 245.
[62] *Malone* v. *United Kingdom* (1984) 7 EHRR 14 at 40, Ect HR para. 86.
[63] *Sunday Times* v. *United Kingdom* (1979) 2 EHRR 245 at 271.
[64] See Chapter 2, p. 38. [65] See Chapter 2, p. 26.
[66] See Cabinet Office, Strategy Unit Report, *Private Action, Public Benefit A Review of Charities and the Wider Not for Profit Sector*, where it recommended that the circumstances when activities can be used as an aid to interpreting purposes should be clarified by statute Annex Z, para. 44.

forms a major part of the law of charitable status.[67] An example of an arbitrary law within the law of public benefit is the rule of law expressed in *Re Compton*[68] and *Oppenheim* v. *Tobacco Securities Trust Co Ltd*[69] (referred to in this book as 'the *Compton* test'). In *Re Compton*, the Court of Appeal held that a trust for the education of children from named families was not a sufficient section of the public. In *Oppenheim* v. *Tobacco Securities Trust Co. Ltd*, the House of Lords ruled that a trust to provide for the education of children of employees or former employees of British-American Tobacco Co. Ltd, or any of its subsidiary or allied companies, would not be a sufficient section of the public either. This was despite the fact that the employees totalled in excess of one hundred thousand.

It is arguable that an educational charity which was removed from the register because it failed to comply with the formulaic *Compton* test, even though in substance it was charitable, could argue that the Commission was in breach of Article 1, Protocol 1: Right to Property[70] which requires any non-compliance to be 'provided for by law'. It will only be 'provided for by law' where the law has the necessary quality and is not therefore of an arbitrary nature.

It could also be argued that the *Compton* test is not proportionate to the legitimate aim of determining between an institution which is charitable and one which is not because it is arbitrary.[71] There is no doubt that the court is competent to decide whether an institution is in substance charitable. The court is used to assessing whether an institution passes the public benefit test, and this involves looking at whether an institution is in substance charitable.[72] The rule cannot therefore be justified.

The idea that an institution could face removal from the register for failing to satisfy the *Compton* test is not as remote a possibility as one might think. One of the grounds for the Commission concluding that the School Fee Planning Charities[73] were not charitable and should therefore be removed from the register was that they failed the *Compton* test. The common connection between the beneficiary children of the School Fee Planning Charities was that their parents had invested in annuities held in the names of the School Fee Planning Charities. The Commission was right that the children could not be said to be a sufficient section of the public. The Commission was therefore entitled to remove the School Fee Planning Charities on that ground alone. Today an institution removed from the register for the same reason could argue that the Commission was in breach of Article 1, Protocol 1: Right to Property. In order

[67] Chapter 2, pp. 34–42. [68] *Re Compton* [1945] Ch 123.

[69] *Oppenheim* v. *Tobacco Securities Trust Co Ltd* [1951] AC 297.

[70] See pp. 137–40 of this chapter. It is also arguable that removal from the register might also breach Article 2, Protocol 1: Right to Education, but for different reasons which are discussed later in this chapter at pp. 152–7.

[71] See pp. 34–42 of this chapter. [72] See Chapter 2, pp. 34–42.

[73] [1996] Ch.Com.A.R. paras. 187–189.

to prevent such a challenge the Commission would have to re-interpret the *Compton* test so that it was not arbitrary.[74]

The Commission has recognised that the *Compton* test can cause anomalies.[75] However, until the decisions in *Compton* and *Oppenheim* are overturned the Commission has gone on record as saying that it will adopt a cautious and flexible approach to deciding what constitutes a sufficient section of the public. The Commission is prepared to look at the facts of each case. It says that there will be limited circumstances in which a large group is not a section of the public – where beneficiaries are determined only by reference to a personal relationship, comprising ties of kin or contract with an individual or company (ies), 'Beyond that there are no clearly formulated criteria.'[76] Where a beneficiary class has an impersonal quality the Commission takes the view:

> that a class whose distinguishing feature is an impersonal quality may be a sufficient section of the community even though its constituent members also happen to share some personal characteristic (e.g. being tenants or related to tenants of a single landlord). This means that on this view we would accept as charities bodies where (even though all potential beneficiaries might actually be connected by kin or contract):
>
> (A) on a general survey of the circumstances and considerations regarded as relevant it is clear that a public class is intended; and
> (B) that class can be (and, as a rule, is in fact) described otherwise than by reference to kin or contractual relationship;
>
> if it is difficult to describe a class using objective and impersonal terms, that would indicate that the body concerned is established for private rather than public benefit; in those cases where the conclusion is that private benefits are intended for a group of individuals who are not together fairly describable as a section of the public or a section of the community, the Compton rule applies to deny the benefits of charitable status.[77]

[74] Notwithstanding a reformulation of the *Compton* test to comply with the Human Rights Act 1998, the *School Fee Planning Charities* would not, under a test of substance rather than form, be saved from being removed from the register for no longer being considered by the Commission to be a charity. They were essentially private trusts and it is unlikely that human rights arguments would have saved them.

[75] RR 8 – *The Public Character of Charity* (February 2001). See also *Public Benefit – the Charity Commission's approach* (January 2005), *Public Benefit – The Charity Commission's Position on how Public Benefit is Treated in the Charities Bill* (July 2005), *Analysis of the Law Underpinning Charity and Public Benefit* (March 2007) and *Charities and Public Benefit The Charity Commission's Guidance on Public Benefit* Part 3. *Public Benefit – Principle 2: Benefit must be to the public, or a section of the public (Section F of Charities and Public Benefit)* (January 2008).

[76] RR 8 – *The Public Character of Charity* (Version February 2001) Annex B, B 9.

[77] *Ibid.* B 10.

The Commission recognises that the law as it currently stands might be open to challenge on human rights grounds.[78] With the adoption of the Commission's policy as set out in RR 8, this seems a less likely prospect.

One final point should be made. The *Compton* test applies to charities for the advancement of education. Although the Commission assumes that the court would apply it to charities generally,[79] the Court has declined to apply the test to charities for the relief of poverty.[80] Whether it applies to other charities is therefore open to doubt but if it does then it is submitted that a court today would probably follow the Commission's approach in RR 8[81] which would limit the ability to remove charities from the register where they fall foul of the *Compton* test.

Necessary in a democratic society

Here the Court must assess:

> Whether the interference complained of corresponded to a pressing social need, whether it was proportionate to the legitimate aim pursued, whether the reasons given by the national authorities to justify it are relevant and sufficient.[82]

The importance of the particular Convention right will be relevant to whether it will be possible to justify limiting the application of Convention rights.[83] Article 9: Freedom of Thought, Conscience and Religion and Article 10: Freedom of Expression are regarded as having particular importance[84] and are discussed later in this chapter.[85]

General and particular Convention rights and the Commission's power to remove charities from the register

There are some Convention rights which are generally relevant to the Commission's power of removal under section 3(4) Charities Act 1993. These are Article 1, Protocol 1: Right to Property and Article 14: Freedom from Discrimination. There are also some particular Convention rights which are relevant to the question of removal. These are Article 9: Freedom of Thought, Conscience and Religion, Article 2, Protocol 1: Right to Education and Article 10: Freedom of Expression.

78 *Ibid.* B 11. 79 RR 8 – *The Public Character of Charity* (February 2001).
80 *Dingle* v. *Turner* [1972] AC 601.
81 RR 8 – *The Public Character of Charity* (February 2001). See also *Public Benefit – the Charity Commission's Approach* (January 2005), *Public Benefit – The Charity Commission's Position on how Public Benefit is Treated in the Charities Bill* (July 2005) and *Charities and Public Benefit: The Charity Commission's General Guidance on Public Benefit* (January 2008).
82 *Sunday Times* v. *United Kingdom* (1979) 2 EHRR 245 at 275.
83 *Lingens* v. *Austria* (1986) 8 EHRR 407 at 418–419. 84 *Ibid.*
85 See pp. 145–52 & 157–67 of this chapter.

These Convention rights could restrict the Commission's powers of removal by widening the application of charitable status.

Article 1, Protocol 1: Right to property

Article 1, Protocol 1 reads as follows:

> Every natural or legal person is entitled to the peaceful enjoyment of his possessions. No one shall be deprived of his possessions except in the public interest and subject to the conditions provided for by law and by the general principles of international law.

This Convention right provides a qualified right to property.[86] The first hurdle that a natural or legal person[87] must overcome is to establish a right or interest in domestic law which can be recognised as a property right under the Convention.[88]

There is little doubt that charities own their property whether it is held on trust[89] or in the case of a charitable company beneficially for its charitable purposes.[90] It is also clear that charities, whether incorporated or unincorporated, will be natural or legal persons within the wording of Article 1, Protocol 1.

Article 1, Protocol 1 comprises three distinct rules:[91]

The peaceful enjoyment of property

This rule applies where some interference with property falls short of confiscation or control of the property but has the effect of disrupting the use and enjoyment of the property.[92] In Chapter 3[93] it was argued that where a charity's objects have become outdated but were originally charitable the appropriate course of action would be for the Commission to modernise the objects and apply the property *cy-pres* by way of a scheme.[94] It is arguable whether a *cy-pres* modernisation of a charity's objects would interfere with a charity's right to the peaceful enjoyment of property. Charity will not be deprived of its property and will still control its use, although the purposes for which the property can be used will have changed.

[86] See pp. 138–40 of this chapter for limitations on this Convention right.

[87] See the wording of Article 1, Protocol 1.

[88] See Application 11716/85: *S* v. *United Kingdom* 47 DR 274 (1986), E Com HR where the occupation of property without a legal right was not protected. On the other hand see *Beyeler* v. *Italy* (2001) 33 EHRR 52, Ect HR where, in a dispute over ownership of a painting, the court found that the applicants dealings with the painting over a period of time could be regarded as 'possession' within the meaning of Article 1, Protocol 1.

[89] See Chapter 5, pp. 104–5. [90] Chapter 5, pp. 108–12.

[91] *Sporrong and Lonnroth* v. *Sweden* (1982) 5 EHRR 35, Ect HR, para. 106.

[92] *Ibid.* at para. 65. [93] Chapter 3, pp. 71–73.

[94] S. 13(1)(e)(ii) Charities Act 1993. See *National Anti-Vivisection Society* v. *IRC* [1948] AC 31.

Deprivation of possessions

Here the property must be expropriated in law or there must be *de facto* appropriation.[95] Where a charity has been removed from the register but its property is schemed[96] to another charity this would amount to a deprivation of possessions if a charity is seen as a distinct institution. However, if a charity is viewed in broader terms[97] than its governing instrument or its institutional status and the focus is on charitable purposes and beneficiaries, then it will be difficult for a charity to argue that a scheme to transfer property to another charity will breach Article 1, Protocol 1. On this analysis there would be no deprivation of possessions within the meaning of Article 1, Protocol 1 where a charity's property is transferred to another charity by way of a scheme and the institution is then removed from the register.

The state is entitled to control the use of property in accordance with the general interest by enforcing such laws as it deems necessary for that purpose

This rule covers measures to secure the payment of taxes.[98] The loss of tax reliefs following removal from the register would, *prima facie*, amount to a breach of Article 1, Protocol 1. However, it is arguable that the taxation of charities would be held to fall within the margin of appreciation allowed to member states as the tax relates to social and economic factors.[99]

Limits on Article 1, Protocol 1

The public or general interest

The text of Article 1, Protocol 1 makes clear that the deprivation of property within the second rule can only be justified if it is in the public interest. When interpreting what is in the general or public interest the state is allowed a wide margin of appreciation in implementing social and economic policies. The state's judgement in these areas will not be interfered with unless it is 'manifestly without reasonable foundation'.[100] The removal of charities from the register which do not qualify for charitable status, or schemes to make charities more efficient, is in the public or general interest because such charities are not concerned with the efficient delivery of social and economic policy.[101]

[95] *Sporrong and Lonnroth* v. *Sweden* (1982) 5 ERHH 35, Ect HR, para. 63.

[96] S. 16(1)(a) Charities Act 1993.

[97] See Chapter 5, pp. 104–5.

[98] *Gous Dosier–Und Fordertechnick* v. *Netherlands* (1995) 20 EHRR 403, Ect HR, para 59.

[99] *R* v. *DPP ex p Kebilene* [2002] 2 AC 326, HL at 381.

[100] *James* v. *United Kingdom* (1986) 8 EHRR 123, Ect HR.

[101] See *ante* at pp. 139–40 of this chapter.

Proportionality

An interference with any of the three rules[102] of Article 1, Protocol 1 must be proportionate. In order to be proportionate, a fair balance must be struck between the general interest of the community and the requirement to protect the individual's Convention rights.[103] The modernisation of objects through *cy-pres* schemes and schemes to transfer property to more efficient charities is a proportionate way of meeting a social and economic policy objective of ensuring the efficient delivery of charitable resources for the benefit of the community.[104] The individual rights of charities are not affected in the case of *cy-pres* schemes because charities will still own the property and will simply apply it for more socially relevant purposes. Even where property is transferred from an inefficient charity to an efficient charity by way of a scheme,[105] leaving the inefficient charity to be removed from the register, it is in the interests of the community that charitable provision is delivered by efficiently run institutions. Charity law focuses on charitable purposes and beneficiaries, rather than the rights of institutions.[106] The interests of the community in the efficient delivery of charitable resources overrides any institutional right to property.

One area where Article 1, Protocol 1 might be relevant is in respect of the loss of tax reliefs following removal from the register. The power of the state to secure the payment of taxes is wide under Article 1, Protocol 1, but the taxing measure must be proportionate.[107] It might therefore be argued that where an institution was mistakenly registered without any fault on the part of the promoters of the institution, it should not be penalised.[108] To avoid this, an institution could be allowed to retain tax reliefs awarded to it in the past. Also, the institution could be allowed to retain tax reliefs in the future. The first approach would be sufficient to satisfy the requirement to act proportionately without the need to continue to confer tax reliefs in the future. If Parliament or the Court were to allow retention of tax reliefs, either wholly or partly, it would have to give greater recognition to the importance of governing instruments and institutional rights than has previously been the case.

Subject to the conditions provided by law

The powers of removal from the register[109] or of making schemes,[110] if they interfere with Article 1, Protocol 1, must be prescribed by law. This means

[102] Pp. 138–40 of this chapter.

[103] *Lithgow* v. *United Kingdom* (1986) 8 EHRR 329, Ect HR, para. 120.

[104] Note the Commission's new charitable resources objective in section 1(B)(2)4 Charities Act 1993.

[105] Pp. 139–40 of this chapter. [106] Chapter 5, pp. 104–5.

[107] *National Provincial Building Society* v. *United Kingdom* (1998) 25 EHRR 127, para. 80.

[108] For details of the tax charges see the discussion of rectification in Chapter 3, pp. 69–71.

[109] S. 3(4) Charities Act 1993. [110] Ss. 13, 14, 16 & 18(2)(ii) Charities Act 1993.

that the Commission's powers must be exercised *intra vires*. It would not, for example, be open to the Commission to take a view that removal from the register is a proportionate way of dealing with an institution which, due to the passage of time, is no longer a charity, rather than to make a *cy-pres* scheme modernising its objects or otherwise providing for its property. Charities are either charitable and should be on the register,[111] regulated if necessary by a scheme, or not charitable and removed from the register. As a matter of law the Commission does not have such discretion.[112] To be compliant with the Human Rights Act 1998, the Commission must act within the law.

The law must also be adequately accessible and sufficiently precise to enable a citizen to regulate his conduct.[113] It was shown earlier in this chapter[114] that the *Compton* test[115] can be described as arbitrary. A charity removed from the register, which is charitable in substance but not charitable in the form required by the *Compton* test, might be able to argue that the Commission is in breach of Article 1, Protocol 1.

Article 14: Freedom from discrimination

If the Commission removes some charities from the register and leaves others on the register then arguably it must avoid discrimination under Article 14. Article 14 reads as follows:

> The enjoyment of the rights and freedoms set forth in this Convention shall be secured without discrimination on any ground such as sex, race, colour, language, religion, political or other opinion, national or social origin, association with a national minority, property, birth or other status.

Article 14 is not an equal treatment guarantee. It only requires equal access to Convention rights. Article 14 can only operate within the ambit of other Convention rights and has been described as parasitic.[116] Whether Article 14 applies to charities removed from the register will depend on whether the other Convention rights discussed in this chapter are relevant. In *Wandsworth London Borough Council* v. *Michalack*[117] the Court of Appeal established a four stage test which has become accepted[118] by the United Kingdom courts.

[111] Unless exempt, excepted or does not qualify for registration. See section 3A(2)(a)–(d) respectively.

[112] S. 3(4) Charities Act 1993 places a duty on the Commission to remove charities from the register.

[113] See pp. 133–6 of this chapter. [114] *Ibid.* [115] *Re Compton* [1945] Ch 123.

[116] See Lester and Pannick, *Human Rights Law and Practice* p. 413.

[117] *Wandsworth London Borough Council* v. *Michalack* [2002] EWCA Civ 271, [2003] 1 WLR 617.

[118] Approved and applied by the Court of Appeal in *A and X* v. *Secretary of State for the Home Department* [2002] EWCA Civ 1502.

Do the facts fall within the ambit of one or more of the substantive Convention rights?

A measure which conforms to a Convention right might still violate Article 14 because it is discriminatory in nature.[119] Furthermore, Article 14 extends not only to Convention rights, but to aspects of the right which the state chooses to guarantee without being obliged to do so under the Convention.[120]

The wording of Article 14 prohibits discrimination on grounds of sex, race, colour, language, religion, political or other opinion, national or social origin, association with a national minority, property, birth or other status. The term 'other status' includes sexual orientation,[121] marital status[122] and professional[123] or military status.[124]

When removing charities from the register, the Commission will need to be careful that it cannot be accused of discrimination on one or more of these grounds, even if the discrimination is unintentional.

Different treatment

A claim by a charity of discrimination contrary to Article 14 would need to show, within the ambit of a Convention right, that it has been treated less favourably[125] on a prohibited ground. For example, if the Commission removed a new religious movement charity simply because it was new, without examining whether it was established for the benefit of the public, and left charities advancing established religions on the register because they had a track record of public benefit over a period of time, this could arguably be prohibited discrimination on the grounds of religion, because the charity advancing the new religious movement would have been treated less favourably.

With the abolition of the presumption of public benefit[126] all charities will have to demonstrate public benefit. Coupled with the new definition of 'religion' for the purpose of charity law in the Charities Act 2006, which extends to polytheistic and non-theistic religious beliefs,[127] the question arises as to how the Commission will justify any difference in treatment between charities with objects for the advancement of religion and charities for the promotion of the mental, moral or spiritual welfare or improvement of the community. This question is particularly relevant in the context of charities being removed

[119] *Belgium Linguistic Case* (1968) (No 2) 1 EHRR 252, Ect HR para. 9.
[120] *Abdulaziz, Cabales and Balkandali* v. *United Kingdom* (1985) 7 EHRR 471, Ect HR, para. 82.
[121] *Dudgeon* v. *United Kingdom* (1981) 4 EHRR 149, Ect HR.
[122] *Satin* v. *Germany* (2003) 36 EHRR 43, [2003] 2 FCR 619, Ect HR.
[123] *Van der Mussele* v. *Belgium* (1983) 6 EHRR 163, Ect HR.
[124] *Engel* v. *Netherlands* (1976) 1 EHRR 647, Ect HR.
[125] *Belgium Linguistic Case* (1968) (No 2) 1 EHRR 252, Ect HR at 256.
[126] S. 3(2) Charities Act 2006.
[127] S. 2(3)(a)(i) & (ii) Charities Act 2006. See pp. 145–9 of this chapter.

from the register where one type of charity is left on the register and another removed. In order to avoid a breach of Article 14, any difference in treatment must have objective and reasonable justification.[128] In *The Church of Scientology* decision,[129] the Commission took the view that the concept of worship provided an objective and reasonable criterion for making such a distinction. Furthermore, the Commission noted that 'worship' was defined by the common law authorities as characterised by reverence for, or veneration of, a supreme being.[130]

It is arguable that to impose an extra requirement of worship in respect of religious charities which is not imposed on belief charities with objects for the promotion of the mental, moral or spiritual welfare or improvement of the community is discriminatory and that as Article 9[131] does not make any distinction between 'religion or belief', nor should the Commission. It follows that if the Commission does remove either religious or fourth head charities from the register, then it should do so on the same basis. If that basis is a lack of public benefit, then in order to avoid a violation of Article 14, the Commission should reinterpret public benefit in a way which is standardised for these two heads of charity. Following the enactment of the Charities Act 2006 and the abolition of the presumption of public benefit in respect of the first three heads of charity, the Commission could avoid discrimination by applying the current test of public benefit for charities providing intangible benefits for both religious and belief charities. This test was set out by Lord Wright in *National Anti-Vivisection Society* v. *IRC*:[132]

> I think the whole tendency of the concept of charity in a legal sense under the fourth head is towards tangible and objective benefits, and at least, that approval by the common understanding of enlightened opinion for the time being, is necessary before an intangible benefit can be taken to constitute a sufficient benefit to the community to justify admission of the object to the fourth class.

There is an element of doubt about indirect discrimination.[133] Indirect discrimination is discrimination resulting from a rule or practice applied equally to all individuals without differentiation, but which has a disproportionate and unjustified adverse impact on members of a particular group or minority. There are few cases which throw light on this issue. One which was successful was

[128] *Belgium Linguistic Case* (1968) (No 2) 1 EHRR 252, Ect HR. See pp. 155–6 of this chapter.
[129] *Decision of the Charity Commissioners for England and Wales 17th November 1999 Application for Registration as a Charity by The Church of Scientology (England and Wales).*See Chapter 4, pp. 95–97 & 99–102.
[130] *The Church of Scientology (England and Wales)* pp. 24–26.
[131] See pp. 145–6 of this chapter.
[132] *National Anti-Vivisection Society* v. *IRC* [1948] AC 31 at 49.
[133] See the conflicting cases of *Abdulaziz, Cabales and Balkandali* v. *United Kingdom* (1985) 7 EHRR 471, Ect HR and *Thilimmenos* v. *Greece* (2000) 31 EHRR 411, Ect HR.

Thilimmenos v. *Greece*.[134] In that case the European Court of Human Rights upheld a claim for discrimination where a Jehovah's Witness who had a conviction for insubordination for refusing to enlist in the army for religious reasons, was then excluded from being a chartered accountant on the ground that he had been convicted of a felony. He argued that the rule that prevented him from being a chartered accountant was a breach of Article 14 taken with Article 9 as it failed to treat people convicted of that offence differently from persons convicted of other offences. The government argued that the authorities had no option but to apply a rule that excluded all persons convicted of a felony, and that such a rule was neutral because of its generality. The court held that there had been a breach of Article 14 because this rule failed to treat differently persons whose situations were significantly different.[135] It concluded that a rule applied without differentiation, but which had a disproportionate and unjustified adverse impact on members of a particular group, can fall within Article 14.

Although the authorities are not clear,[136] the better view is that Article 14 does protect against indirect discrimination[137] because considering the balance and development of Convention jurisprudence,[138] the fact that it is established in European Community law[139] and domestic anti-discrimination law and elsewhere,[140] it seems more likely that the court will interpret Article 14 as prohibiting indirect discrimination. Therefore, if a number of charities were removed from the register, say, on the grounds that they were being used to fund personal loans to members, and it was shown that this was a cultural issue amongst an ethnic group which made up a large proportion of the charities' membership, then this could lead to an argument that there had been indirect discrimination. If Article 14 applies, the Commission must take into account any possible indirect discrimination when interpreting charity law.

Comparable situation

The burden lies on the charity to establish[141] that it has been treated less favourably than others in comparable circumstances, and that the basis for the different treatment was a prohibited ground.[142] It might be difficult, as a matter

[134] *Thilimmenos* v. *Greece* (2000) 31 EHRR 411, 9 BHRC 12, Ect HR. [135] *Ibid.* para. 44.

[136] See *Abdulaziz, Cabales and Balkandali* v. *United Kingdom* (1985) 7 EHRR 471, Ect HR and *Thilimmenos* v. *Greece* (2000) 31 EHRR 411, Ect HR.

[137] See Lester and Pannick, *Human Rights Law and Practice* p. 428.

[138] For example, see *McShane* v. *United Kingdom* (2002) 35 EHRR 23, Ect HR at 135.

[139] For example, see Case 170/84: *Bilka-Kaufhaus GmbH* v. *Weber von Hertz* [1986] ECR 1607, [1987] ICR 160, ECJ.

[140] For example, see section 1(1)(b) Sex Discrimination Act 1975 and section 1(1)(b) Race Relations Act 1976. Indirect discrimination is expressly prohibited in the USA and Canada: see Lester and Pannick, *Human Rights Law and Practice* p. 428, fn 4.

[141] *Selcuk and Asker* v. *Turkey* (1998) 16 EHRR 477, Ect HR para. 102.

[142] See pp. 141–3 of this chapter.

of evidence, to prove that those who have been more favourably treated are in an analogous situation to their own.[143] In the case of charities being removed from the register, the Commission could try to defeat a claim for violation of Article 14 by citing why the situation is not analogous. Although theoretically all charities are the same in terms of charitable status, the charity sector is diverse.[144] This diversity might make it difficult for charities to prove that they are being treated less favourably than others in analogous situations.

Justification

A difference in treatment will only be discriminatory if it has no objective and reasonable justification.[145] The Commission would therefore have to prove that the difference in treatment pursues a legitimate aim and that there is a reasonable relationship of proportionality between the means employed and the aim to be realised.[146] The burden of proof falls on the Commission to justify differential treatment.[147]

Legitimate aim

The Commission needs to show a rational basis for differential treatment.[148] The need to maintain an accurate register of charities so that the public and, more particularly, donors[149] can have confidence that institutions on the register provide public benefit is a legitimate aim for removing institutions from the register which do not qualify as charities. The efficient delivery of an aspect of social and economic policy would be compromised if the register of charities was not charitable. So long as there is a legal basis for removal on principles applicable to all charities then removal can be justified as a legitimate aim.

Proportionality

If differential treatment is shown to promote a legitimate aim, then the court will go on to consider whether differences in treatment strike a fair balance between the protection of the interests of the community and respect for the rights and freedoms safeguarded by the Convention.[150] Where an institution does not qualify as a charity, it would be proportionate to remove it from the register. It is in the interests of the community that an accurate register of charities is kept.[151]

[143] *R (Hooper, Withey, Naylor and Martin)* v. *Secretary of State for Work and Pensions* [2003] EWCA Civ 813, [2003] 1 WLR 2623 CA at para. 84.

[144] Chapter 1, pp. 7–10.

[145] *Belgium Linguistic Case* (1968) (No. 2) 1 EHRR 252, Ect HR para. 9 at para. 32.

[146] *Darby* v. *Sweden* (1990) 13 EHRR 774, Ect HR, para. 31.

[147] *Carson and Reynolds* v. *Secretary of State for Work and Pensions* [2003] EWCA Civ 797, [2003] 3 All ER CA para. [72].

[148] *Darby* v. *Sweden* (1990) 13 EHRR 774, Ect HR.

[149] See Chapter 1, p. 10.

[150] *Rasmussen* v. *Denmark* (1984) 7 EHRR 371, Ect HR para. 40.

[151] P. 138 of this chapter.

Margin of appreciation

Although contracting states enjoy a margin of appreciation in the delivery of social and economic policy, including the regulation of charities, some types of discrimination require greater justification than others. 'Very weighty reasons' will be required to justify discrimination on grounds of sex[152] and religion.[153] Discrimination on grounds of race will also be difficult to justify.[154] It is in these areas that the Commission will need to be especially careful to avoid triggering a claim for discrimination when removing charities from the register.

Article 9: Freedom of thought, conscience and religion

This section considers the effect of Article 9 on the Commission's powers of removal.[155] The broad scope of this Article has the potential to severely limit the Commission's powers. The effect of Article 9 is considered in respect of the removal of charities registered with objects for the promotion of the mental, moral or spiritual welfare or improvement of the community, which under the Charities Act 2006 could now qualify as a 'religion which does not believe in a god'.[156] It also considers the limits of Article 9 in the context of the promotion of religious worship.

Article 9 (1) reads as follows:

> Everyone has the right to freedom of thought, conscience and religion; this right includes freedom to change his religion or belief and freedom, either alone or in community with others and in public or in private, to manifest his religion or belief, in worship, teaching, practice or observance.

The freedoms of thought, conscience and religion under Article 9(1) are absolute rights and may not be subject to any form of limitation or restriction.[157] It is only the manifestation of religion or beliefs which may be subject to the limitations set out in Article 9(2).[158] Removal from the register will not restrict the freedom to adhere to a religion or belief, but the loss of tax reliefs and the ability to fund-raise may restrict the manifestation of religion or belief thus leading to a breach of Article 9(1). Whether that can be justified will depend on the wording of Article 9(2) which is discussed later.[159]

[152] *Abdulaziz, Cabales and Balkandali* v. *United Kingdom* (1985) 7 EHRR 471, Ect HR, para. 78.

[153] *Hoffmann* v. *Austria* (1993) 17 EHRR 293, Ect HR at 36.

[154] Not only because it can amount to Article 14 discrimination but also because it can amount to degrading treatment contrary to Article 3. See *East African Asians* v. *United Kingdom* (1973) 3 EHRR 76 Ect HR.

[155] Article 14 in relation to Article 9 was discussed in pp. 146–9 of this chapter.

[156] S. 2(3)(a)(ii) Charities Act 2006.

[157] *Kokkinakis* v. *Greece* (1994) 17 EHRR 397, Ect HR, para. 33.

[158] See pp. 149–51 of this chapter. [159] *Ibid.*

Although Article 9(1) cannot be enjoyed by corporate entities[160] or non-natural persons such as associations,[161] because they are incapable of exercising a right to freedom of conscience,[162] it is enjoyed by institutions such as churches on the basis that a church is a collection of its adherents.[163] It is therefore submitted that if Article 9(1) applies to charities being removed from the register, then religious charities will be protected even when the charity holds the property and the church is separately governed by canon law.[164]

Religion or belief

The terms 'religion or belief' have been given a wide interpretation by the European Court of Human Rights.[165] During the debates[166] on the Charities Bill,[167] Lord Lester pointed out that the purpose set out in the Bill, 'the advancement of religion',[168] as was interpreted by the common law,[169] was not compliant with Article 9(1). Judicial statements on the definition of religion for the purposes of the law of charitable status was, prior to the Charities Act 2006, defined as having two essential attributes: faith in a god and worship of that god.[170] The wording of Article 9(1) is broader than monotheistic religions and broader than religious belief itself. Lord Lester pointed out that the common-law definition for the purposes of charitable status does not cover non-religious beliefs or religions of the non-theistic or polytheistic kind.

The Charities Act 2006 provides a definition of religion for the purposes of charity law which includes polytheistic and non-theistic religions and which is compliant with Article 9(1).[171] It follows that it would be unlawful for the Commission to remove an institution because it was not advancing a mono-theistic religion.

Prior to the Charities Act 2006, the court had sometimes side-stepped the issue of whether an institution qualified as a 'religion' by holding them to be charitable under the old fourth head of charity for the promotion of the mental, moral or spiritual welfare or improvement of the community (as explained in the paragraph below). On occasion the Commission has followed the approach of

160 *Application 3798/68: Church of X v. United Kingdom* 12 YB 306 (1968), E Com HR.

161 *Verein Kontakt-Information-Therapie v. Austria 57 DR 81* (1988), E Com HR.

162 *Vereniging Rechtswinkers Utrecht* v. *Netherlands* 46 DR 200 (1986), E Com HR.

163 *X and Church of Scientology* v. *Sweden* 16 DR 68 (1979), E Com HR.

164 As in the case of the Roman Catholic Church whose property in England and Wales is held by Diocesan Trusts. For example the RC Diocese of Hexham and Newcastle, registered charity number 234071.

165 *Kokkinakis* v. *Greece* (1983) 17 EHRR 397, Ect HR, para. 31. It includes both a religious dimension and also includes atheists, agnostics, sceptics and the unconcerned.

166 Lords Hansard 20 January 2005; cols. 918–920.

167 Charities Bill [HL] 15 2004. 168 Clause 2(2)(c).

169 *Re South Place Ethical Society* [1980] 1 WLR 1565.

170 *Ibid.* 171 S. 2(3)(a)(i) & (ii) Charities Act 2006.

the court.[172] Charities such as the British Humanist Association are registered with objects for 'the mental and moral improvement of the human race'.[173] The problem with registration under this category of the old fourth head of charity is that the legal authorities are very specific and do not provide a general authority for charitable status.

There are four main legal authorities which need to be considered. *Re Scowcroft* is concerned with the furtherance of conservative principles and religious and mental improvement and the promotion of temperance.[174] *Re Hood*[175] is concerned with the promotion of temperance. *Re Price* involved the promotion of the teachings of Dr Rudolf Steiner[176] and *Re South Place Ethical Society* the 'study and dissemination of ethical principles and the cultivation of a rational religious sentiment'.[177] The latter two cases are ambiguous.[178] In both the comments on qualification under the fourth head were *obiter*. Furthermore, in *Re Price*[179] (the Dr Rudolf Steiner case) Cohen J referred to a case involving the advancement of religion.[180] This would not appear to be permissible because the old third and fourth heads of charity have different tests for public benefit.[181] In *Re South Place Ethical Society*[182] (the case about ethical principles and the cultivation of religious sentiment), the court decided that the institution was charitable by way of advancing education or by analogy with the cases promoting temperance. Alternatively, on the basis of *Re Price*,[183] it was charitable under the old fourth head as promoting the moral and spiritual welfare of the community. However, Dillon J did not explain why the charity could qualify under the fourth head and his comments can be regarded as *obiter*.

Even if this line of cases were not ambiguous, they are limited to their own particular facts and provide no general basis for being charitable under the category of the mental, moral or spiritual welfare or improvement of the community. A charity with such objects would appear to be in a weak position if it was removed from the register. Yet following the Human Rights Act 1998, such charities might seek to argue that Article 9 protects 'religion or belief' and that charities registered under this category would therefore be protected if not as religions then as beliefs. For example, although the British Humanist

172 *Re South Place Ethical Society* [1980] 1 WLR 1565. 173 Registered number 285987.

174 *Re Scowcroft* [1898] 2 Ch 638. 175 *Re Hood* [1931] 1 Ch 240.

176 *Re Price* [1943] Ch 422. 177 *Re South Place Ethical Society* [1980] 1 WLR 1565.

178 See *Decision of the Charity Commissioners for England and Wales 17th November 1999 Application for Registration as a Charity by The Church of Scientology (England and Wales)* where the ambiguities are fully explained.

179 *Re Price* [1943] Ch 422. 180 *Thorton* v. *Howe* (1862) 31 Beav 13.

181 Previously under the advancement of religion public benefit was presumed although the presumption could be rebutted. Under the old fourth head public benefit had to be demonstrated. See *National Anti-Vivisection Society* v. *IRC* [1948] AC 31. Note that section 3(2) Charities Act 2006 abolishes the presumption of public benefit.

182 *Re South Place Ethical Society* [1980] 1 WLR 1565. 183 *Re Price* [1943] Ch 422.

Association is registered with objects for 'the mental and moral improvement by the human race',[184] it has argued[185] that it is protected by Article 9 because it is promoting a 'religion or belief'.[186] As the British Humanist Association says:

> Humanism is a life stance that fulfils for its adherents many of the same functions that a religion does for its believers[187]

If the British Humanist Association was removed from the register because the Commission no longer considered that it was charitable under the old fourth head of charity, it could argue that it was a religion within the definition set out in Article 9 and that the definition of 'religion' for the purposes of charity law has been widened to include 'beliefs' such as humanism.

Another example is the Pagan Hospital and Funeral Trust which was registered as a charity in 1995 and removed from the register in 1998 on the ground that it had ceased to exist.[188] The objects of the Pagan Hospital and Funeral Trust under the fourth head were:

> The relief of sickness and suffering particularly by providing physical emotional and spiritual support, guidance, counselling and assistance for those who are terminally ill particularly but not exclusively those who are pagan or subscribe to pagan beliefs and by extending such spiritual support, guidance, counselling and assistance to such persons' families and carers.

The Commission decided to remove the Pagan Hospital and Funeral Trust from the register because it concluded that the Trust was carrying out too many activities for the benefit of pagans and the advancement of paganism.[189] Following the Human Rights Act 1998, it is arguable that Article 9 might have protected paganism. Certainly paganism recognises a higher force, so in that sense it is comparable with other religions.[190]

In the *Church of Scientology* decision[191] the Commission, in the face of ambiguous legal authorities, adopted a Convention rights approach to determining the charitable status of charities with objects for the mental, moral or

[184] Registered charity number 285987.

[185] Submission on promotion of religious harmony, September 2002, letter to John Stoker, Chief Commissioner, the Charity Commission, 26 September 2002. www.humanism.org.uk.

[186] Article 9. Belief is defined as: *'more than just 'mere opinions or deeply held feeling'; there must be a holding of spiritual or philosophical convictions which have an identifiable formal content'.* See *McFeely* v. *UK* (1981) 3 EHRR 161.

[187] Submission on promotion of religious harmony, September 2002, letter to John Stoker, Chief Commissioner, The Charity Commission 26 September 2002. www.humanism.org.uk.

[188] S. 3(4) Charities Act 1993.

[189] www.freedom.org.uk (a Scientology-run website). A letter from the Charity Commission dated 21 June 1996.

[190] www.freedom.org.uk.

[191] *Decision of the Charity Commissioners for England and Wales 17th November 1999 Application for Registration as a Charity by The Church of Scientology (England and Wales).*

spiritual welfare or improvement of the community. In doing so, it decided that the necessary characteristics for this charitable object are that the doctrines, beliefs and practices of the institution are accessible to the public and capable of being applied by members of the public according to individual judgement or choice in such a way that the mental, moral or spiritual welfare or improvement of the community may result.[192] It is therefore unlikely that the Commission would seek to remove a charity with objects for the mental, moral or spiritual welfare or improvement of the community just because it was not squarely within the facts of one of the decided cases. The Commission's generous approach to interpretation is in line with Article 9 and Article 14 which protects both 'religion or belief' and protects against discriminatory access to Article 9.

If the Commission removes charities because they do not fall within the facts of one of the decided cases for the promotion of the mental, moral or spiritual welfare or improvement of the community, then it is arguable that such an approach might well amount to a breach of Articles 9 and 14.[193]

Limits on Article 9

Article 9 is subject to limits set out in the wording of Article 9(2):

> Freedom to manifest one's religion or beliefs shall be subject only to such limitations as are prescribed by law and are necessary in a democratic society in the interests of public safety, for the protection of public order, health or morals, or for the protection of the rights and freedoms of others.

The right to religion or belief under Article 9(1) is an absolute right without limitation. The power to interfere with the freedoms under Article 9(1) is limited to manifestation of religion or belief. For example, in *Kokkinakis* v. *Greece*[194] the applicants were Jehovah's Witnesses who had been convicted under Greek law of the offence of proselytism. The court held that the right to manifest one's religion by trying to convince one's neighbours of the merit of one's sect, fell within Article 9, as long as such attempts at proselytism could not be characterised as improper. The court described improper proselytism as a 'corruption or deformation of [bearing Christian Witness] which was not compatible with respect for freedom of thought, conscience and religion'. On the facts, the court held that the Greek Government had not justified the interference with the applicants' rights under Article 9 by a pressing social need. An example of how a potential breach of Article 9(1) may be justified by Article 9(2) can be seen by considering private religious worship.

The wording of Article 9(1) – '… either alone or in community with others and in public or in private, to manifest his religion or belief, in worship, teaching, practice and observance' – raises the question of whether the

192 See Warburton, J. 'Human Rights and Charity Law' S.J. 144 (17) Supp 2000 24–26.

193 See pp. 146–9 *ante* for a discussion of Article 14.

194 *Kokkinakis* v. *Greece* (1993) 17 EHRR 397, Ect HR.

Commission can remove charities from the register on the ground that they do not provide sufficient public access to 'worship'. Article 9 protects private religious practice and manifestation of a religion or belief through a way of life. In *Kokkinakis* v. *Greece*,[195] the court observed that freedom to manifest one's religion is not only exercisable in community with others or with a circle of those who share the same faith but also alone or in private.

Private religious worship was examined in *Gilmour* v. *Coats*,[196] where the question arose as to whether an enclosed Roman Catholic priory was charitable. The priory consisted of a community of cloistered nuns who devoted their lives to prayer, contemplation, penance and self-sanctification within their convent and engaged in no exterior works. The House of Lords determined that the purposes of the priory were not charitable because they did not demonstrate public benefit. The benefit of intercessory prayer to the public was not in their Lordships' opinion susceptible to legal proof. Further, they ruled that edification by example was too vague and intangible to satisfy the test of public benefit.

Cardinal Griffin gave evidence that the Roman Catholic Church believed that there was public benefit both in intercessory prayer and also that the practice of religious life by the nuns was a source of edification to other members of the Roman Catholic faith.[197] That evidence was rejected by the House of Lords. Lord Simonds quoted Wickens V-C in *Cocks v. Manners*:[198]

> It is said in some cases, that religious purposes are charitable, but that can only be true as to religious services tending directly or indirectly towards the instruction or the edification of the public; an annuity to an individual, so long as he spent his time in retirement and constant devotion, would not be charitable, nor would a gift to ten persons, so long as they lived together in retirement and performed acts of devotion, be charitable. Therefore the gift to the Dominican Convent is not, in my opinion, a gift on a charitable trust.

The width given to the meaning of manifestation of worship in Article 9(1) means that there is a potential breach of that article if the Commission denies charitable status to a religion which is an enclosed order. Although it is arguable that removal from the register does not breach Article 9 because it will not prevent people from adhering to a 'religion or belief', nevertheless it might affect people's ability to manifest their 'religion or belief' through, for example, religious services and proselytism. This is because the loss of tax reliefs and the enhanced ability to fund-raise using a registered charity number might impede an institution's ability to fund these activities.

Breach, however, may be justified under Article 9(2). There are four conditions that need to be satisfied. First, it must be prescribed by law. Second, it

[195] *Kokkinakis* v. *Greece* (1994) 17 EHRR 397, Ect HR. [196] *Gilmour* v. *Coats* [1949] AC 426.
[197] *Ibid.* 441–442. [198] *Cocks* v. *Manners* (1871) LR 12 Eq 574.

must be necessary in a democratic society. Third, it must be for the protection of the rights and freedoms of others. Fourth, it must be for the protection of health and morals.

Prescribed by law

As previously discussed,[199] when looking at the general principles and limitations, where the wording of an article requires the limitation to be prescribed by law, not only must it have some basis in domestic law, but it must also not be arbitrary and must therefore be precise and accessible.[200] The removal of charities from the register is prescribed by domestic law. Section 3(4) Charities Act 1993 provides the statutory power of removal. If the ground for removal is that there is insufficient public benefit from the inception of a charity, then it is clear that the criterion for public benefit is the need to demonstrate that it is good for the public to have and practise a religion, and that it is not non-beneficial or harmful to the public and there is sufficient public access to worship.[201]

Necessary in a democratic society

It was shown, earlier in this chapter,[202] when looking at general principles and limitations, that to be necessary in a democratic society the intervention with a Convention right must correspond to a pressing social need, be proportionate to the legitimate aim pursued and the reasons given must be relevant and sufficient.[203] Article 9 has placed great importance on the need to secure religious pluralism as an inherent feature of a democratic society.[204] However, it can still be argued that, where an institution lacks public benefit, that is sufficient reason to remove it from the register. Article 9(2) appears to support this argument because it imposes a limit on Article 9(1) 'for the protection of the rights and freedoms of others' and 'for the protection of health and morals'.

For the protection of the rights and freedoms of others

It could be argued that removing charities from the register which have not satisfied the public benefit criterion of public access to worship protects the rights and freedoms of those charities which are entitled to be registered. It ensures that tax reliefs are only given to those charities which provide benefit to the public.[205]

For the protection of health and morals

The limit in Article 9(2) of 'for the protection of health and morals' would allow the Commission to remove a religious institution from the register on the

[199] See pp. 132–6 of this chapter. [200] *Sunday Times* v. *United Kingdom* (1979) 2 EHRR 245.
[201] Chapter 4, pp. 97–99. [202] Pp. 132–6 of this chapter.
[203] *Sunday Times* v. *United Kingdom* (1979) 2 EHRR 245.
[204] *Manoussakis* v. *Greece* (1996) 23 EHRR 387, para. 44. [205] *Ibid*. p. 10.

grounds that the religion or belief promoted failed the public benefit test as a result of being contrary to public policy, as involving, for example, a corruption of moral standards or the break-up of the family through the use of brainwashing techniques.[206] These types of objects would not be protected by Article 9(1) as they would fall within the limits set out in Article 9(2).

Article 2, Protocol 1: Right to education

The removal of independent schools from the register could lead to a breach of the right to education contained in Protocol 1, Article 2 if it led to the closure of those schools through the loss of tax reliefs, and the ability to fund-raise using a registered charity number and/or through the *cy-pres* application of the school's property.[207] If the closure of these schools or application of their property *cy-pres* led to a loss of pluralism, including the right of parents to ensure that the education and teaching for their children was in conformity with their own religious and philosophical convictions, then it is arguable that there might be a breach of Protocol 1, Article 2 and discrimination under Article 14.

Protocol 1, Article 2 reads as follows:

> No person shall be denied the right to education. In the exercise of any functions which it assumes in relation to education and teaching, the state shall respect the right of parents to ensure such education and teaching in conformity with their own religious and philosophical convictions.

The negative wording in the opening sentence indicates the qualified scope of the right to education. The principle affirmed in the second sentence of Article 2 is accepted by the United Kingdom only in so far as it is compatible with the provision of efficient instruction and training, and the avoidance of unnecessary public expenditure.[208]

Article 2, Protocol 1 provides, *inter alia*, a right of access to such educational establishments as exist.[209] However, states are under no duty to establish educational institutions at their own expense or to subsidise education of any particular type or at any particular level.[210] In *W & DM and M & HI* v. *United Kingdom*[211] the applicants' children were refused places at selective grammar schools where there was a set quota, and the children had to go to non-selective comprehensive schools. The claim was rejected because there was no lack of pluralism. Pluralism is important because, without it, respect for the religious and philosophical convictions of parents might not be given[212] and

[206] See Chapter 2, pp. 37–38. [207] See Chapter 5, pp. 108–12.

[208] See pp. 138–40 of this chapter for the limits on Article 2, Protocol 1.

[209] *Belgium Linguistic Case* (1968) (No. 2) 1 EHRR 252 Ect HR. [210] *Ibid.*

[211] *W & DM and M & HI* v. *United Kingdom Applications* 10228/82 and 10229/82.

[212] See pp. 152–5 of this chapter.

a lack of pluralism in the provision of education amounts to discrimination under Article 14.[213]

There are some tensions in the law. States are under no obligation to fund private and independent schools so long as this does not lead to discrimination.[214] Nevertheless, if the removal of charitable status and/or the *cy-pres* application of its property leads to the closure of independent charitable schools, or to their property being applied *cy-pres* and, as a result, a loss of educational pluralism, then this could arguably lead to a breach of Article 2, Protocol 1.[215]

If charitable schools are removed from the register and/or their property applied *cy-pres*, it is likely to be because they are charging fees that are so high that their intake of pupils is unacceptably narrow for the purposes of public benefit and pupils on low incomes are excluded.[216] Even though the existing case law supports charitable schools having a narrow beneficiary class which, in practice, excludes the poor[217] it looks as though the Commission might choose to reinterpret the law of public benefit to place greater emphasis on access by members of the general public on low incomes.[218] Leaving aside the legality of this approach from a charity law perspective, if the loss of charitable status and / or the *cy-pres* application of property led to the closure of schools[219] then this could, because of a loss of pluralism, amount to a breach of Article 2, Protocol 1 and Article 14. Therefore when reinterpreting public benefit, the Commission will need to take into account Article 2, Protocol 1. As a result the Commission's scope for interpreting public benefit might be limited.

[213] See pp. 156–7 of this chapter.

[214] *Application 10476/83: W and KL* v. *Sweden* 45 DR 143 (1985) at 148–149.

[215] See 'A Joint Opinion by Anthony Lester QC and David Pannick' (ISIS document no. 11) April 1987.

[216] See Chapter 4, pp. 90–93. See also *Charities and Public Benefit The Charity Commission's General Guidance on Public Benefit F 11. Principle 2 c: People in poverty must not be excluded from the opportunity to benefit* (January 2008).

[217] *Re Resch's Will Trusts* [1969] 1 AC 514.

[218] See *Charities and Public Benefit The Charity Commission's General Guidance on Public Benefit F 11. Principle 2 c: People in poverty must not be excluded from the opportunity to benefit* (January 2008). But note the evidence given to the *Joint Committee on the Draft Charities Bill in a Memorandum from the Independent Schools Council* ('ISC') (DCH 9) 30 September 2004: www.publications.parliament.uk where evidence is provided of public access. ISC represents 506,000 children attending 1,278 schools. 83 per cent of those schools are charities (1,061in total). According to the ICS, 31.5 per cent of children at ICS schools receive help with their fees, 23 per cent of them from the school itself. Furthermore, evidence was also presented of partnership activities between ISC schools and maintained schools.

[219] But note the evidence given to the *Joint Committee on the Draft Charities Bill* in a *Memorandum from the Independent Schools Council* (DCH 9) 30 September 2004. It is unlikely that the loss of tax reliefs will lead to the closure of charitable schools because ISC claim that they give back directly £2.30 for each £1 gained as a result of charitable status. Furthermore, unlike maintained schools, charitable schools suffer the burden of irrecoverable VAT on buildings, maintenance and other costs paid by ISC schools at £170 million per annum. This is about double the amount of fiscal benefits from charitable schools.

The safer course of action would be for the Commission to work with schools to increase their public benefit and this appears to have been recognised by the Strategy Unit Report,[220] and subsequently the Commission.[221] Ironically, the loss of charitable status along with charity tax reliefs and the enhanced ability to fundraise, where the property is not applied *cy-pres*,[222] could lead to a substantial increase in the fees charged by deregistered schools and as a consequence an even greater restriction on access.

It could be argued that many independent schools with charitable status provide for special needs children who would not otherwise be provided for by the state. It is estimated that 12 per cent of children at Independent Schools Council ('ISC') schools have special educational needs including dyslexia, dyspraxia and special educational needs as gifted children.[223] Furthermore, ISC schools include specialist schools for children who are deaf, blind or who have exceptional musical gifts or performing talents. The ISC claims its schools provide education which would otherwise not be available.[224] It is also estimated that 20 per cent of all children have special educational needs or learning difficulties.[225] 17–18 per cent of such children have specific, possibly temporary and relatively minor special needs.[226] These children will have their needs met by a state school's delegated budget. The others have severe complex learning difficulties, which will usually be met by the local education authority following a statement of special educational needs. Financial pressure on schools' delegated budgets[227] means that many children who do not qualify for a statement do not receive the amount of support that their parents would wish. As a result there are many children at independent charitable schools who would not qualify for a statutory statement of special needs and who would not have their special needs fully met from a delegated budget. Their parents might well select an independent charitable school for their small class sizes and access to a learning support unit.[228] These facilities would not usually be available, to the same extent, in the state school sector. Charitable schools with learning support units typically charge additional fees for access to a learning support unit.[229] Access is therefore potentially more restrictive to the general public. Yet the removal of these schools from the register, with the

[220] Cabinet Office, Strategy Unit Report, *Private Action, Public Benefit A Review of Charities and the Wider Not-for-Profit Sector* paras. 4.26–4.30.

[221] *Public Benefit Checks-how will we carry them out* September 2004.

[222] This would be where the institution was never a charity and its property is not charitable. See Chapter 5, pp. 104–5.

[223] See the evidence given to *the Joint Committee on the Draft Charities Bill in a Memorandum from the Independent Schools Council* (DCH 9) 30 September 2004.

[224] *Ibid.*

[225] See R. Gold with N. Evans and D. Coleman, *Running a School 2004/5: Legal Duties and Responsibilities*, 2nd edn (Bristol: Jordans, 2005), Chapter 5.

[226] *Ibid.* [227] Gold, *Running a School 2004/5*, Chapter 5.

[228] For an example of such a school see www.stokecollege.co.uk. [229] *Ibid.*

consequential loss of tax reliefs, where the property is not applied *cy-pres*,[230] might lead to fees becoming even more unaffordable or to the school closing. In such circumstances it is arguable that the right to education is denied and that there would be a breach of Article 2, Protocol 1.

Article 2, Protocol 1 and Article 14 together

In conjunction with Article 14, there is a right not to be discriminated against without objective and reasonable justification.[231] An important point to make is that Article 14 extends not only to Convention rights but also to aspects of a Convention right which a state chooses to guarantee, without being obliged under the Convention to do so.[232] Therefore, although states are under no obligation to fund or subsidise charitable schools, once they do so they must not do so in a discriminatory way.[233] It follows that the Commission may need to be careful when removing charitable schools from the register in case it is accused of discrimination. There will be discrimination if there is less favourable treatment than those of comparable charities. In order to show justification, the Commission would need to show that the difference in treatment pursues a legitimate aim and that there is a reasonable relationship of proportionality between the means employed and the aim sought to be realised. These principles are well illustrated by the *Belgium Linguistic Case*.[234] In this case the applicants were French-speaking parents who wanted their children to be educated in French and who objected to having to send their children outside the area where they lived for that purpose, when the children of the Flemish speaking majority suffered no such discrimination. The European Court of Human Rights held that the Belgian government's policy of assimilation of the majority language, Flemish, was objectively and reasonably justified. It pursued the legitimate aim of creating unilingual regions in most of the country by reasonably proportionate means and did not violate Article 2, Protocol 1 when read in isolation, or when read together with Article 14, because the material characteristic was language, and not religious or philosophical conviction.

If the Commission does remove charitable schools from the register and/or applies their property *cy-pres* it will need to ensure that it does not lay itself open to a claim of discrimination on one of the prohibited grounds.[235] Many schools have a particular religious or philosophical ethos and if they are removed from the register and/or their property applied *cy-pres* and other schools are

[230] This would be where the institution was never a charity and its property is not charitable. See Chapter 5, pp. 104–5.

[231] *Belgium Linguistic Case* (1968) (No. 2) 1 ERHH 252, Ect HR, para. 9, para. 32. See pp. 140–5 of this chapter.

[232] *Ibid.* [233] *Application 10476/83: W and KL* v. *Sweden* 45 DR 143 (1985) at 148–149.

[234] *Belgium Linguistic Case* (1968) (No 2) 1 EHRR 252, Ect HR.

[235] See pp. 140–5 of this chapter.

not, the Commission will need to ensure that they are not treated differently without objective and reasonable justification.[236] Even where the Commission applies a test of public benefit which applies to all schools, it will need to be careful that it does not have the effect of indirectly discriminating against one particular section of the community on prohibited grounds.[237]

Respect for the religious and philosophical convictions of parents

The second sentence of Article 2, Protocol 1 reads as follows:

> the state shall respect the right of parents to ensure such education and teaching in conformity with their own religious and philosophical convictions.

The criteria upon which access to education is granted must be consistent with the parents' right to ensure their child's education conforms with their own religious or philosophical convictions. A breach of this requirement will usually go hand in hand with a claim under Article 14.[238] This applies to both state schools and independent charitable schools.[239] A conviction is more than an opinion or an idea. It is akin to a belief.[240] The types of conviction which qualify are narrowly interpreted.[241]

'Respect' means more than 'take account of' or 'acknowledge' but less than 'comply with'.[242] It implies a positive obligation on contracting states.[243] Each state has a choice of means to respect parents' rights unless in practice there is only one effective remedy available.[244] For example, in *Campbell and Cosans* v. *United Kingdom*[245] the European Court of Human Rights endorsed the exemption of certain pupils from corporal punishment, rather than their removal to another school. Similarly, the removal of charitable status of a school, coupled with an offer of *cy-pres* funding for pupils at that school in accordance with their religious or philosophical convictions if they transfer to a state school, would arguably not involve a breach of Article 2, Protocol 1.

There are some schools in the charity sector which provide for particular religious and philosophical convictions which are not specifically provided by the state sector. If the removal of a charitable school led to its closure, as a result

236 *Belgium Linguistic Case* (1968) (No 2) 1 EHRR 252, Ect HR.

237 See pp. 140–5 of this chapter.

238 For example, *Belgium Linguistic Case* (1968) (No. 2) 1 EHRR 252, Ect HR.

239 *Campbell and Cosans* v. *United Kingdom* (1982) 4 EHRR 293, Ect HR paras. 36–41 (opposition to corporal punishment).

240 *Campbell and Cosans* v. *United Kingdom* (1982) 4 EHRR 293, Ect HR at para. 36.

241 *Belgium Linguistic Case* (1968) (No. 2) 1 EHRR 252, Ect HR, para. 5, p. 32 (a preference for language did not qualify).

242 Lester and Pannick, *Human Rights Law and Practice* p. 487.

243 *Campbell and Cosans* v. *United Kingdom* (1982) 4 EHRR 293, Ect HR at para. 37.

244 *Kjeldsen, Busk Madsen and Pedersen* v. *Denmark* (1976) 1 EHRR, Ect HR, para. 50.

245 At para. 37.

of a loss of tax reliefs and/or the *cy-pres* application of its property, it could be argued that there was a violation of Article 2, Protocol 1. More generally, it could be argued that the desire to educate one's children at an independent school was a philosophical conviction which would be denied if the removal of charitable status and/or the *cy-pres* application of the property of significant numbers of schools led to their closure, and thereby restricted access to such schools.

Limits on Article 2, Protocol 1

An important limit on Article 2, Protocol 1 is contained in the United Kingdom's reservation:

> ... the principle affirmed in the second sentence of Protocol 1, art. 2 is accepted by the United Kingdom only so far as it is compatible with the provision of efficient instruction and training and the avoidance of unreasonable public expenditure.

It might be argued that the provision of tax reliefs to charitable schools involves unreasonable public expenditure. As state schools are generally available free of charge, it might be argued that it is more cost-effective to educate pupils in those schools where the overheads have already been largely provided. However, as parents are paying fees and fund-raising for their charitable schools, this argument is unlikely to limit the effect of Article 2, Protocol 1, where a charitable school is being removed from the register and/or its property applied *cy-pres*. Furthermore, there is a counterargument that charitable schools actually relieve the public purse in real terms.[246]

Article 10: Freedom of expression

It is arguable that the rule of law,[247] which says that charities cannot have political objects, conflicts with the wording of Article 10 which confers a right to freedom of expression. An illustration of this in relation to removal is think tanks, which are often accused of having political bias[248] and thus falling foul of the rule against charities having political objects.[249] If think tanks are threatened with removal, then it could be argued that removal from the register would be a breach of Article 10, which confers a right to freedom of expression and discrimination, which would breach Article 14 if the Commission leaves some think tanks on the register but removes others.

246 See *Memorandum from the Independent Schools Council* (DCH 9) *Joint Committee on the Draft Charities Bill – Minutes of Evidence*, where it was estimated that their schools saved the public purse £1.98 million and that the fiscal benefits of charitable status amounted to £88 million.

247 See *McGovern* v. *AG* [1982] Ch 321.

248 See for example *Statement on the Charity Commission and The Smith Institute 19th February 2001*.

249 For a discussion of the power of the court to look at the underlying objects see Chapter 2, pp. 27–31.

Article 10(1) reads as follows:

> Everyone has the right to freedom of expression. This right shall include freedom to hold opinions and to receive and impart information and ideas without interference by public authority and regardless of frontiers. This Article shall not prevent States from acquiring the licensing of broadcasting, television or cinema enterprises.

Freedom of speech has been described as a primary right in a democracy.[250] Lord Nichols of Birkenhead described freedom of expression in the following terms:

> The high importance of freedom to impart and receive information and ideas have been stated so often and so eloquently that this point calls for no elaboration in this case. At a pragmatic level, freedom to disseminate and receive information on political matters is essential to the proper functioning of the system of parliamentary democracy cherished in this Country.[251]

The Human Rights Act 1998 does not establish principles different from those already found in the common law. The Human Rights Act 1998 reinforces and gives weight to the principles of freedom of speech and expression recognised in the common law.[252] As Lester and Pannick point out,[253] the principal change in judicial approach necessitated by the Human Rights Act 1998 is the application of the principle of proportionality when used in scrutinising the legitimacy of interference with freedom of speech.[254] The application of the principle of proportionality has given the principle of freedom of speech a much higher protected status than that enjoyed under United Kingdom domestic law prior to the Human Rights Act 1998.[255] Lord Nicholls summed up the position by saying in *Reynolds* v. *Times Newspapers*[256] that any curtailment of freedom of expression must be:

> convincingly established by a countervailing consideration, and the means employed must be proportionate to the end sought to be achieved.

A vital aspect of Article 10 is the freedom to receive information and ideas.[257] This is an important right in relation to the think tank charities which will be reviewed later in this chapter.

Political expression enjoys the highest degree of protection under the Convention, given the role Article 10 plays in modern democratic society.[258]

[250] *R* v. *Secretary of State for the Home Department ex p Simms* [2000] 2 AC 115, HL, per Lord Steyn at 125.
[251] *Reynolds* v. *Times Newspapers* [2001] 2 AC 127, HL at 2000.
[252] *Douglas* v. *Hello! Ltd* [2001] QB 967 CA. [253] *Human Rights Law and Practice* p. 337.
[254] See pp. 132–3 of this chapter for a discussion on the principle of proportionality.
[255] *Human Rights Law and Practice* p. 337.
[256] *Reynolds* v. *Times Newspapers* [2001] 2 AC 127, HL at 200.
[257] *Sunday Times* v. *United Kingdom* (1979) 2 EHRR 245, Ect HR, paras. 65–66.
[258] *Lingens* v. *Austria* (1986) 8 EHRR 407, Ect HR.

Political expression includes any form of communication on a matter of public interest.[259] For example an academic lecture on an important aspect of constitutional law would be of public interest.[260] Where a speaker seeks to criticise governmental actions, the European Court of Human Rights has stressed that restrictions on free speech will only be allowed in the most exceptional circumstances.[261]

On the face of it, the rule of law against charities having political objects conflicts with the wording of Article 10. As a matter of law, an institution will not be charitable if it has purposes which are, on construction, predominantly political[262] rather than educational.[263] Where the objects are construed to be propagandist,[264] the objects will not be charitable.

A classic statement of the rule against charities having political objects was given by Slade J in *McGovern* v. *AG*[265] when he ruled that the institution created by Amnesty International was not a charity. His reasons were twofold. First, because objects which advocate a change in the law are political and not charitable. Second, because an object to press for changes in government policies or administrative decisions is also political, and not charitable.

An important qualification to the rule against charities having political objects is where they carry out political activities which are incidental to charitable objects. There are no specific cases of this, but the rule is consistent with the general principle that non-charitable activities carried out in furtherance of charitable purposes are permissible as long as they are incidental.[266]

Unless there is justification, the rule against political objects and the constraint on political activities so that they are incidental to political objects, are arguably breaches of Article 10. This is because the wording of Article 10 is that 'everyone has a right' to freedom of expression. It does not exempt any person or organisation, including charities. It follows that unless there is justification, it is arguable that charities should not have their freedom of expression restricted.

The position is not entirely clear, as there are some arguments against this proposition.[267] It could be argued that if charities were allowed to have political objects and to campaign without restraint, the logical outcome would be for political parties to be allowed to have charitable status. This would completely change the face of charity, as organisations with party-political purposes have

[259] *Wingrove* v. *UK* (1986) 24 EHRR 1, Ect HR, para. 58.

[260] *Wille* v. *Liechtenstein* (2000) 30 EHRR 558, Ect HR.

[261] *Castells* v. *Spain* (1992) 14 EHRR 445, Ect HR.

[262] *National Ant-Vivisection Society* v. *IRC* [1948] AC 31 at 61, 76–77. See generally J. Warburton, *Tudor on Charities*, 9th edn (London: Butterworths, 2003) pp. 59–61.

[263] *Anglo-Swedish Society* v. *IRC* (1931) 16 TC 34.

[264] *Re Hopkinson* [1949] 1 All ER 346 at 348.

[265] *McGovern* v. *AG* [1982] Ch 321.

[266] For example, see *Incorporated Council of Law Reporting for England and Wales* [1972] 1 Ch 73. See CC9 – *Campaigning and Political Activities by Charities* (September 2004).

[267] See Moffat, G. 'Charity, Politics and the Human Rights Act 1998: Chasing a Red Herring?' 4 IJNL 1, September 2001.

not been accepted as charitable, because their purposes do not further recognise charitable objects.[268] However, to comply with Article 10, charity law does not need to change that radically. Arguably compliance would only require a change in the law to allow charities to carry out political activities in direct furtherance of their objects, without the need for such activities to be incidental or ancillary to those objects. For this to happen charities would need to be allowed to have a political object amongst their charitable objects.[269]

There are some reasons[270] why Article 10 might not affect the rule against political objects and restricted political activities. First, political campaigning is allowed to a certain extent, so long as it is incidental to charitable purposes. Nevertheless, it is still a restriction and is arguably a breach of Article 10 so this argument is limited. Second, it is only if an institution decides to be a charity that it has to accept the rules. Again, this argument is limited because it ignores the tax reliefs and status which accompany charitable status.[271] The case of *Bowman* v. *UK*[272] offers support for the proposition that Article 10 is concerned with financial impediments on freedom of speech. In this case, the European Court of Human Rights held that a statutory limit of £5 on electoral expenditure by third parties was the equal to a total ban on them being able to communicate information to the electorate. The court rejected the government's argument that Mrs Bowman could have used alternative means. Although she could have stood for election and become entitled to the statutory amount of expenses allowed for candidates she would have been required to pay a deposit of £500 which she would have probably lost.[273]

It could be argued that the removal of charitable status on grounds of having political purposes, with the consequential loss of tax relief, could hinder an institution's ability to campaign and thus breach Article 10. Although, ironically, the removal of the institution from the register on the ground that it was no longer considered to be a charity[274] could pave the way for an institution to adopt political objects and carry out unrestricted political campaigning.

Think tanks

The debate about the application of Article 10 to save charities from removal from the register has most relevance in relation to think tanks. Under existing charity law some think tanks are arguably not charitable because they present a perspective which is biased.[275] This begs the question whether those think tanks could be saved from removal as a result of Article 10.

The Commission has registered a number of think tanks which appear to have political leanings. For example the Institute of Economic Affairs[276] and

[268] See *McGovern* v. *AG* [1982] Ch 321.
[269] See Moffat G 'Charity, Politics and the Human Rights Act 1998'. [270] *Ibid*.
[271] See Chapter 1, p. 10. [272] *Bowman* v. *UK* (1998) 26 EHRR 1. [273] *Ibid*, para. 46.
[274] S. 3(4) Charities Act 1993. [275] *Re Bushnell* [1975] 1 WLR 1596.
[276] Registered charity no. 235351.

the Adam Smith Institute, both of which are described by another charity, the Policy Studies Institute,[277] as right-of-centre think tanks.[278] Both charities have objects for the advancement of education in economics and politics. On the other side of the political divide, the Institute for Public Policy Research has also been registered as a charity.[279] The IEA describes this charity as 'Britain's leading centre-left think tank'.[280] Its aim is to promote and contribute to a greater understanding of key social, economic and political questions.[281]

These think tanks have, on occasion, been challenged about their political bias. In 1984 the Labour Research Department complained to the Commission about the IEA's political activities. However, the Commission concluded that their publications were research publications and the fact that they were right wing was incidental.[282]

A complaint was, however, upheld against the British Atlantic Committee which had been established to 'advance public education in the aims of the Atlantic Treaty and NATO, and the duties and responsibilities of the government and people under the Treaty'. It issued leaflets against CND but undertook not to do so again.[283]

There are some signs that the Commission might take a closer look at the activities of think tanks. In 1991 the Margaret Thatcher Foundation[284] applied for charitable status with objects for:

> the education of the general public and in particular, without prejudice to the generality of the foregoing, the increase of knowledge, understanding and appreciation of the principles of freedom under a rule of law, of democracy and of responsibility towards both the ethical and physical environment.

The Commission cited *Re Bushnell (deceased) Lloyds Bank* v. *Murray*[285] as authority for the rule of law that 'education' is defined as a process to equip the persons being educated, through subjects of educational merit, to 'choose for themselves, starting with neutral information, to support or oppose' any given position.

The Commission considered that the words in the objects clause which indicated that the education would be focused upon certain areas – 'responsibility towards both the ethical and physical environment' – were imprecise and, as a result, they had to look at extrinsic evidence and the proposed activities to determine public benefit.

277 Registered charity no. 313819. 278 www.psi.org.uk. 279 www.ippr.org.uk.
280 www.psi.org.uk. 281 www.psi.org.uk.
282 See I. Williams, *The Alms Trade: Charities Past, Present and Future*, 1st edn, (London: Harper Collins, 1989) pp. 166–170.
283 See [1982] Ch.Com.A.R. and I. Williams, *The Alms Trade*, pp. 167–168.
284 *The Margaret Thatcher Foundation* [1991] Ch.Com.A.R. 39–40 App D(a). More recently see *Inquiry into the Smith Institute, 18 July 2008*.
285 *Re Bushnell* [1975] 1 WLR 1596.

It was proposed that the Foundation would take a close interest in the progress made towards freedom, democracy and prosperity in Eastern Europe, the Soviet Union and South Africa. The objects would be achieved by making grants to set up or sustain foreign journalists; sponsoring missions by western businessmen and technical advisers. The Commission concluded that this was not educational in a neutral sense and therefore declined to register the Foundation as a charity. There may be some think tanks on the register which might be threatened with removal on the ground that their 'educational purposes' are in reality political purposes.

A think tank removed from the register could argue that under the existing law its objects were educational and not political. There is sufficient ambiguity in the law of charitable status[286] to allow think tanks to argue this point. Alternatively, it could argue that Article 10 in combination with Article 14 and Protocol 1, Article 1[287] would protect it from removal.

Limits to Article 10: Freedom of expression

Article 10(2) sets out the limits to the application of Article 10. Article 10(2) reads as follows:

> The exercise of these freedoms, since it carries with it duties and responsibilities, may be subject to such formalities, conditions, restrictions or penalties as are prescribed by law and are necessary in a democratic society, in the interests of national security, territorial integrity or public safety, for the prevention of disorder or crime, for the protection of health and morals, for the protection of the reputation or rights of others, for preventing the disclosure of information received in confidence, or for maintaining the authority and impartiality of the judiciary.

The interference with free speech through a prior restraint, such as the rule against charities having political objects and only conducting incidental campaigning, requires a very high level of justification.[288] Any restriction on free speech must pass three distinct tests.[289] It must be prescribed by law, it must further a legitimate aim, and the interference must be shown to be necessary in a democratic society. In assessing whether it is 'necessary' in a democratic society, there is a need to consider whether the interference complained of corresponds to a pressing social need, whether it is proportionate to the legitimate aim pursued and whether the reasons for justification are relevant and sufficient under Article 10(2).

Prescribed by law

The key to fulfilling this condition is foreseeability.[290] The law must be of sufficient precision to enable the charity trustees to understand the qualification

[286] See Chapter 2, pp. 32–34. [287] See pp. 140–5 of this chapter.
[288] *Association Ekin* v. *France*, Judgment of 17 July 2001, Ect HR.
[289] *Handyside* v. *United Kingdom* (1976) 1 EHRR 737, 754, para. 48. See pp. 162–5 of this chapter.
[290] *Sunday Times* v. *UK* (1979) 2 EHRR 245, Ect HR.

for being a charity. It is arguable that the rule of law prohibiting charities from having political objects, and requiring campaigning to be conducted in a way which is ancillary to their charitable objects, is not sufficiently clear. For example, objects for the 'furtherance of conservative principles and moral and mental improvement' were held charitable,[291] whereas objects to teach and propagate 'Socialised Medicine' to demonstrate 'that the full advantage of Socialised Medicine can only be enjoyed in a Socialist State' was held not to be charitable as the objects were construed as essentially political rather than educational.[292] The lack of clarity in the law allows the Commission to argue that educational institutes such as think tanks are not charitable because they cross the dividing line between what is charitable and what is non-charitable.

Some of the cases involve points of emphasis. In *Re Strakosch*,[293] although Lord Greene ruled that a trust to appease racial feelings within the community was a political object, he did comment, *obiter*, that it might have been possible for the trust to have been charitable had the emphasis been more clearly placed on education.

As Santow[294] pointed out, the line between educational and political has become blurred with matters of tone and style playing a larger part than acknowledged. Choice of speaker and subject matter can subtly influence the outcome. To quote Santow:[295]

> … how is an educative purpose to be appraised where there is a didactic element in the programme? Accepting that education must involve an objective pursuit of knowledge, can education ever be entirely value free? When does education merge into propaganda? … It is here judges have to be careful to keep out their own prejudices, but without avoiding those critical questions for educational trusts.

One can argue that the law is not sufficiently precise to enable charity trustees to understand the requirements for being a charity in all but the clearest cases.

Legitimate aims

The wording of Article 10(2) provides three specific restrictions relevant to the rule that charities cannot have political objects and that any political activities must be incidental. First, it must be shown that such a rule is for the protection of the rights of others. Second, it must be shown that the rule helps maintain the authority and impartiality of the judiciary. Third, it must be shown that imposing such restrictions on charities is necessary in a democratic society.

[291] *Re Scowcroft* [1898] 2 Ch 638.

[292] *Re Bushnell* [1975] 1 WLR 1596. [293] *Re Strakosch* [1949] 1 Ch 529.

[294] Santow, G. F. K. 'Charity in its Political Voice – a Tinkling Cymbal or a Sounding Brass' 18 Aus.Bar.Rev. 225, 1999.

[295] *Ibid.*

For the protection of the rights of others

In *Bowman* v. *UK*[296] the issue was whether the statutory limit of £5 on third-party funding of candidates in UK elections was a breach of Article 10. In the joint dissenting opinion of Judges Loizou, Baka and Jambreck (who held that the spending limit was not disproportionate) it was stated:

> There can be no doubt that limits on election campaign spending maintain equality of arms as between candidates, a most important principle in democratic societies and in the electoral process.[297]

It could be argued that the tax advantages and status a charity enjoys gives an unfair advantage in political campaigning and therefore the restriction on political objects and campaigning can be justified on that basis.[298] This argument ignores the fact that other organisations receiving subsidies from the government are not subject to the same restrictions as charities.[299]

Maintaining the authority and impartiality of the judiciary

This limitation appears to be squarely in line with the reasons put forward to justify the rule against political objects by Slade J in *McGovern* v. *AG*.[300] The court would have no means of judging whether changes in laws, government policies or administrative decisions would be for the public benefit, and to decide that the law is not right as it stands would usurp the functions of the legislature. The justification for the rule against political objects and restricted political activities would appear to be justified as a legitimate aim.

It has been argued[301] that this stance is less tenable following the Human Rights Act 1998, and therefore that Article 10 could have a bearing on the rule against charities having political objects and restriction on their activities. Following the Human Rights Act 1998, the judiciary does involve itself in political controversy as the judiciary has to decide whether legislation or government policy is a breach of a Convention right.

Furthermore, following the Human Rights Act 1998 the courts have the power to interpret domestic legislation with reference to Convention rights. Judgments can conflict with government policy, which undermines the doctrine of separation of the judicial and legislative arms of government. Under section 4 of the Human Rights Act 1998, the court can declare legislation to be incompatible with Convention rights. It is therefore arguable that the rule against political objects and restricted political activities can no longer be sustained.

296 *Bowman* v. *UK* (1998) 26 EHRR 1. 297 *Ibid.* at p. 23.

298 See Morris, D. 'Charities Politics and Freedom of Speech' 5 CL & PR 3, 1999.

299 Birt, E. 'Charities and Political Activity: Time to Re-think the Rules' [1998] The Political Quarterly 23, at p. 27.

300 *McGovern v. AG* [1982] Ch 321 at 333–337.

301 See Moffat, G. 'Charity, Politics and the Human Rights Act 1998: Chasing a Red Herring?' 4 IJNL 1 pp. 25–26.

Alternatively, one could argue that the Human Rights Act 1998 maintains the rule of law and does not give the court the power to overrule legislation. A declaration of incompatibility does not affect the validity of primary or subordinate legislation until the government amends it[302] and primary legislation will prevail in the courts over Convention rights.[303]

Necessary in a democratic society

As previously discussed in this chapter[304] the word 'necessary' implies the existence of a pressing social need to protect the competing interest.[305] Furthermore, the courts must apply the principle of proportionality when exercising their jurisdiction in respect of a legitimate aim.[306] As previously discussed, charity law already allows for ancillary political activities and it could be argued that this is a proportionate way of protecting the reputation and rights of others, in this case, charities.

Article 10 and Article 14 together

If the Commission removes some think tanks from the register it needs to ensure that it is not guilty of political discrimination. As the court has found it difficult to distinguish between educational and political charities when determining charitable status,[307] it will not be any easier for the Commission when determining whether to remove charities from the register. There are charities on the register with arguably political purposes such as the Lord's Day Observance Society Incorporated[308] and the Howard League for Penal Reform.[309] Both of these charities' objects are in a charitable form but it is clear that they are concerned with law reform. The Lord's Day Observance Society has recently been involved in campaigning against unrestricted licensing hours,[310] and the Howard League for Penal Reform has recently been involved in a range of campaigns including prison overcrowding.[311] If the Commission decides to remove some charities with political objects it will be difficult for it to show objective and reasonable justification[312] for leaving others with political objects on the register.

A difference in treatment will only be discriminatory if it has no objective and reasonable justification.[313] In order to prove justification, the Commission would have to show that the difference in treatment pursues a legitimate aim and there is a reasonable relationship of proportionality between the means

302 S. 4(2) Human Rights Act 1998.

303 S. 3(2)(b) Human Rights Act 1998. 304 P. 136 of this chapter.

305 *Sunday Times* v. *United Kingdom* (1979) 2 EHRR 245, Ect HR, para. 59.

306 *Handyside* v. *United Kingdom* (1976) 1 EHRR 737 para. 50.

307 See pp. 162–4 of this chapter. 308 Registered charity number 233465.

309 Registered charity number 251926. 310 See www.lordsday.co.uk.

311 See www.howardleague.org. 312 See pp. 140–5 of this chapter for limits on Article 14.

313 *Belgium Linguistic Case* (1968) (No. 2) 1 EHRR 252, Ect HR para. 9 at para. 32.

employed and the aim sought to be realised.[314] It is arguable that the legitimate aim of maintaining an accurate register of charities does not provide sufficient objective and reasonable justification for impeding an institution's freedom of expression under Article 10 (where the benchmark is higher), through the loss of tax reliefs and charitable recognition that result from removal from the register. It might not therefore be proportionate to remove charities with political objects.

Reinterpretation of the rule against political objects

A case can be made for using Article 10 to reinterpret the rule against political purposes and restricted campaigning.[315] This could lead to charities being allowed to have a political object alongside their charitable objects with the result that political campaigning would no longer have to be incidental to the charitable objects. As Tudor[316] points out, it can also be argued that the charitable status of a purpose to advocate a change in the law and encourage debate is analogous with the already accepted purposes of educating the public in forms of government[317] and encouraging political awareness.[318] If such a purpose was accepted as charitable, then an institution seeking to argue that it should not be removed from the register would still have to demonstrate that it passed the public benefit test from its inception.[319] A reinterpretation of the law along these lines might save some charities from being removed.

Developments in some Commonwealth jurisdictions point the way for an interpretation of the law which would accommodate Article 10. *Public Trustee* v. *AG of New South Wales*[320] concerned a trust with objects for the removal, by legislation, of racial discrimination. Most of the Australian states had already legislated to remove racial discrimination. Santow J commented, *obiter*, that a purpose to introduce a new law consistent with the way the law is developing and reinforced by treaty obligations should be charitable.[321] Here a distinction can be made between a trust for purposes contrary to the established law and those whose object is to introduce new law consistent with the way the law is tending.[322]

The judge in *Re Collier (Deceased)*,[323] while upholding the rule of law in New Zealand that a trust to change the law was not charitable, expressed the

[314] See pp. 140–5 for the discussion of Article 14. [315] See pp. 162–4 of this chapter.

[316] J. Warburton, *Tudor on Charities*, 9th edn (London: Butterworths, 2003), para. 2-040.

[317] *Re The Trusts of the Arthur McDougal Fund* [1957] 1 WLR 81.

[318] *AG* v. *Ross* [1986] 1 WLR 252.

[319] To satisfy the Commission the arguments would have to be sound and well founded. See CC, *The Promotion of Human Rights* (2002) paras. B3-B6.

[320] *Public Trustee* v. *AG of New South Wales* (1997) 42 NSWLR 600.

[321] See Santow, G. F. K. 'Charity in its Political Voice – a Tinkling Cymbal or a Sounding Brass?' (1999) 18 Aus.Bar.Rev. 225.

[322] *Ibid.* [323] *Re Collier (Deceased)* [1998] 1 NZLR 81.

opinion,[324] *obiter*, that a court could recognise an issue as worthy of debate even though the result of that debate could lead to a change in the law.

These cases allow for freedom of expression on a more realistic basis than the existing demarcation between what is political and what is educational.[325] A development of the law along these lines might accommodate Article 10 and the freedom of expression and in turn save many charities with political objects from being removed from the register.

The Charities Act 2006

Quite apart from the Human Rights Act 1998 the Charities Act 2006 has implications for charities on the register. The Charities Act 2006 widens the scope of charitable status in some respects. This in turn will limit the Commission's power to remove charities from the register.

An example is the new head of charity: 'the advancement of human rights, conflict resolution,[326] or reconciliation, or the promotion of religious or racial harmony, or equality and diversity'.[327] Previously, it was unclear whether all or any of these objects were charitable. Indeed, there were authorities which suggested otherwise.[328] This new head was included in the Charities Act 2006 to remove any doubt.[329]

The Charities Act 2006 amends the Recreational Charities Act 1958 so that recreational charities with a beneficiary class solely restricted to men can be charitable.[330] Previously, the Recreational Charities Act 1958 could have been held to be incompatible with Article 14 European Convention on Human Rights in that it contemplated a beneficiary class restricted solely to women.[331] The widening of the scope of the 1958 Act will make it more difficult for the Commission to remove recreational charities from the register.

324 *Ibid.* 90. 325 Pp. 162–4 of this chapter.

326 The Commission have accepted that the promotion of conflict resolution in a national and international context can be charitable where the activities are limited to those which are carried out on an impartial and non-partisan basis. See *Application For Registration of Concordis International Trust Decision of The Commission made on 23rd July 2004*.

327 S. 2(2)(h) Charities Act 2006.

328 *Re Harwood* [1936] Ch 285, a dubious authority which has been cited as an authority for the proposition that the promotion of peace is a charitable object. It was not followed in *Re Koeppler's Will Trusts* [1985] Ch 243. Also, the rejection by the court of the assertion by Amnesty International that it was a charity (prior to the Human Rights Act 1998) in *McGovern v. AG* [1981] 3 All ER 493. Note that the Commission has accepted that the promotion of human rights is charitable. See RR 12 – *The Promotion of Human Rights* (April 2005).

329 Cabinet Office, Strategy Unit, *Private Action, Public Benefit A Review of Charities and the Wider Not-for-Profit Sector* (2002) para. 4.40.

330 Ss. 1(2) & (2A) Recreational Charities Act 1958, as substituted by section 5(2) Charities Act 2006.

331 S. 1(2) Recreational Charities Act 1958.

Finally, there was clear legal authority for the proposition that the promotion of mere sport was not charitable.[332] It was mentioned in Chapter 3[333] that the Commission issued RR 11 – *Charitable Status and Sport,*[334] which recognised two new charitable objects which do not directly promote particular sports but allow sports to be used as a means to promote other previously recognised charitable objects. As a result, the promotion of community participation in healthy recreation by the provision of facilities for playing particular sports and the advancement of physical education of young people not undergoing formal education were both considered by the Commission to be charitable. However, as Parliament or the Court had not determined the issue the position was unclear. The advancement of amateur sport is now contained in the Charities Act 2006 in its list of charitable purposes.[335] Sport is defined by section 2(3)(d) Charities Act 2006 as meaning sports or games which promote health and involve physical or mental skill or exertion. This widens the scope of charitable status.

On the other hand, the Charities Act 2006 takes away the statutory right of miners' welfare trusts to charitable status under the 1958 Act.[336] In future they will have to demonstrate that they are charitable by satisfying the public benefit requirement. Furthermore, registered sports clubs[337] with charitable objects will not be charities following the Charities Act 2006.[338] To the extent that the Charities Act 2006 narrows the scope of charitable status, there will be an increased chance that the Commission will need to consider removing charities from the register.

Under the Charities Act 2006, it is a requirement that to be a charity an institution must have purposes which are for the public benefit.[339] There is no longer a presumption of public benefit for a head of charity.[340] However, the Charities Act 2006 does not alter the law of public benefit as it currently stands.[341] It specifically places a duty on the Commission to issue guidance[342] in pursuance of its public benefit objective.[343] This objective is to promote 'awareness and understanding of the operation of the public benefit requirement'.[344]

As the guidance will be based on the existing law and will come about following consultation,[345] it is not expected to radically affect charities on the

[332] *Re Nottage* [1895] 2 Ch 649. [333] Chapter 3, pp. 65–67.

[334] RR 11 – *Charitable Status and Sport* (Version 2003). [335] S. 2(2)(g) Charities Act 2006.

[336] S. 2 Recreational Charities Act 1958.

[337] Registered under Schedule 18 to the Finance Act 2002 relief for community amateur sports clubs.

[338] S. 5(4) Charities Act 2006. [339] S. 3(1) Charities Act 2006.

[340] S. 3(2) Charities Act 2006. [341] S. 3(3) Charities Act 2006.

[342] S. 4(1) Charities Act 2006. [343] S. 1B(2)1 Charities Act 1993.

[344] S. 1B(3)2 Charities Act 1993.

[345] S. 4(4) Charities Act 2006. See *Consultation on Draft Public Benefit Guidance* (February 2007) and *Charities and Public Benefit: The Charity Commission's General Guidance on Public Benefit* (January 2008).

register. Any interpretation of the existing law of public benefit by the Commission will have to be objective and reasonable if it is to comply with Article 14.[346] The guidance issued will not be legally binding.[347]

Conclusion

There are two ways in which the Human Rights Act 1998 can affect the Commission's power of removal. First, by the application of Convention rights potentially of general relevance to charities being removed from the register, namely; Article 1, Protocol 1: Protection of Property and Article 14: Prohibition against Discrimination. Second, by particular Convention rights which may have the effect of broadening the scope of charitable status, namely; Article 9: Freedom of Thought, Conscience and Religion, Article 2, Protocol 1: Right to Education and Article 10: Freedom of Expression.

The conclusion reached in this chapter was that Article 1, Protocol 1: Protection of Property might be relevant to the question of removal where it is not proportionate for charities which were mistakenly registered, through no fault of the promoters, to lose their charity tax reliefs.[348] Furthermore, it was concluded that it would not be proportionate for the Commission to take the view that a charity with dated objects should be removed from the register rather than have its objects modernised by a *cy-pres* scheme.[349] Finally, it was shown that because the law must be of sufficient quality it is arguable that if the Commission removed a charity which was in substance charitable but in form non-charitable according to the *Compton* test[350] this could amount to a breach of Article 1, Protocol 1.[351]

It was shown[352] that Article 14, which prohibits discrimination, might be breached in respect of the Convention rights discussed in the chapter, if the Commission removes some charities from the register, but leaves others remaining. It was concluded that the Commission needs to be careful that, in particular, it does not discriminate directly or indirectly on grounds of sex and religion.[353]

It was also shown that there are particular Convention rights which have the effect of broadening the scope of charitable status and thereby restricting the power of the Commission to remove institutions. In the case of Article 9, which protects freedom of thought, conscience and religion, it was concluded that there are two ways in which the Commission's power of removal might be limited. First, Article 9 has already led to a wider definition of religion than under the common law[354] to include polytheistic and non-theistic religions in the Charities Act 2006.[355] It was concluded that Article 9 will not only provide

346 *Tsirlis and Kouloumpas* v. *Greece* (1997) 25 EHRR 198, para. 116.
347 S. 4(6) Charities Act 1993. 348 P. 139 of this chapter. 349 *Ibid.*
350 *Re Compton* [1945] Ch 123. 351 Pp. 133–6 of this chapter.
352 Pp. 140–5 of this chapter. 353 See p. 141 of this chapter.
354 *Re South Place Ethical Society* [1980] WLR 1565. 355 Pp. 146–9 of this chapter.

greater protection for religious charities but also charities with objects for the mental, moral or spiritual welfare or improvement of the community. Second, it was concluded that the loss of tax reliefs and ability to fundraise as a charity following removal might breach Article 9 if this affects their ability to hold services and evangelise.[356] This is because an important feature of a democratic society is religious pluralism.[357]

The chapter examined Article 2, Protocol 1, which protects the right to education and, in particular, the obligation on the state to respect the right of parents to ensure such education and teaching in conformity with their own religious and philosophical convictions. It was concluded that the closure of a school as a result of the application of a school's property, *cy-pres*, or removal and the loss of tax reliefs and the ability to fundraise might be a breach of Article 2, Protocol 1, and therefore the law of charitable status might need to be interpreted more widely to accommodate this Convention right.

It was argued that the rule of law[358] against charities having political objects and restricted campaigning breaches the wording of Article 10 which confers a right to freedom of expression.[359] Think tanks provide an illustration of a category of charities which might be threatened with removal.[360] They are often accused of having political bias[361] and thus falling foul of the rule against charities having political objects.[362]

The chapter also looked at areas of charitable status[363] which will be broadened as a result of the Charities Act 2006. These areas include the advancement of human rights, conflict resolution, or reconciliation, or the promotion of religious or racial harmony, or equality and diversity, the Recreational Charities Act 1958 and the promotion of amateur sport.

This chapter illustrates two of the basic propositions[364] of this book. First, the Human Rights Act 1998 will arguably limit the Commission's powers of removal, both in terms of how it exercises its powers, and through a broader definition of charity. In some respects the Charities Act 2006 has also led to a broader definition of charitable status. These conclusions support the basic proposition that the Commission's powers of removal are limited. Second, it is not clear to what extent the Human Rights Act 1998 will impact on the Commission's powers of removal and the law of charitable status until the Court determines these issues. These conclusions support the basic proposition that there is a need for clarification of the Commission's powers of removal.

356 P. 150 of this chapter. 357 *Manoussakis* v. *Greece* (1996) 23 EHRR 387, para. 44.

358 Pp. 162–4 of this chapter. 359 Pp. 48–53 of this chapter.

360 Pp. 160–2 of this chapter.

361 See for example *Inquiry into the Smith Institute 18 July 2008*.

362 For a discussion of the power of the court to look at the underlying objects see Chapter 2, pp. 27–32.

363 See pp. 167–9 of this chapter. 364 Chapter 1, pp. 1–4.

8
Grounds for appeal

Introduction

It is one of the basic propositions[1] of this book that there is a need for charities removed from the register to have access to justice. It will be shown in this chapter that charities do not have effective access to justice because the appeal process is unsatisfactory.[2] When it comes to an appeal, the Commission is in a position of strength.

The chapter looks at appeals against removal from the register under section 3(4) Charities Act 1993, which are referred to as direct removal, and appeals against orders made under sections 18 and 19 Charities Act 1993 (which can indirectly lead to removal under section 3(4) Charities Act), which are referred to as indirect removal.

Appeals are especially important in the context of direct and indirect removal because the Commission does not always allow charities to make more than limited representations as to why they should not be removed, or why orders under sections 18 and 19 Charities Act 1993 should not be made. In the case of direct removal, the Commission does not generally contemplate any correspondence other than establishing whether charities qualify for removal and notifying trustees (where they can be traced) that their charity is being removed.[3] In the case of indirect removal, the Commission contemplates inviting trustees to make representations prior to making its orders under sections 18 and 19 Charities Act 1993, but it states that in some serious cases it may be necessary to take action before raising concerns with the trustees.[4] It is therefore important that trustees are given the opportunity to test the correctness and lawfulness of the Commission's actions before an independent and impartial tribunal or court.

[1] Chapter 1, pp. 1–4.

[2] For a general review of these problems see *Power Without Accountability: The Charity Commission as Regulator* (Association For Charities Report-June 2004), www.association4charities.org.uk.

[3] *OG 17 A2-6th February 2006 The Law, Final Accounts and Reinstatement.*

[4] *CC 47 – Complaints about Charities* (version May 2003).

There are a number of problems with appeals against direct removal. Where the Commission uses section 3(4) to remove an institution because it no longer considers that it is a charity, or it has ceased to exist, or it no longer operates, the extent of these powers of removal are not clearly established by law.[5] The Charity Tribunal does not have lawmaking powers and like the Commission it is bound by the general law.[6] As there are so few modern decisions of the Court[7] on charitable status this will limit the power of the Charity Tribunal to decide that charities can be removed from the register. This means that charities will need to appeal[8] from the Charity Tribunal to the Court if they wish to have a legal decision. Such appeals will usually be test cases because of the lack of common law decisions on charitable status[9] and this uncertainty of outcome will deter many institutions from appealing.

Even if an appellant is successful the Commission may, notwithstanding the decision of the tribunal on appeal, consider the matter afresh, if the Commission considers that there has been a change in circumstances, or that the decision is inconsistent with a later judicial decision.[10] These exceptions to the *res judicata* rule could work against an appellant.

There are interrelated problems with appeals against indirect removal.[11] Following the appointment of an interim manager or additional trustees (forming a majority), there will be a loss of control by the original trustees. This loss of control could prevent them accessing charity assets to pay for the cost of an appeal.

Charities facing direct or indirect removal may wish to challenge the Commission by way of appeal, judicial review or common-law actions. An appeal[12] against direct removal under section 3(4) Charities Act 1993 will be on the basis that the institution is a charity for the purposes of registration.[13] An appeal against indirect removal will be an appeal against the making of an order under sections 18 and 19 Charities Act 1993. The ground for the appeal would be that the order had not been correctly made.[14] Whereas an appeal deals with the question of whether the Commission is right or wrong, judicial review considers whether the decision to remove is lawful or unlawful.[15] Potential grounds for judicial review in the context of direct removal include: the right to be heard,[16] legitimate expectation[17] and estoppel.[18] Potential grounds for judicial review in the context of indirect removal include: *ultra vires*, Wednesbury unreasonableness and bias,[19] a right to a fair hearing and Article 6,[20] natural

[5] Chapter 3, pp. 45–52. [6] Pp. 5–7 of this chapter. [7] Chapter 3, pp. 45–52.
[8] S. 2C(1) Charities Act 1993. [9] Chapter 3, pp. 45–52.
[10] S. 4(5) Charities Act 1993. See pp. 5–7 of this chapter. See also Chapter 3, pp. 45–52.
[11] See pp. 7–11 of this chapter. [12] Schedule 1C1(1) Charities Act 1993.
[13] Pp. 174–5 of this chapter. [14] Pp. 175–7 of this chapter.
[15] Pp. 177–9 of this chapter. [16] P. 180 of this chapter.
[17] Pp. 180–2 of this chapter. [18] Pp. 182–3 of this chapter.
[19] Pp. 184–5 of this chapter. [20] Pp. 185–6 of this chapter.

justice[21] and estoppel.[22] Quite apart from an appeal or judicial review, a charity might decide to initiate common-law actions which, in the case of direct removal, could include estoppel[23] or negligent misstatement[24] and, in the case of indirect removal, could also include these types of actions.[25]

Judicial review and common-law actions are not available to charities against the Commission when being directly removed.[26] The statutory right of appeal[27] is by way of rehearing and not by way of review.[28] The combination of these factors means that the conduct of the Commission will not be taken into account on appeal against direct removal to either the Tribunal[29] or the Court.[30] Although judicial review and common-law remedies are not currently available in this context, it is arguable[31] that they should be and for this reason they are explored.

For the reasons outlined above, except in the case of an appeal against the decision to institute an inquiry under section 8 Charities Act 1993, where judicial review is available in the Charity Tribunal,[32] judicial review and common-law actions will not be available against the Commission in the case of indirect removal either, but again it is arguable that these remedies should be generally available[33] and, for that reason, they are explored to see the extent to which they would provide charities with remedies. In addition, it will be shown that although the Commission can seek an advanced ruling as to whether it is acting within public law charities do not have the same opportunity.[34]

The chapter also looks at the issue of costs for appeals in respect of direct and indirect removal.[35] Costs are a problem for a number of reasons. First, access to justice is expensive.[36] Second, access to charity funds may be difficult because it is normally advisable for trustees to seek the consent of the Commission to use charity funds to pay for costs.[37] Third, it is likely that costs will still be an issue for appeals to the Charity Tribunal.[38]

Given these problems, alternatives to the appeal process such as the Commission's internal review procedure (which reviews the correctness of decisions) and the complaints procedure, including the Independent Complaints Reviewer,[39] and the Ombudsman[40] (who review the Commission's conduct) assume greater importance. However, these alternatives either lack independence,

[21] Pp. 186–7 of this chapter. [22] P. 187 of this chapter.
[23] Pp. 182–3 of this chapter. [24] P. 183 of this chapter.
[25] P. 187 of this chapter. [26] Pp. 177–9 of this chapter.
[27] Schedule 1C1(1) Charities Act 1993. [28] Schedule 1C1(4) Charities Act 1993.
[29] Schedule 1C1(4)(a) & (b) Charities Act 1993.
[30] *Weth* v. *AG* [1999] 1 WLR (CA) 686 *per* Nourse LJ at 694.
[31] See pp. 177–9 of this chapter. [32] Schedule 1C3(2)(a) & (b) Charities Act 1993.
[33] See pp. 177–9 of this chapter. [34] *Ibid.* [35] Pp. 188–91 of this chapter.
[36] *Ibid.* [37] *Ibid.* [38] *Ibid.*
[39] See the Independent Complaints Reviewer's website: www.icrev.demon.co.uk.
[40] See pp. 191–3 of this chapter.

in the case of the Commission and the Independent Complaints Reviewer,[41] or lack teeth in the case of the Ombudsman.

Appealing against direct removal under section 3(4) Charities Act 1993

Section 3(4) Charities Act 1993 places a statutory duty on the Commission to remove an institution from the register which it no longer considers is a charity, or has ceased to exist, or does not operate.[42] If the Commission removes an institution from the register which is entitled to be registered, then the charity will have a right of appeal[43] on a point of law, i.e. that the institution is a charity for the purposes of registration and must therefore be registered.

The statutory basis for an appeal against direct removal is set out in the Table in Schedule 1C to the Charities Act 1993. Where the appeal is successful, the Charity Tribunal has the power to quash the decision and (if appropriate) remit the matter to the Commission and direct the Commission to rectify the register. The appeal will be by way of rehearing,[44] and therefore the conduct of the Commission when making the decision will be irrelevant.[45]

When determining the issue of entitlement to registration the Charity Tribunal will, itself, be bound by the general law when making decisions.[46] As shown in Chapter 3,[47] there are very few modern decisions of the court on the question of charitable status, which means that the Charity Tribunal will face the same difficulty as the Commission when deciding questions of charitable status. This will limit its power when deciding whether charities should be removed from the register. It follows that charities seeking a legal ruling will still need to appeal to the Court.[48] Appeals from the Charity Tribunal to the Court can only be on a point of law[49] with attendant risk on costs which come with test cases.[50]

Following the outcome of the appeal, the Commission may, notwithstanding the decision of the Charity Tribunal, consider the matter afresh, if the Commission considers that there has been a change in circumstances, or that the decision is inconsistent with a later judicial decision.[51] The *res judicata* rule does not apply in these two instances. This rule prevents parties from litigating

[41] See the Independent Complaints Reviewer's website: www.icrev.demon.co.uk 'Frequently Asked Questions'.

[42] See Chapter 3, pp. 45–52. [43] Schedule 1C1(1) Charities Act 1993.

[44] Schedule 1C1(4) Charities Act 1993. For example, see *Incorporated Council of Law Reporting for England and Wales* v. *AG* [1972] Ch 73.

[45] Removal is not a reviewable matter: see Schedule 1C3(1) Charities Act 1993. See *Incorporated Council of Law Reporting for England and Wales* v. *AG* [1972] Ch 73.

[46] The Charity Tribunal has no law making powers under the Charities Act 2006 and is, like any public body, bound by the general law. See Chapter 3, pp. 45–52.

[47] *Ibid.* [48] S. 2C(1) Charities Act 1993.

[49] S. 2C(2) Charities Act 1993. [50] Pp. 188–91 of this chapter.

[51] S. 4(5) Charities Act 1993. See *National Anti-Vivisection Society* v. *IRC* [1948] AC 31.

the same question again following a judicial determination even though the determination is shown to be wrong.[52] Other than these two grounds, the *res judicata* rule will apply and the Commission will not be able to re-examine the case. It should rarely be the case that the Commission will be able to re-examine a decision of the Charity Tribunal. The purpose of the *res judicata* rule is to impose a finality on proceedings and unless the Commission has strong grounds for re-examining a decision of the Charity Tribunal, it could itself face an appeal with the risk that the Charity Tribunal would merely restate its decision. Nevertheless, it remains an obstacle for appellants.

Appealing against indirect removal

As shown in Chapter 6[53] the Commission sometimes exercises its powers under sections 18 and 19 Charities Act 1993 in a way that indirectly leads to charities being removed from the register under section 3(4) Charities Act 1993. An appeal could arise against the institution of an inquiry,[54] or the subsequent making of orders[55] under sections 18 and 19 Charities Act 1993, prior to the charity being removed under section 3(4) Charities Act 1993. The statutory basis for an appeal is set out in the Table in Schedule 1C to the Charities Act 1993.[56] An appeal from the Charity Tribunal may be made to the court[57] but only on a point of law.[58]

In the case of a decision by the Commission, under section 8 Charities Act 1993, to institute an inquiry into a class of charities, the Charity Tribunal has the power to direct the Commission not to consider a particular institution and, in the case of all inquiries, to direct the Commission to end the inquiry.[59] In respect of appeals against decisions by the Commission to make orders under sections 18 and 19 Charities Act 1993, the Charity Tribunal has the power to (a) quash the order in whole or in part and (if appropriate) remit the matter to the Commission, (b) substitute for all or part of the order any other order which could have been made by the Commission, and/or (c) add to the order anything which could have been contained in an order made by the Commission. An additional power is available to the Charity Tribunal in the case of a decision of the Commission to (i) discharge an order following a review under section 18(13) Charities Act 1993, or (ii) not to discharge an order following such a review. In these cases the Charity Tribunal also has the power to (d) discharge the order in whole or in part (whether subject to any savings or other transitional provisions or not).

The Commission has been given new powers under the Charities Act 2006 to direct a person to take any action[60] and direct a person to apply the property in

[52] See *The Duchess of Kingston's Case* (1776) 20 St.Tr. 355, 538 n.
[53] Chapter 6, p. 114. [54] Schedule 1C3(2)(a) & (b) Charities Act 1993.
[55] Schedule 1C1(1) Charities Act 1993. [56] *Ibid.*
[57] S. 2C(1) Charities Act 1993. [58] S. 2C(2) Charities Act 1993.
[59] The Table to Schedule 1C Charities Act 1993. [60] S. 19A(2) Charities Act 1993.

the specified manner.[61] In such cases the Charity Tribunal can quash the order and (if appropriate) remit the matter to the Commission.

The ground for appeal against the Commission making an order under sections 18 or 19 Charities Act 1993 (other than section 19B which is explained below) would be that the order was not correctly made. To make such an order the Commission must be satisfied,[62]

> that there has been misconduct or mismanagement in the administration of the charity; or that it is necessary or desirable to act for the purpose of protecting the property of the charity or securing a proper application for the purposes of the charity of that property or of property coming to the charity.

The conditions that need to be fulfilled are on an either/or basis except[63] when the Commission wish to make an order to remove[64] any trustee, charity trustee, officer, agent or employee of the charity who has been responsible for or privy to the misconduct or mismanagement, or has by his conduct contributed to it or facilitated it and/or, by order, establish a scheme[65] for the administration of the charity. Where the Commission wish to make either of these orders both conditions must be met.

In the case of section 19B, which confers power on the Commission to direct the application of charity property, there is no requirement, as in the case of the other powers in sections 18 and 19, to open an inquiry first or to meet the conditions described (above). Instead, the Commission must be satisfied:

> (a) that a person or persons in possession or control of any property held by or on trust for a charity is or are unwilling to apply it properly for the purposes of the charity, and
> (b) that it is necessary or desirable to make an order under this section for the purpose of securing a proper application of that property for the purposes of the charity.

It will not be difficult for the Commission to satisfy any of the conditions for sections 18, 19 and 19B in order to justify making an order. Charities are not generally run by professionals and most charities, if scrutinised by the Commission, would fail some aspect of management. The Commission's published inquiry reports[66] reveal that most inquiries involve a failure of governance and a consequential lack of efficiency rather than a direct risk to charity property. It follows that the ease with which the Commission can make their orders makes it difficult for an appellant to succeed in showing that those orders were incorrectly made.

[61] S. 19B(2) Charities Act 1993. [62] S. 18(1)(a) and (b) Charities Act 1993.

[63] S. 18(2)(a) and (b) Charities Act 1993. [64] S. 18(2)(i) Charities Act 1993.

[65] S. 18(2)(ii) Charities Act 1993.

[66] See Chapter 6, pp. 121–4 for an examination of the Inquiry reports for 2003–2004.

Prior to the Charities Act 2006, an appeal against indirect removal to the court was by rehearing.[67] Other than an appeal against a decision by the Commission to institute an inquiry,[68] an appeal against an order being made under sections 18 or 19 of the Charities Act 1993 to the Charity Tribunal continues to be by way of rehearing.[69] The Charity Tribunal would examine whether, on the evidence, the order should be made. As the appeal is by rehearing, the actions of the Commission will be irrelevant. Public law remedies relating to the Commission's conduct will not therefore be available.

There are two interrelated problems with an appeal against indirect removal from the register. The first problem relates to a loss of control where additional trustees forming a majority of the trustees or an interim manager are appointed. Usually when exercising its power under section 18, the Commission will appoint so many additional trustees that they will outnumber the original trustees.[70] As charity trustees act by majority, the new trustees will have control of the charity. Loss of control also occurs where an interim manager is appointed because, in most cases, the Commission will specify in the order that the interim manager will have all the powers and duties of a charity trustee to the exclusion of the original trustees.[71] The original trustees will, in effect, be powerless in such circumstances. The second problem is that the original charity trustees will not have access to charity funds where they are no longer in control whether they are appealing against an order under sections 18 or 19 Charities Act 1993 or subsequent removal under sections 3(4) Charities Act 1993. The issue of costs is explored later in the chapter.[72]

Direct and indirect removal, judicial review and common-law action

One of the main problems faced by charities appealing against either direct removal or indirect removal, other than against a decision by the Commission to institute an inquiry,[73] is that the appeal will be by way of rehearing and not review.[74] For example, in *Rule* v. *Charity Commissioners*[75] the Exclusive Brethren sought certain declarations and injunctions against the Commission on the ground that the conduct of an inquiry by the Commission had, *inter alia*, been unfair and contrary to natural justice. In that case, Fox J said:

67 See *Weth* v. *AG* [1999] 1 WLR 686 (CA) *per* Nourse LJ at 693.

68 Schedule 1C3(2)(a) & (b) Charities Act 1993.

69 Schedule 1C1(4)(a) & (b) Charities Act 1993.

70 See Chapter 6, pp. 116–17.

71 S. 19(3)(a) & (b) Charities Act 1993.

72 See pp. 188–91 of this chapter.

73 Schedule 1C3(2)(a) & (b) Charities Act 1993.

74 Schedule 1C1(4) Charities Act 1993. For examples, see *Incorporated Council of Law Reporting for England and Wales* v. *AG* [1972] Ch 73; *McGovern* v. *AG* [1982] Ch 321; *Weth* v. *AG* [1999] 1 WLR 686 (CA); *Jones* v. *AG* [1974] Ch 148.

75 *Rule* v. *Charity Commissioners* (High Court, 10 December 1979); [1979] Ch.Com.A.R. pp. 12–16.

> It seems to me that the Court will not normally make a declaration in the air. There must be practical consequences to justify making the declaration.[76]

Since, in that case, the Exclusive Brethren could bring appeal proceedings to the High Court[77] against the making of an order[78] or the removal from the register[79] and because the appeal would be by way rehearing the conduct of the Commission was irrelevant.[80]

Review by the Charity Tribunal is only available for an appeal against a decision by the Commission to institute an inquiry.[81] However, in the case of section 19B, which confers the power on the Commission to direct the application of charity property, there is no such requirement for an inquiry to first be instituted.[82] This means that there is no scope for review when this power is exercised.[83]

An appeal by way of rehearing considers whether a decision is right or wrong. It does not review the Commission's conduct in relation to the decision to examine whether the decision is lawful. On appeal the question is 'right or wrong'; on review the question is 'lawful or unlawful'.[84] Currently charities will have difficulty in applying for judicial review because where there is a statutory appeal to the Charity Tribunal[85] and from the Charity Tribunal to the Court[86] under the Charities Act 1993, it is this procedure that charities must use, and not separate proceedings such as judicial review, or common-law actions such as negligence proceedings.[87] The court has taken the decision that it is not in the interests of charities to have multiple legal actions on grounds of cost.[88]

Theoretically, it would be open to a charity refused an application for judicial review or a common law action to challenge[89] the Court by way of an application for judicial review that such a refusal amounted to a breach of Article 6(1) of the European Convention on Human Rights, which provides a right to a fair hearing. Article 6(1) reads as follows:

[76] *Rule* v. *Charity Commissioners* [1979] Ch.Com.A.R. para 31.

[77] At that time under section 5(3) Charities Act 1960.

[78] Under what are now sections 18 & 19 Charities Act 1993.

[79] S. 3(4) Charities Act 1993.

[80] *Weth* v. *AG* [1999] 1 WLR 686.

[81] See Schedule 1C3(2)(a) & (b) Charities Act 1993.

[82] S. 18(1) Charities Act 1993.

[83] Chapter 6, pp. 120–1.

[84] See H. W. R. Wade and C. F. Forsyth, *Administrative Law*, 8th edn (Oxford University Press, 2000) p. 33.

[85] Schedule 1C1(1) Charities Act 1993. The limited access to judicial review available in the Charity Tribunal is explained in pp. 175–7 of this chapter.

[86] S. 2C(1) Charities Act 1993.

[87] See *Weth* v. *AG* [1999] 1 WLR 686 (CA) *per* Nourse LJ at 694 and *Mills* v. *Winchester Diocesan Board of Finance* [1989] Ch 428 per Knox J at 452.

[88] *Per* Knox J in *Mills* v. *Winchester Diocesan Board of Finance* [1989] Ch 428 at 452.

[89] The appeal would have to be made to the Court by way of judicial review if it was in respect of a decision by the Commission which was not a 'reviewable matter' as defined by Schedule 1C3 because the Tribunal has the power to apply judicial review principles in respect of these matters. As to why Article 6 will not be of assistance see pp. 185–6 of this chapter.

> In the determination of his civil rights and obligations or of any criminal charge against him, everyone is entitled to a fair and public hearing within a reasonable time by an independent and impartial tribunal established by law

A refusal by the court to allow charities to challenge the lawfulness of the Commission's decisions, or to allow a common law action, is a denial of the right to be heard.[90] The need to challenge the court to be allowed access to judicial review or common-law rights of action presents another hurdle for charities. The Charity Tribunal will not assist in this respect as in the context of removal the only relevant reviewable matter is the decision by the Commission to institute an inquiry.[91] It will be shown later in the chapter that charities can complain to the Commission[92] and to the Ombudsman,[93] but what is needed is a statutory right of appeal to both the Charity Tribunal and the Court to review the Commission's decisions generally.

Charities face a further disadvantage. It is open to the Commission to make a reference,[94] with the consent of the Attorney General,[95] in relation to the exercise by the Commission of any of its functions,[96] which involves either the operation of charity law in any respect or its application to a particular state of affairs.[97] A reference may therefore be made in respect of a direct or indirect removal and, in doing so, the Commission may seek an advanced ruling not only on these issues, but also in relation to its duties when performing these functions. Section 1D(2)4 Charities Act 1993 reads as follows:

> In performing its functions the Commission must, so far as relevant, have regard to the principles of best regulatory practice (including the principles under which regulatory activities should be proportionate, accountable, consistent, transparent and targeted only at cases in which action is needed).

These general duties would include a duty to act 'fairly and reasonably'.[98] This means that the Commission has the opportunity to seek an advance ruling as to whether it is acting within public law but charities do not. Given the restricted access to the Charity Tribunal and the Court for judicial review by charities[99] of Commission this additional restriction is particularly unfair.

Direct removal, judicial review and common-law action

Except in the case of an appeal against a decision to institute an inquiry where judicial review is available in the Charity Tribunal, judicial review and common law rights of action against the Commission will not be not available in the

90 See *Holy Monasteries* v. *Greece (*1994) 20 EHRR 1, Ect HR, para. 83; *Devlin* v. *United Kingdom* (2001) 34 EHRR 1029. Article 6(1) is discussed later in the chapter at pp. 185–6.

91 Schedule 1C3 Charities Act 1993.

92 See pp. 191–2.

93 See pp. 192–3.

94 Schedule 1D1(1)(a) & (b) Charities Act 1993.

95 Schedule 1D1(2) Charities Act 1993.

96 Schedule 1D(1)(a) Charities Act 1993.

97 Schedule 1D1(1)(b) Charities Act 1993.

98 Lords Hansard 12 October 2005; col. 335.

99 See pp. 177–9 of this chapter.

context of removal.[100] Nevertheless,[101] it is arguable that these actions should generally be available to charities. They are discussed for this reason and because their current unavailability serves to highlight how charities are at a disadvantage. In the context of direct removal these actions are the right to be heard and Article 6,[102] legitimate expectation,[103] estoppel[104] and negligent misstatement.[105]

The right to be heard and the Human Rights Act 1998: Article 6: A right to a fair trial

It is fundamental to fair procedure that both parties should be heard.[106] Failure by the Commission or the court to allow a charity to put forward its legal arguments should provide grounds for judicial review for failure to hear the charity's case. The Commission provides limited opportunity[107] for charities to make representations in the context of removal and it is therefore arguable that, on occasion, the Commission might be in breach of the requirement to provide charities with a right to be heard.

Article 6 of the European Convention on Human Rights,[108] which provides a right to a fair trial, will not provide a remedy in this context because when the Commission removes charities under section 3(4) Charities Act 1993 it does not act in a judicial capacity.[109] Furthermore, access to 'an independent and impartial tribunal established by law' is provided by the Charity Tribunal[110] and the Court[111] through the right of appeal.

Legitimate expectation

Where the Commission gives an undertaking not to remove a charity from the register, and then breaches that undertaking, the appellant might wish to argue that there has been a breach of legitimate expectation. It is currently unclear whether legitimate expectation is part of public law[112] and therefore a ground for judicial review, or whether it belongs to the common law of estoppel.[113]

In the context of direct removal, an argument for legitimate expectation[114] could result from an undertaking given by the Commission not to remove a charity from the register provided that certain conditions will be fulfilled. An

[100] Schedule 1C3(2)(a) & (b) Charities Act 1993. See *Mills* v. *Winchester Diocesan Board of Finance* [1989] Ch 428; *Weth* v. *AG* [1999] 1 WLR 686 and *Rule* v. *Charity Commissioners* (High Ct, 10 December 1979); [1979] Ch.Com.A.R. pp 12–16.

[101] Pp. 177–9 of this chapter.

[102] P. 180 of this chapter.

[103] Pp. 180–2 of this chapter.

[104] Pp. 182–3 of this chapter.

[105] P. 183 of this chapter.

[106] *Ridge* v. *Baldwin* [1964] AC 40.

[107] Pp. 171–9 of this chapter.

[108] Pp. 185–6 of this chapter.

[109] See Chapter 3, pp. 45–52.

[110] Schedule 1C1(1) Charities Act 1993.

[111] S. 2C(1) Charities Act 1993.

[112] *O'Reilly* v. *Mackman* [1983] 2 AC 237; *Council of Civil Service Unions* v. *Minister for the Civil Service* [1985] AC 374 at 408.

[113] *R* v. *Jockey Club, ex parte RAM Racecourses Ltd* [1993] 2 All ER 225 at 236.

[114] For a review of legitimate expectation see R. Thomas, *Legitimate Expectations and Proportionality in Administrative Law*, 1st edn (Oxford University Press, 2000).

example of how this situation might arise is the case of the *School Fee Planning Charities*.[115] The Commission had threatened to remove these charities from the register. However, in exchange for an undertaking to restructure their operations so that the non-charitable annuity investments were hived off to a non-charitable investment company, the Commission agreed not to remove these charities from the register.

What would the position be if the Commission had changed its mind and removed these charities from the register, regardless of the undertaking they had given? The answer to this question is particularly relevant at the moment because the Strategy Unit Report[116] which paved the way for the enactment of the Charities Act 2006 concluded that, in most cases, where public benefit was regarded by the Commission as insufficient, the Commission would work with charities to increase it. The Commission has subsequently confirmed that this will be its approach.[117] It is not difficult, therefore, to imagine a scenario where a charity has agreed to increase the level of public benefit but the Commission then removes the charity from the register.

It is unlikely that an institution could be able to successfully appeal on the ground of legitimate expectation where an undertaking had been breached in the circumstances described above. There has been a reluctance on the part of the judiciary to accept a right of legitimate expectation, other than in terms of a right for those affected to be heard when an undertaking is breached, in other words as a procedural right rather than a substantive one.[118] There is also a reluctance on the part of the judiciary to accept a legitimate expectation as a substantive right, because they think it would be an unacceptable fetter on the power of a public authority to change its policy when it considers it to be necessary.[119]

Regardless of the difficulty of raising the legitimate expectation argument in English law, the reason, above all else, why it would not succeed is that it must be a 'legitimate' expectation. In other words, the undertaking must be lawful. It is institutions that are not charitable which are relevant in this context. In such circumstances the Commission's duty[120] is to remove the institution from the register rather than to enter into undertakings to allow the institution to stay on the register if its trustees take steps to make the institution become charitable.

A good comparative example of this principle is the case of *Al Fayed* v. *Advocate General for Scotland*.[121] In this case, for administrative convenience, the Inland Revenue agreed with the taxpayer that he would pay a set amount of tax rather than be taxed according to an assessment. Subsequently, the Inland

[115] See [1996] Ch.Com.A.R. paras 187–191.

[116] Cabinet Office, *Strategy Unit Report, Private Action, Public Benefit A Review of Charities and the Wider Not-for-Profit Sector* para. 4.30.

[117] See cc *Public Benefit Checks-How Will We Carry Them Out?* September 2004.

[118] *R* v. *Secretary of State for Transport , ex p Richmond upon Thames London Borough Council* [1994] 1 All ER 577.

[119] *Ibid.* [120] S. 3(4) Charities Act 1993.

[121] *Al Fayed* v. *Advocate General for Scotland* 2004 SLT 798.

Revenue received advice that this agreement was *ultra vires* and terminated it. The taxpayer appealed unsuccessfully to the court on various grounds, including legitimate expectation. In particular, the legitimate expectation argument failed because the agreement was not lawful. In determining the appeal The Lord President (Cullen), Lords Kirkwood and Maclean jointly ruled[122] that:

> under our domestic law a legitimate expectation can only arise on the basis of a lawful promise, representation or practice. There can be no legitimate expectation that a public body will continue to implement an agreement when it has no power to do so … While the petitioners may well have had an expectation, it was not, in the particular circumstances of the case and according to our common law, a legitimate expectation.

Similarly an institution which was not charitable would not be able to hold the Commission to an agreement not to remove it from the register if its trustees took certain steps to make it charitable. The proper course of action would be for the Commission to remove[123] the institution from the register and then invite the trustees to take steps to make it charitable and then reapply for registration.[124]

Estoppel

Alternatively, it might be argued that the Commission should be estopped from breaching its undertaking not to remove an institution from the register if certain steps are taken to make it charitable. It is unclear whether there is any distinction between estoppel and legitimate expectation.[125] It is also unclear whether legitimate expectation and estoppel are grounds for judicial review or common-law actions.[126] Although there are some decisions which suggest that the court will estop a public authority from reversing a decision, where it is incorrect and has been relied on to the detriment of a member of the public,[127] these decisions are regarded as doubtful.[128] In *Howell* v. *Falmouth Boat Construction Co. Ltd*[129] the House of Lords rejected an estoppel argument based on the wrongful assumption of authority by a public body, on the basis that it conflicted with the rule that estoppel cannot give a public authority power that it does not possess. Even if charities could challenge the Commission either by way of judicial review, or through a common-law action, it would not be open to a charity to argue that the Commission should be estopped from removing it from the register. Registration does not guarantee that the conclusive presumption[130] will

[122] *Ibid.* at 820–821. [123] S. 3(4) Charities Act 1993. [124] S. 3A(1) Charities Act 1993.
[125] See pp. 174–5 of this chapter. [126] *Ibid.*
[127] *Robertson* v. *Minister of Pensions* [1949] 1 KB 227; *Lever Finance Ltd* v. *Westminster London Borough Council* [1971] 1 QB 222.
[128] H. W. R. Wade and C. F. Forsyth, *Administrative Law*, 8th edn (Oxford University Press, 2000) pp. 339–344.
[129] *Howell* v. *Falmouth Boat Construction Co. Ltd.* [1951] AC 837; *Western Fish Products* v. *Penwith District Council* [1981] 2 All ER 204.
[130] S. 4(1) Charities Act 1993.

continue, as the Commission has a power to rectify the register[131] and remove an institution under section 3(4) Charities Act 1993.[132]

Negligent mis-statement

Finally, it might be argued that the Commission should be held accountable where it negligently allows a charity to rely on assurances that if it takes certain steps, it will not be removed. This would involve a common-law action of negligent mis-statement and would entail the court reviewing all the evidence including the Commission's conduct. The court answered this question in *Mills* v. *Winchester Diocesan Board of Finance*.[133] Although the case was involved with written advice given under what is now section 29 Charities Act 1993 (and was not concerned with the removal of a charity from the register), the decision of the court is wide enough to cover advice which is not written under that section. The reasons why the court dismissed the notion that there could be a right of action against the Commission apply equally to a situation where the Commission enters into an agreement not to remove a charity from the register, subject to the trustees taking certain steps to make the institution charitable, and then in breach of that agreement removes the institution from the register.

The first reason (by analogy in this context) is that, as a matter of law, there is a right of appeal[134] against removal from the register which should be exhausted, rather than seeking to sue the Commission for negligently mis-stating that the institution could remain on the register whilst being converted into a charity.

The second reason is also relevant (by way of analogy) to the question of removal from the register. A concurrent exercise of rights in negligence at common law, and a right of appeal could only multiply legal costs to the detriment of the institution (and ultimately charity if the institution successfully converted itself into a charity).[135]

Even if a charity could bring an action for negligent mis-statement in respect of a statement by the Commission that if it took certain steps it would not be removed from the register, as in the case of legitimate expectation[136] and estoppel,[137] a charity would be unlikely to succeed because the Commission's duty is to remove institutions from the register where they qualify for removal under section 3(4) Charities Act 1993.

Having discussed grounds for appeal in respect of direct removal under public law by way of judicial review, or alternatively actions under the common law on the basis that charities should enjoy such rights, a similar analysis is required in respect of indirect removal.

[131] *Ibid.* [132] S. 3(4) Charities Act 1993.

[133] *Mills* v. *Winchester Diocesan Board of Finance* [1989] Ch 428.

[134] Schedule 1C(1) Charities Act 1993. See *Mills* v. *Winchester Diocesan Board of Finance* [1989] Ch 428 *per* Knox J at 452.

[135] *Mills* v. *Winchester Diocesan Board of Finance* [1989] Ch 428 *per* Knox J at 452.

[136] Pp. 180–2 of this chapter. [137] Pp. 182–3 of this chapter.

Indirect removal, judicial review and common-law action

In the context of indirect removal, the Charity Tribunal can only apply the principles of judicial review in respect of an appeal against a decision by the Commission to institute an inquiry.[138] It will be difficult to challenge such a decision on appeal.[139] There are also problems where appellants wish to appeal the Commission's decisions under sections 18 and 19 Charities Act 1993.[140]

Unless the current bar on judicial review proceedings and common-law actions[141] is successfully challenged, these actions will not be available to charities, in the context of removal, other than in the case of the review of a decision by the Commission to institute an inquiry where judicial review is available.[142] Again it is arguable[143] that judicial review and common-law actions should be generally available to charities and for this reason possible grounds are explored. Their unavailability also demonstrates how charities are currently at a disadvantage. In the context of indirect removal the grounds and actions which require consideration are *ultra vires*, Wednesbury unreasonableness and bias,[144] the right to be heard and Article 6,[145] natural justice,[146] estoppel and negligent mis-statement.[147]

Ultra vires, Wednesbury unreasonableness and bias

A good hypothetical example of how the lawfulness of the Commission's conduct could be challenged by judicial review would be if the Commission *fed* an interim manager or additional trustees (who then formed a majority) with their hidden agenda to dissolve a charity, and applied to have it removed from the register once the assets had been transferred to another charity. The Commission is precluded by statute from exercising the functions of a charity trustee,[148] or otherwise from directly being involved in the administration of a charity,[149] so any use of an appointee to indirectly control and administer a charity would be unlawful because it was *ultra vires* and/or because it was *Wednesbury*[150] unreasonable and/or because there was bias. To avoid exercising a discretion *Wednesbury* unreasonably the public authority must consider those matters that it is bound to consider, disregard any absurd considerations

[138] Schedule 1C3(2)(a) & (b) Charities Act 1993. [139] See pp. 175–7 of this chapter.

[140] *Weth* v. *AG* [1999] 1 WLR 686.

[141] *Mills* v. *Winchester Diocesan Board of Finance* [1989] Ch 428; *Weth* v. *AG* [1999] 1 WLR 686 and *Rule* v. *Charity Commissioners* (High Court, 10 December 1979); [1979] Ch.Com.A.R. 12–16.

[142] Schedule 1C3(2)(a) & (b) Charities Act 1993. [143] Pp. 175–7 of this chapter.

[144] Pp. 184–5 of this chapter. [145] Pp. 185–6 of this chapter.

[146] Pp. 186–7 of this chapter. [147] P. 187 of this chapter.

[148] S. 1E(2)(a) Charities Act 1993. [149] S. 1E(2)(b) Charities Act 1993.

[150] *Associated Provincial Picture Houses Ltd* v. *Wednesbury Corporation* [1948] 1 KB 223.

and act in good faith.[151] Acting in good faith would include the avoidance of any bias.[152] The rule against bias is that justice should not only be done but also be seen to be done.[153] Amongst the causes of bias is a commercial relationship.[154] It is arguable that the appointment and reappointment of paid interim managers could give rise to judicial review, on the ground that the interim managers are biased and merely follow the Commission's instructions because they wish to be considered for further paid interim managerships.

The issue surfaced in *Weth* v. *AG*.[155] Although there was no evidence that the receiver and manager had merely carried out the Commission's instructions, Neuberger J outlined what would be acceptable and unacceptable conduct by the Commission and the appointee, and how appointments of professional advisers ran the risk of allegations of unfairness:

> it does appear to me that there would be much to be said for the Commissioners not running the risk of appearing to encourage a prospective or actual Receiver and Manager to take one course or another, on the basis of a particular view of the relevant issues or facts. There is a real danger, as I see it, that an accountant appointed by the Commissioners would hope to please his clients, possibly with a view to obtaining further appointments, by providing recommendations which the Commissioners have indicated in advance they would like to receive.

The same issue could arise where additional trustees are appointed from rival charities to act for charities which the Commission regards as failing.[156] If there was evidence of the Commission colluding with an interim manager or additional trustees, then it is arguable that an application for judicial review should be made on the grounds of *ultra vires*, *Wednesbury* unreasonableness or bias.

The right to be heard and the Human Rights Act 1998: Article 6: Right to a fair trial

It is fundamental to a fair process that both parties are given a hearing.[157] Although the Commission generally gives charities the opportunity to make representations, it states that in some serious cases it may be necessary to take action before raising concerns with the trustees.[158] It is arguable that this might amount to a denial of the right to be heard.

[151] For a more up-to-date test see Lord Diplock's explanation in *Council of Civil Service Unions* v. *Minister for the Civil Service* [1985] AC 375 at 310 '… a decision which is so outrageous in its defiance of logic or accepted moral standards that no sensible person who had applied his mind to the question to be decided could have arrived at it'.

[152] See *R* v. *Sussex Justices ex p McCarthy* [1924] 1 KB 256 at 259.

[153] *Per* Atkin LJ in *Shrager* v. *Basil Dighton Ltd* [1924] 1 KB 274 at 284.

[154] *R* v. *Rand* (1866) LR 1 QB 230 at 232–3.

[155] *Weth* v. *AG* Unreported Transcript 29 April 1999.

[156] See Chapter 6, pp. 116–17. [157] See pp. 186–7 of this chapter.

[158] *CC 47 – Complaints about Charities* (version May 2003).

For indirect removal, the relevant Article of the European Convention on Human Rights to consider in the context of the right to a fair hearing will be Article 6: Right to a Fair Trial. Article 6 reads as follows:

> In the determination of his civil rights and obligations or of any criminal charge against him, everyone is entitled to a fair and public hearing within a reasonable time by an independent and impartial tribunal established by law

Can the Commission be said to be 'an independent and impartial tribunal established by law'? A distinction needs to be made on the one hand between the Commission opening an inquiry under section 8 Charities Act 1993 and investigating charities which are administrative acts, and on the other hand where it consequentially makes orders under sections 18 and 19 Charities Act 1993 which are judicial functions. In the former case the Commission could not be challenged under Article 6 even though it could not be described as *'impartial'* because it both investigates and decides the outcome.[159] As charities can appeal[160] to the Charity Tribunal which is 'an independent and impartial tribunal established by law' there will be no breach of Article 6.[161] In the later case, where the Commission is acting in a judicial capacity then arguably it will be in breach of Article 6 because it will not be 'an independent and impartial tribunal established by law' because it will be acting as both judge and jury[162] although the right of appeal to the Charity Tribunal might make reparation for the breach of Article 6.[163]

Natural justice

Another ground for judicial review is a breach of natural justice. Natural justice comprises: that a person or institution may not be judge in his or its own cause and a person's defence must be fairly heard.[164] Currently natural justice does not offer any relief to appellants feeling aggrieved by the Commission acting as both judge and jury.[165] Where, the Commission is obliged by statute to act as an investigator and in a judicial capacity in making orders under sections 18 and 19 Charities Act 1993, the court will see necessity as overriding any natural justice argument. Without giving support to the statutory provisions, the Commission would have no means of making decisions and the machinery of justice or

[159] See *Runa Begum* v. *Tower Hamlets London Borough Council* [2003] 2 AC 430 at 461–462.
[160] Schedule 1C3(2)(a) & (b) Charities Act 1993. See *Human Rights Act 1998 Article 6 – Right to a Fair Trial* OG 71 C1 (18 September 2000).
[161] *Runa Begum* v. *Tower Hamlets London Borough Council* [2003] 2 AC 430; *Albert and Le Compte* v. *Belgium* (1983) 5 EHRR 533, Ect HR, para. 29.
[162] *De Cubber* v. *Belgium* (1984) 7 EHRR 236, Ect HR, para. 32.
[163] *Ibid.* at para. 33.
[164] *Spackman* v. *Plumstead District Board of Works* [1885] 10 AC 229.
[165] As discussed in pp. 186–7 of this chapter.

administration would break down.[166] Even so it might be argued that the Commission still has a duty to do its best to act fairly and in particular must give those subject to an inquiry or orders an opportunity to comment on statements which are prejudicial to them.[167] In some serious cases the Commission states that it may be necessary to take action before raising concerns with the trustees.[168] In such circumstances, it is arguable that an action for a breach of natural justice should be available.

Estoppel and negligent mis-statement

As in the case of direct removal, the Commission could make statements that it will not open an inquiry or exercise its powers under sections 18 or 19 Charities Act if the charity takes certain steps. If the Commission renege an action for estoppel[169] or negligent misstatement[170] by the charity, it would be unlikely to succeed because the Commission has no power to enter into such arrangements. Its general function is to identify and investigate apparent misconduct or mismanagement in the administration of charities, and to take remedial or protective action.[171] Even though the Commission has a general duty[172] to act proportionately, it does not have the power to enter into such agreements.[173]

Conclusion

Grounds for judicial review ought to be relevant where there is very clear evidence that the Commission are colluding in bad faith (this will be rare)[174] with an interim manager or additional trustees or where the Commission does not give charities the opportunity to make representations.[175] If the Commission makes statements about charities remaining on the register which give rise to common law actions of estoppel or negligent misstatement then, even if such actions were permitted,[176] the Court would be unlikely to uphold them because the Commission has a duty to remove charities under section 3(4) which qualify for removal. It has no power to bargain with charities if they take certain steps.[177]

[166] *Great Charte* v. *Kennington* (1730) 2 Str. 1173. In that case there were no justices who were not ratepayers and allowing them to decide would prevent a failure of justice. See also *London and Clydeside Estates Ltd* v. *Secretary of State for Scotland* 1987 SLT 459 at 463.

[167] *Rule* v. *Charity Commissioners* (High Court, 10 December 1979); [1979] Ch.Com.A.R. 12–16.

[168] *CC 47 – Complaints about Charities* (version May 2003). [169] Pp. 182–3 of this chapter.

[170] See p. 183 of this chapter. [171] S. 1C(2)3 Charities Act 1993.

[172] S. 1D(2)4 Charities Act 1993. Note that the Commission's general duty under this section is an expression of its public law duties under the general law. See Lords Hansard, cols 809–810, 7 June 2005, *per* Lord Swinfen.

[173] See pp. 16–19 of this chapter for a discussion of *Al Fayed* v. *Advocate General for Scotland* 2004 SLT 798.

[174] Pp. 23–24 of this chapter. [175] Pp. 171–4 of this chapter.

[176] *Mills* v. *Winchester Diocesan Board of Finance* [1989] Ch 428.

[177] See pp. 180–2 of this chapter.

Costs

Costs will be a major issue when a charity appeals to the Court from the Charity Tribunal[178] in respect of direct or indirect removal, applies for judicial review, or initiates common law proceedings. Expense will not be the only concern. It may be difficult to access to charity funds to pay the costs, or there may be a risk of personal liability where litigation is not within the charity's powers.

A prudent trustee would seek the protection of a Commission order under section 26 Charities Act 1993, confirming that proceedings were 'expedient in the interests of the charity' or advice under section 29 Charities Act 1993 that the trustees are acting within their powers by taking legal proceedings. Failure to act within the charity's powers when litigating unsuccessfully and, as a result, causing financial loss to the charity, could result in personal liability.[179] For example, in *Weth* v. *AG*[180] Mr Weth appeared in person to save costs when he appealed against the appointment of a receiver and manager.[181] This appeal failed and he was ordered to pay three-quarters of the Commission's taxed costs.[182] Where additional trustees who then form a majority of the trustees or an interim manager have been appointed, the original trustees will be unable to access charity funds.

Alternatively, if the Commission refused to make an order authorising proceedings under section 26 Charities Act 1993 or to give advice under section 29 then the trustees could apply to the Court for a *Beddoe*[183] order authorising legal proceedings. Any proceedings which are 'charity proceedings'[184] requires the consent of the Commission or failing that the Court. An application for a *Beddoe* order is 'charity proceedings'[185] so the trustees would need the consent of the Commission or the Court to apply for the order. Furthermore, the cost of appealing can be prohibitive.[186] For these reasons although, in theory, an appeal process is open to appellants, in practice it is rarely used.

Trustees will face considerable difficulties in terms of costs and procedure before they can make an application for judicial review. The cost of litigation tends to be prohibitively high for an individual without legal aid and the chance

178 S. 2C(1) Charities Act 1993. 179 *Bahin* v. *Hughes* (1886) 31 Ch D 390.

180 *Weth* v. *AG* [1999] 1 WLR 686 (CA). 181 *Ibid.* 182 *Ibid.* at 694.

183 See *Re Beddoe* [1893] 1 Ch 547. Note that a refusal to allow the trustees to bring legal proceedings, or to have access to charity funds to pay for the costs of bringing legal proceedings, might amount to a breach of Article 6(1) ECHR. See *Pine* v. *Law Society* [2002] UK HRR 81, para. 11.

184 Ss. 33(2) & 33(5) Charities Act 1993. 185 Warburton, J. *Tudor on Charities* p. 389.

186 The cost of the appeal by Mr Weth was estimated to be £500,000 and he was not legally represented. For a general review of these problems see *Power Without Accountability The Charity Commission as Regulator* (Association For Charities Report-June 2004) pp. 75–76, www.association4charities.org.uk.

of a charity applying for judicial review is remote. A search[187] of reported applications to the court for judicial review of the Commission's decisions revealed only one attempt which ended in failure. An application for judicial review of the Commission's decision to make an order under sections 18 and 19 Charities Act 1993 will not be 'charity proceedings'[188] because it will not be concerned with 'the administration of a trust for charitable purposes'.[189] This is not beyond doubt and resolving the issue will present another hurdle for trustees when contemplating judicial review.[190]

It would help if charities were automatically granted a 'protective costs order'[191] when they challenged the Commission in judicial review proceedings. This would mean that charities could take legal proceedings without having to pay costs if they lost so long as the proceedings were in the public interest. This would give greater access to justice.

The problem of costs is likely to remain an issue in the context of the Charity Tribunal. The scepticism of the Joint Committee on the Draft Charities Bill about an assertion by the Commission that the Charity Tribunal will be a low-cost forum should be noted.[192] When the Joint Committee on the Draft Charities Bill published its report, formal minutes and evidence,[193] the issue of costs featured quite prominently. The Joint Committee recommended that the Charity Tribunal should have the power to award compensation and/or costs against the Commission;[194] that the Commission should formally state that it will not seek to recover costs against an unsuccessful appellant except where the Charity Tribunal decides that the appeal amounted to an abuse of process;[195] that consideration be given to including in the Charities Bill a residuary power for Ministers to make regulations enabling financial assistance to be given to parties to the Charity Tribunal, if it becomes apparent in the light of experience, that access to the Charity Tribunal is being limited by costs,[196] and that the rules to be made by the Lord Chancellor on appeals to the Charity Tribunal should

[187] A search of the Charity Commission's Annual Reports on Westlaw only revealed one application for judicial review which also ended in failure. See *The Queen* v. *Charity Commissioners for England and Wales ex p Lynda Lucille Baldwin* [2001] WTLR 137. A search of Commission annual reports only revealed one application for judicial review which also ended in failure. See *Rule* v. *Charity Commissioners* (High Ct, 10 December 1979); [1979] Ch.Com.A.R. 12–16.

[188] S. 33 Charities Act 1993.

[189] S. 33(8) Charities Act 1993. See *The Queen on the Application of the London Borough of Brent* v. *Fed 2000 (a Board of Trustees of the formerly independent school, The Avenue School) The Temporary Governing Body of The Avenue School Case No: CO/4376/2005* 2005 WL 3027228 (QBD Admin Ct).

[190] See *R v. National Trust for Places of Historic Interest or Natural Beauty ex p Scott & Others* [1998] 2 All ER 705.

[191] *R (on the application of Corner House Research)* v. *Secretary of State for Trade and Industry* (2005) EWCA Civ 192.

[192] *Joint Committee on the Draft Charities Bill* (HC 660 ix), 7 July 2004 Qs 707–708.

[193] HL Paper 167–1, HC 660–1. [194] *Ibid.* para. 232.

[195] *Ibid.* para. 239. [196] *Ibid.* para. 240.

include provision for either the Attorney General or the Commission to refer matters to the Charity Tribunal for interpretation, without the individual charities having to bear the costs of pursuing a particular case.[197]

The Commission equivocal response was:[198]

> The Charity Commissioners will not routinely ask for costs but the position would be very much governed by the facts of the individual case and the circumstances of the individual.

In the event the government did not consider that the Charities Act 2006 should contain a residuary power for Ministers to make regulations to enable financial assistance to be given to parties if it became apparent that access to the Charity Tribunal was being restricted due to costs. The government concluded that the Charity Tribunal, like other Tribunals, would be inquisitorial and, therefore, there would be no need for the parties to present an argument. The Government thought that most parties could represent themselves. Furthermore, it pointed out that, in exceptional cases where it was in the interests of justice that a party needs to be legally represented, public funds could be made available under the Access to Justice Act 1999. In other cases, where the issue is complex but the party cannot afford legal representation, the Attorney General could, at his discretion, decide to become a party to proceedings.[199]

The government's response ignores the fact that although most tribunals are supposed to be accessible to lay people, often the parties are legally represented. It also fails to recognise that the Commission will always be legally represented. Correcting this inequality will usually involve legal costs. As the government's view is that the Charity Tribunal will be a low-cost forum, it will be difficult to persuade the Commission to authorise the expenditure of charity funds on legal costs under sections 26 or 29 Charities Act 1993 where an appeal is made to the Charity Tribunal. The government subsequently gave a commitment to review the effectiveness of the Charity Tribunal and attempt to address any major problems of access to justice.[200]

The Charities Act 2006 does make provision for the Charity Tribunal to make an order for one party to pay another party the whole or part of the costs of proceedings if one party has acted vexatiously, frivolously or unreasonably.[201] This ground for the award of costs might, in exceptional cases, offer redress to parties who are aggrieved by the Commission's conduct. Of greater assistance is the power of the Charity Tribunal to award costs where it considers that

[197] *Ibid.* para. 241.

[198] *The Government's Reply to the Joint Committee on the Draft Charities Bill* Session 2003–2004 HL Paper 167/HC 660 para. 25.

[199] *Ibid.* para. 26.

[200] Charities Bill [Lords] Standing Committee A; col. 141 *per* Edward Miliband.

[201] S. 2B(6) Charities Act 1993.

a decision, direction or order of the Commission which is the subject of the proceedings was unreasonable,[202] although the relevance of this power is likely to be restricted to '*reviewable matters,*'[203] which will be of limited assistance to charities being removed from the register, as the only available reviewable matter in this context is a decision by the Commission to institute an inquiry.[204]

Alternatives to an appeal to the court

Given the problems with appeals to the Charity Tribunal and the court the effectiveness of the alternatives are all the more important. These range from the Commission's internal review and complaints procedure to the Parliamentary Commissioner for Administration, otherwise known as the Ombudsman. The internal review procedure deals with the correctness of a decision.[205] It is an internal version of the statutory appeal processes for direct and indirect removal.[206] The complaints procedure, the Independent Complaints Reviewer and the Ombudsman deal with the Commission's conduct when making decisions. They are non-judicial versions of judicial review proceedings.

Although there is no objective data to indicate how successful these alternative processes are, it is perhaps significant that the Strategy Unit recommended[207] that there should be an independent Charity Tribunal and provision has been made for this by the Charities Act 2006.[208]

The Commission's internal review procedure

The internal review procedure allows the Commission's decisions to be reviewed by another officer at the Commission.[209] This process will be of little use to a person requesting a review where the original decision involved carrying out the Commission's policy, as in the case of charities removed from the register on the basis that they do not operate, because of governance issues.[210]

[202] S. 2B(7) Charities Act 1993. Note that rule 25(3) of the Draft Charity Tribunal Rules 2007 to be made under section 2B Charities Act 1993 provides for the award of costs where the Commission's decision is irrational.

[203] Schedule 1C3(1)(a) & (b) Charities Act 1993.

[204] *Ibid.*

[205] *Requests For A Decision To Review* OG 94 A1 (16 July 2003). See *Consultation Paper: Decision Review-Reconsidering the Commission's Decisions* (2007).

[206] See pp. 174–7 of this chapter.

[207] Cabinet Office, Strategy Unit Report, *Private Action, Public Benefit A Review of Charities and the Wider Not-for-Profit Sector* (2002) paras 7.76–7.80.

[208] S. 8 Charities Act 2006.

[209] *Requests For A Decision To Review* OG 94 A1 (16 July 2003).

[210] See Chapter 6, pp. 121–3 for an examination of charities removed under section 3(4) Charities Act 1993 on the basis that they do not operate.

The Commission's complaints procedure

Quite separately, the Commission has also introduced a complaints procedure, which can lead to a referral to the Independent Complaints Reviewer.[211] There is no indication how the system is working but the fact that only 11.5 per cent of complaints which were reviewed were fully or partly upheld,[212] suggests that the chance of making a successful complaint is remote. Although called 'independent' the office of the Independent Complaints Reviewer is partly funded by the Charity Commission.[213]

The Ombudsman

In addition to the complaints procedure charities can also complain to the Ombudsman.[214] The essence of the Ombudsman's method is to investigate a complaint and then make recommendations which will usually be accepted by a government department. The Ombudsman has no formal legal sanctions under the Parliamentary Commissioner Act 1967. He has complete discretion as to whether to investigate a complaint[215] and there are no legal means to compel him to act if he decides not to.[216]

Despite these drawbacks, the indications are that the Ombudsman has remedied many injustices which would otherwise have gone unchecked. A search on the Ombudsman's website[217] revealed two Commission cases. One involved a loss of remuneration due to the Commission's delay in providing authorisation. The complaint was upheld and the Commission was asked to consider ways to authorise the remuneration. The second case involved a complaint about the Commission's refusal to release information about a charity. This complaint was only partially upheld. The Ombudsman found that the Commission could have handled the request better, but at the same time, the complainant was partly to blame as she had failed to tell the Commission that she had authority from the founder and former trustee of the charity.

These complaints appear to have been fairly handled and, as Wade[218] comments, the Ombudsman has investigated cases where the complainant has been misled and suffered loss, and has persuaded the government department to make monetary compensation. It might well be the case that the trustees of a

[211] *The Role of The Independent Complaints Reviewer* (ICR) OG 93 B3 (2003). See *Consultation Paper: Review of the Commission's Complaint and Customer Feedback Procedures* (2007).

[212] *Independent Complaints Reviewer to the Charity Commissioner for England and Wales Annual Report 2005/06: Seeking a Fair Resolution.*

[213] See the Independent Complaints Reviewer's website: www.icrev.demon.co.uk 'Frequently Asked Questions'.

[214] Governed by the Parliamentary Commissioner Act 1967.

[215] S. 5(5) the Parliamentary Commissioner Act 1967.

[216] *Re Fletchers' Application* [1970] 2 All ER 527.

[217] www.ombudsman.org.uk.

[218] H. W. R. Wade and C. F. Forsyth, *Administrative Law*, 8th edn (Oxford University Press, 2000) pp. 98–99.

charity which was mistakenly registered and then removed might decide to complain to the Ombudsman when it suffers a monetary loss as a result of being led to believe it was a charity. Whereas the Independent Complaints Reviewer can only recommend that the Commission awards modest compensation[219] the Ombudsman can recommend any level of financial redress caused by maladministration.[220]

Conclusion

Due to problems with the appeals system charities do not have effective access to justice. The overall thesis is that the Commission's powers of removal are limited. On the other hand charities have problems accessing justice when appealing therefore although the Commission's powers of removal are limited the Commission is in a position of strength.

[219] www.icrev.demon.co.uk. [220] See Lords Hansard, 12 October 2005; col 381.

9

Conclusion

Introduction

In Chapter 1 it was explained that there are five basic propositions: the Commission's powers of removal are limited; there is a distinction between the governing instrument of a charity and its property; there is a problem of legality for the Commission when exercising its powers of removal; there is a need to clarify the Commission's powers of removal; and there is a need for charities to have greater access to justice in the context of removal.[1] The conclusion to this book suggest ways in which the law could be reformed to solve the problems raised by the basic propositions.

Law reform

Each of the basic propositions has raised problems associated with the removal of charities from the register which will now be discussed in terms of proposals for law reform.

The Commission's powers of removal are limited

It was shown in Chapter 3[2] that the Commission's powers of removal are limited. It could be argued that the Commission should have no powers of removal.[3] According to this argument, the Commission should retain charities on the register so that it can use its protective powers to cure any breaches of trust.

It could also be argued that the Commission's powers of removal should be widened by tightening the qualification for registration to include additional requirements such as good governance, efficiency and viability.[4] According to this argument, the Commission should remove more charities.

[1] Chapter 1, pp. 1–4. [2] Chapter 3, pp. 45–52.
[3] P. 195 of this chapter. [4] Pp. 196–7 of this chapter.

Alternatively, it could be argued that in addition to the Commission's powers of removal it should have powers to protect the property of a removed institution.[5] Currently, where the Commission removes an institution from the register which it 'no longer considers is a charity'[6] it is difficult for it to exercise its powers of protection under sections 18 and 19 Charities Act 1993 because these powers are only exercisable in respect of 'charities'.

Finally, it could be argued that the Commission's powers of removal should be further restricted by giving the Commission a statutory power to determine that an institution is a charity, where it is holding charitable property irrespective of whether its governing instrument is in a charitable form.[7]

No powers of removal

The approach of not removing charities from the register has been adopted in the Indian states of Maharashtra and Gujarat, which have a Charity Commissioner established by the Bombay Public Trust Act 1950.[8] Under that Act, the Charity Commissioner does not have the power to remove charities from the register but he does have powers of inquiry where there are fiscal or management irregularities. The general approach is therefore to correct wrongs rather than to remove. Although, a trust may be extinguished or terminated if 'its purpose becomes unlawful'.[9]

It could be argued that there is some merit in this approach because it is clear that the Charity Commissioner must take responsibility for the institutions which he registers. Furthermore, the public can be assured that institutions on the register will remain accountable.

One of the side effects of registration as a charity in England and Wales is that registration is seen by the general public as a stamp of approval.[10] Therefore, it is submitted that, if the non-removal approach is adopted there ought to be a system of kite-marking those charities which maintain certain basic standards, such as low administration and fund-raising costs, so that public confidence is maintained and charities are encouraged to improve their performance.

The drawback with the non-removal approach is that there will be occasions when removal is appropriate where, for example, an institution is a front for serious criminal activities such as paedophile rings and terrorist organisations. In such cases it will be desirable to deprive such institutions of charitable status to prevent them being able to pass themselves off as charities, and prevent them furthering their unlawful purposes.

[5] P. 197 of this chapter. [6] S. 3(4) Charities Act 1993. [7] Pp. 196–7 of this chapter.

[8] www.gujlegal.gov.in/english/charity/gujarati/act7.htm. See also Daruvala N. B. 'Charitable Trusts in India' *Offshore Investment* May 1995.

[9] S. 77 Indian Trusts Act 1882.

[10] See Barker, C. R, 'Public Charitable Collections: Are they a Worthwhile Cause?' 63(6) *MLR* 791–812 2000.

Greater powers of removal

It could be argued that the Commission should have greater powers of removal by tightening the qualification for registration[11] so fewer institutions are registered and more are removed. The qualification for registration could be tightened by imposing additional requirements such as good governance, efficiency and viability. In this context, 'viability' means not having objects which are duplicated by other charities in circumstances where there was no efficacy in having other charities carrying out the work of already established and efficient charities.

In respect of the argument that charities should display good governance to qualify for registration it could be argued that the distinction between a breach of trust and grounds for removal should become one and the same if trustees do not take steps to remedy the breach of trust. A similar approach has been taken in New Zealand which has recently passed the Charities Act 2005.[12] This Act established a Charity Commission and provides for the removal of charities which significantly and persistently fail to comply with the obligations under the Charities Act 2005 or any other enactment.[13] An approach along these lines in England and Wales would enable the Commission to refuse to register charities which did not meet a more general statutory criteria for charitable status and, consistent with that, enable the Commission to remove charities which no longer met that criteria. This would require a statutory definition of charitable status along these lines in England and Wales. The English Charities Act 2006 provides for a statutory list of charitable purposes[14] but it could be argued that what is needed in addition is a more general statutory criteria of good governance setting out what is required to qualify as a charity under those heads of charity.

The Commission has set out its own thoughts on the basic requirements for a charity in *The Hallmarks of an Effective Charity*.[15] It is not a legal requirement to follow these principles[16] but through the publication of Standard Information Returns[17] and inquiry reports,[18] which taken together judge charities against these principles, there is pressure on trustees to conform. The Commission's approach has been criticised as overstepping the mark between regulation and interference in the governance of charities.[19] The counter argument is that the Commission should be given the power to take a strategic role in determining which charities should be on the register according to whether they can effectively respond to social and economic need.[20]

[11] Under section 3A(1) & (2) Charities Act 1993. See Chapter 2, pp. 12–14 for the essential indicia of charitable status.

[12] This Act came into force on 1 July 2005. [13] S. 32 The Charities Act 2005.

[14] S. 2(2) Charities Act 2006. [15] See CC 60 – *The Hallmarks of an Effective Charity* (2006).

[16] *Ibid.* [17] See www.charity-commission.gov.uk. [18] *Ibid.*

[19] Aldridge, N. 'Super Charities charter', *Society Guardian*, 3 June 2004.

[20] See R. Meakin, *Charity in the NHS: Policy and Practice*, 1st edn (Bristol: Jordans, 1998) pp. 16–17.

It could be argued that the Commission should have a power to merge charities which do not attain the wider criteria for charitable status after a reasonable period of time on the register. In Chapter 6[21] it was shown that some inquiries were resulting in charities being merged where there was an efficient charity and an inefficient charity operating with similar objects. This can happen through the appointment of additional trustees or interim managers.[22] There is no evidence, for the moment, of an agenda[23] by the Commission to bring about mergers in the charity sector. Nevertheless, the Commission's new power to give directions on the application of charity property[24] could lead to the enforced take over of inefficient charities by efficient charities, leaving the inefficient decanted charity to be removed from the register. As the Commission will have more information about the efficiency of larger charities through the introduction of the Standard Information Return[25] this is a plausible scenario.

The argument that the Commission's powers of removal should be widened by tightening the definition of charitable status might, at first sight, be attractive from a regulatory perspective, but there is a need to bear in mind that the more difficult it is to qualify for charitable status the harder it will be for the Commission to force institutions to register as charities and become subject to its regulation. Furthermore, making it harder to qualify for charitable status might stifle charitable initiative. For these reasons, it is not proposed in this thesis that the qualification for registration should be tightened to allow charities to be more easily removed from the register.

Powers to protect the property of removed institutions

This approach has been taken in Scotland. The Charities and Trustee Investment (Scotland) Act 2005 makes provision for a body called the Office of the Scottish Charity Regulator,[26] which is similar to the Commission for England and Wales. The OSCR will continue to have powers of inquiry and supervision in respect of a removed institution's property and income regardless as to whether it is charitable.[27] This is a pragmatic approach which makes it easier to protect the donors' position, but it only protects the position of institutions which have been registered and then removed. It does not address the question of protecting the charitable property of institutions which do not qualify for charitable status even though they are charitable in substance. This is now explained.

[21] Chapter 6, pp. 116–18. [22] Ss. 18 and 19 Charities Act 1993.

[23] In fact the Commission has gone on record saying that it will not force charities to merge. See RS4 a-*Collaborative Working and Mergers: Summary* (March 2003).

[24] S. 19B Charities Act 1993. [25] See www.charity-commission.gov.uk.

[26] S. 1 The Charities and Trustee Investment (Scotland) Act 2005.

[27] S. 19 The Charities and Trustee Investment (Scotland) Act 2005.

The Commission's powers of removal should be further restricted by widening the qualification for registration as a charity

In order to avoid the problem of protecting the charitable property of an institution which does not have charitable status it is argued that the qualification for registration as a charity should be widened to include any institution exclusively holding charitable property. It is therefore submitted that the Commission should be given a statutory power to determine that an institution is a charity where it is exclusively holding charitable property, irrespective of whether the governing instrument is charitable in form. This would also address the problem of the distinction between the governing instrument of a charity and its institution.[28]

Having made that determination, it could be argued that the current ground for removal on the basis that the Commission no longer considers an institution to be a charity[29] would no longer be necessary, as the obligation would be on the Commission to use its powers of protection over the charitable property under sections 18 and 19 Charities Act 1993, and only remove charities which no longer operate or cease to exist once the property has been secured for charitable purposes. Currently sections 18 and 19 Charities Act 1993 can only be used in respect of a 'charity'[30] whether registered or not. This solution would remove the problem of the Commission removing institutions from the register on the basis that they no longer appear to be a 'charity' which effectively prevents the Commission from using its powers of protection under sections 18 and 19 Charities Act 1993.

Sometimes organisations will be deliberately structured in a non-charitable form to avoid registration.[31] The court has adopted a flexible approach to the determination of charitable status in such circumstances by looking at substance over form. For example, it has determined that where funds are raised for charitable purposes by a non-charitable person or institution such as a fundraiser, that the fundraiser is accountable for any unauthorised remuneration.[32] Furthermore, the court has construed an institution's objects to be charitable, even where it is affiliated to a non-charitable organisation.[33]

On occasion the Commission will argue that form should triumph over substance. In the *Mariam Appeal*[34] inquiry the Commission decided that the stated objects of an appeal were charitable, even though one of the underlying purposes was not charitable. In this case, one of the activities of the Appeal was to bring a named child to the UK to receive medical treatment,

[28] Note that it would also assist in the prevention of a human rights challenge. See Chapter 7, pp. 133–6.
[29] S. 3(4) Charities Act 1993.
[30] Ss. 18(1) & 19(1) Charities Act 1993. 'Charity' is defined in section 1 Charities Act 1993.
[31] See T. Levene, 'Charity Cheats Laid Bare-By You', *The Guardian*, 25 August 2007.
[32] *Jones v. AG* ,The Times, 10th November 1976.
[33] *AG v. Ross* [1986] 1 WLR 252; [1976] Ch. Com. Dec, p. 33.
[34] *The Mariam Appeal* 28 June 2004, www.charity-commission.gov.uk.

which is not a charitable purpose.[35] The Commission will therefore argue that form should triumph over substance if it wants to protect funds which are partly charitable.[36] If the Commission had a statutory power to determine that an institution was charitable if it exclusively holds charitable property it would make the protection of charitable property easier in the context of removal.[37]

Conclusion: More or less removal?

In conclusion, the argument supported in this book is that the Commission should be given the power to determine that institutions which are holding charitable property are charitable in law. It would follow that the ground for removal on the basis that an institution is no longer charitable should be abolished, and that any removals should only be on the basis that charities cease to operate or cease to exist. This would ensure easier and better protection of charitable property.

There is a distinction between a governing instrument of a charity and its property

As the powers of removal[38] make no distinction between a charity's governing instrument and its property, when the Commission removes a charity's governing instrument from the register it has to use its powers[39] to provide for the charitable property separately. Sometimes this will involve the Commission constructing arguments to justify safeguarding charitable property.[40] A solution to this problem was discussed in the previous paragraph of providing the Commission with the power to determine that institutions which are holding charitable property are charitable.

Alternatively, the protection of charitable property would be made easier if there was a statutory provision deeming all the property of the institution removed from the register to be charitable. In the case of a charitable incorporated organisation[41] its general property will be automatically vested in the Official Custodian to be held at the discretion of the Commission for such charitable purposes as it shall determine by scheme if removed from the register. A more general application of this provision for all charities would have the advantage of deeming property to be charitable (as opposed to the institution) and would avoid the need for the Commission to seek evidence of charitable intention to enable it to use its *cy-pres* power[42] in respect of property where the institution was never charitable in law.

[35] See *Re Compton* [1945] Ch 123.

[36] See Chapter 3, pp. 54–56 for a discussion of *Re Esteem Settlement* [2003] JRC 092 para. 60.

[37] For a discussion of the problem of legality see Chapter 3, pp. 45–52.

[38] S. 3(4) Charities Act 1993.

[39] Ss. 13, 16(1)(a) & 18(2)(ii) Charities Act 1993.

[40] Pp. 198–9 of this chapter.

[41] See para. 5(6) & (10) of the Draft Regulations dated 19 May 2005.

[42] See Chapter 5, pp. 104–5.

The problem of legality

One of the major problems for the Commission, which has been explored in this book, is its inability to make law in the field of charitable status.[43] Even after the Charities Act 2006, which lists twelve specific heads of charity,[44] it must always second-guess what the court might decide when deciding novel questions of charitable status. It is submitted that the Commission should be given the same power as the court to decide questions of charitable status. It is not such a radical proposal because, for example, the Commission already has concurrent power with the High Court when making schemes for the administration of charities.[45]

It would provide legal certainty if removal from the register actually meant that the institution was not a charity in law. Currently registration confers a conclusive presumption that an institution is a charity[46] but only the court or Parliament can confirm that this is in fact the case.[47] Similarly when an institution is removed from the register it merely loses its presumption of charitable status.

The need for clarification

It has been shown in this thesis that there is a lack of certainty about the essential indicia of charitable status for the purpose of registration which contributes to a lack of certainty about the Commission's powers of removal.[48] It is argued in this book[49] that the Commission should have concurrent powers with the court to decide questions of charitable status. The Commission can now refer questions of removal to the Charity Tribunal,[50] but the Charity Tribunal itself is bound by the common law,[51] as decided by the Court. The Charity Tribunal will, like the Commission, have to second-guess the Court due to the dearth of modern case law.[52] For this reason the Charity Tribunal does not provide an entirely satisfactory solution.

Where the Commission wishes to decide questions of charitable status strategically then arguably neither the Charity Tribunal nor the court can assist as the right of appeal appears to be in respect of an institution affected by a particular decision of the Commission.[53] It is therefore argued that the Commission should be given the power to issue legally binding guidance on strategic issues of charitable status.

Access to justice

There is a need for charities removed from the register to have access to justice in the context of direct and indirect removal. It was explained in Chapter 8[54] that

[43] See Chapter 1, pp. 1–4. [44] S. 2(2) Charities Act 2006. [45] S. 16(1)(a) Charities Act 1993.
[46] S. 4(1) Charities Act 1993. [47] Chapter 3, pp. 45–52. [48] See Chapter 2, pp. 12–14.
[49] See pp. 10–11 of this chapter. [50] Schedule 1D1(1)(a) & (b) Charities Act 1993.
[51] Chapter 8, pp. 171–4. [52] Chapter 3, pp. 45–52.
[53] See Schedule 1D1(1)(a) & (b) Charities Act 1993. [54] Chapter 8, pp. 188–91.

because of the high cost of appealing to the court or the Charity Tribunal, and problems for trustees in accessing funds, charities are effectively denied their right to appeal against direct[55] and indirect[56] removal. To provide for access to justice, charities need to be financially assisted when appealing against the Commission's decisions relating to removal.[57] The Joint Committee on the Draft Charities Bill recommended that a suitors' fund be established or that access to legal aid be provided.[58] The rejection by the government[59] of this proposal on the ground that the Charity Tribunal will be accessible by lay people without the need for lawyers is not borne out by the experience of other Tribunals.[60]

In the context of judicial review under the general law, there is the possibility of obtaining a protective costs order.[61] This type of order allows charities to take legal proceedings without having to pay legal costs, so long as it is in the public interest. It would greatly assist access to justice if charities were granted protective costs orders in relation to direct and indirect removal.

In addition to providing funding for appeals by charity trustees affected by a decision of the Commission, there is a need to allow charities greater access to judicial review. The current bar by the court[62] on judicial review needs to be lifted, along with the restricted access to judicial review in the Charity Tribunal.[63]

Finally, there is a need to allow the public, including donors, the opportunity to make representations to the Commission why a charity should not be removed. Currently there is a statutory right[64] for persons who are, or may be, affected by the registration of an institution as a charity to apply to the Commission for it to be removed, but there is no statutory right for such persons to object to an institution's removal. Removal from the register is such an important issue that it is surprising that the Commission is not under a general statutory obligation to give notice to the public and invite representations before removing a charity from the register. This will be the case for a charitable incorporated organisation which is removed from the register, where three months publication of notice will have to be given, along with an invitation to the public to make representations to show cause why it is not to be removed

[55] Under section 3(4) Charities Act 1993.

[56] As a consequence of the Commission using its protective powers under sections 18 & 19 Charities Act 1993.

[57] Chapter 8, pp. 188–91.

[58] *Report from The Joint Committee on the Draft Charities Bill Session 2003–04 HL Paper 167/HC 660*, para. 237.

[59] *The Government Reply to the Report from The Joint Committee on the Draft Charities Bill Session 2003–04 HL Paper 167/HC 660 Cm 6440*, para. 26.

[60] 'CBI Criticises Complexity of Tribunal System' *Com.Law.* 2005, 26 (12), 368–369.

[61] *R (on the application of Corner House Research)* v. *Secretary of State for Trade and Industry* (2005) EWCA Civ 192.

[62] Chapter 8, pp. 171–4. [63] See Schedule 1C3(2)(a) & (b) Charities Act 1993.

[64] S. 4(2) Charities Act 1993.

from the register.[65] An extension of this requirement to cover all charities would assist access to justice.

Overall conclusion

The overall conclusion to this book is that the powers of the Commission to remove charities from the register are limited. Looking to the future, if the Commission ever tries to remove swathes of charities from the register, it not only runs the risk of having its powers of removal challenged in law, but it also runs the risk of damaging public perception that charities are on the register because they are charitable in law. Neither scenario would enhance confidence in the Commission.

At a time when it is government policy to increasingly rely on charities to deliver public services[66] and to encourage the public to donate more to charity,[67] it is important that there is a belief that institutions on the register are entitled to be registered as charities.

[65] See para. 5(6) & (10) of the Draft Regulations dated 19 May 2005.
[66] Chapter 1, pp. 7–10. [67] Chapter 1, p. 10.

Bibliography

Claricoat, J. and Phillips, H. *Charity Law A-Z Key Questions Answered*, 2nd edn (Bristol: Jordans, 1998)

Dicey, A. V. *An Introduction to the Study of the Constitution* (1885), 10th edn (London: Macmillan, 1959)

Dunn, A. *The Voluntary Sector, the State and the Law*, 1st edn (Oxford: Hart, 2000)

Gold, R. with Evans, N. and Coleman, D. *Running a School 2004/5 Legal Duties and Responsibilities*, 2nd edn (Bristol: Jordans, 2005)

Hems, L. and Passey, A. *The Voluntary Sector Almanac* (London: NCVO, 1998/9)

Lester and Pannick *Human Rights Law and Practice*, 2nd edn (London: LexisNexis UK, 2004)

Lewis, C. *Judicial Remedies in Public Law*, 2nd edn (London: Sweet and Maxwell, 2000)

Luxton, P. *The Law of Charities*, 1st edn (Oxford University Press, 2001)

Maxwell *Interpretation of Statutes*, 12th edn (London: Sweet and Maxwell, 1969)

Meakin, R. *Charity in the NHS: Policy and Practice*, 1st edn (Bristol: Jordans, 1998)

Moffat, G. *Trusts Law: Text and Materials*, 3rd edn (Cambridge University Press, 1999)

Morris, D. *Charities and the Contract Culture: Partners and Contractors? Law and Practice in Conflict* (Liverpool University Charity Law Unit, 1999)

Schools – An Education in Charity Law, 1st edn (Aldershot: Dartmouth, 1996)

Nathan *The Charities Act 1960*, 1st edn (London: Butterworths, 1962)

Picarda, H. *The Law and Practice Relating to Charities*, 3rd edn (London: Sweet and Maxwell, 1999)

Riddall, J. G. *The Law of Trusts*, 6th edn (Oxford University Press, 2002)

Thomas, R. *Legitimate Expectations and Proportionality in Administrative Law*, 1st edn (Oxford University Press, 2000)

Venables, R. and Kessler, J. *Tax Planning and Fundraising for Charities*, 5th edn (London: Key Haven, 2003)

Wade, H. W. R. and Forsyth, C. F. *Administrative Law*, 8th edn (Oxford University Press, 2000)

Wainwright, Clark, Griffith, Jochum & Wilding *The UK Voluntary Sector Almanac 2004*, 5th edn (London: NCVO, 2006)
Warburton, J. *Tudor on Charities*, 9th edn (London: Butterworths, 2003)
West, E. *Companies Limited by Guarantee*, 2nd edn (Bristol: Jordans, 2004)
Williams, I. *The Alms Trade: Charities Past, Present and Future*, 1st edn (London: Harper Collins, 1989)

Articles

'A Joint Opinion by Anthony Lester and David Pannick' (ISIS document no.11) April 1987
'Administration of Justice A Time for Everything Under the Law: Some Reflections on Retrospectivity' Roger, A. *LQR* 2005, 121 (Jan) 57–79
'Blair to Assign NHS Role to the Voluntary Sector' *Third Sector* 21 June 2006
'CBI Criticises Complexity of Tribunal System' *Com.Law.* 2006, 26 (12) 368–369
'Charitable Companies Ceasing to be Charitable' Dutton, J. 7, *CL & PR*, 1, 2001
'Charitable Trusts in India' Duruvala, N. B. *Offshore Investment* May 1995
'Charitable Trusts-Unique' Warburton, J. (1999) 63 *Conv*, Jan/Feb
'Charities and Political Activity: Time to Re-think the Rules' Birt, E. *The Political Quarterly*, 23, 1998
'Charities and the Contract Culture: Partners or Contractors? Law and Practice in Conflict?' Morris, D. Liverpool University Charity Law Unit, 1992
'Charities and the State' Garton, J. 14 *Tru LI* 93, 2000
'Charities, Politics and Freedom of Speech' Morris, D. 5, *CL & PR*, 3, 1999
'Charities that Charge: The Impact of the Strategy Unit Report and the Charities Bill 2004' Christopher McCall QC and Guy Newey QC, Maitland Chambers, 6 July 2004
'Charity Appeals in the High Court: Practice Problems and Reform' Fryer, J.M. 36 *NLJ* (Ann. Charity. Rev.) 20, 1986
'Charity Cheats Laid Bare – By You' Levine, T. *The Guardian* 25 August 2007
'Charity in its Political Voice – a Tinkling Cymbal or a Sounding Brass?' Santow G.F.K., 18 *Aus. Bar. Rev.* 225, 1999
'Charity, Politics and the Human Rights Act 1998: Chasing a Red Herring?' Moffat, G. 4, *IJNL*, 1, 2001
'Compact Table of Shame' Plummer, J. *Third Sector*, 14 February 2007
'Conflicts of Interest in Charity Law' Luxton, P. *The Voluntary Sector, the State and the Law* ed. Dunn, A. (Hart Publishing, 2000)
'Drawing a Line', *Third Sector* 8 February 2006
'Endowed Charities: A Total Return Approach to Investment?' Dutton, J. 7, *CL & PR*, 2, 2001
'Human Rights and Charity Law' Warburton, J. S. J. 144 (17) *Supp* 24–26, 2000
'Legal Issues in Charity Mergers' Morris, D. Liverpool University Charity Law Unit 2001
'New Religions and Ethical Movements as Charities' Picarda, H. 131 *NLJ* 436, 1981

'Permanent Endowment and Total Return' Hill, J. and Smith, J. 7, *CL & PR*, 2, 2001
'Poor Little Rich Schools' *Guardian Education*, 23 April 2002
'Power Without Accountability The Charity Commission as Regulator' (Association For Charities Report 2004)
'Public Benefit in Charities' Atiyah, P.S. 21 *MLR* 138, 1958
'Public Charitable Collections: Are they a Worthwhile Cause?' Barker, C. R. 63 (6) *MLR* 791–812, 2000
'Retirement and Removal of Trustees' Phillips, A. *Trusts and Estates Law Journal*, July/August 1999
'Sector is Losing Out to Private Bids' *Third Sector*, 31 January 2007
'Super Charities Charter' Aldridge, N. *Society Guardian*, 3 June 2004
'The Charitable Status of Rifle Clubs: the Explosion Occurs' Clarke, P. 2, *CL & PR*, 2, 1993/4
'The Draft Charities Bill Public Benefit and the Advancement of Religion' Quint, F. Charity Law Association, 9 July 2004
'The Judge as Law Maker' Lord Reid 12 *J.S.P.T.L. (N.S)* 22, 1972–1973
'The Trustees Right to Silence-Lessons from the Guiness Trial' Wilson, T. and Meakin, R. 6 *NGO Finance*, Feb/March 1996
'Watch Out There's A Charity About' King, J. *The Spectator*, 28 October 2000, 30–31
'What are the Boundaries between "Public Sector" and "Charity"?' Cairns, E. *Charitable Schools and What Needs to be Done?* ed. Mountfield. *Directory of Social Change* 1992

Government Publications

Charities and Not-for-Profits A Modern Legal Framework: The Government's Response to Private Action, Public Benefit (Home Office, 2003)
Compact: Getting It Right Together (Cm 4100, 1998)
Consultation on the Review of Charities Administration in Northern Ireland in 2005 (Department for Social Affairs, 2005)
Efficiency Scrutiny of the Supervision of Charities (HMSO, 1987)
Getting Britain Giving: Inland Revenue Guidance Note (2000)
Higher Standards, Better Schools For All: More Choice for Parents and Pupils (Cm 6677, 2005)
Independent Complaints Reviewer to the Charity Commissioner for England and Wales Annual Report 2005/06: Seeking a Fair Resolution
Private Action, Public Benefit: A Review of Charities and the Wider Not-for-Profit Sector (Cabinet Office, Strategy Unit 2002)
Racial Disadvantage (Cm 8476, 1982)
Report, Formal Minutes and Evidence (Joint Committee on the Charities Bill, HL Paper 167–1, HC 660–1, 2004)
Rights Brought Home (Cm 3782, 1997)
The Future Role of the Third Sector in Social and Economic Regeneration: Final Report, July 2007 (Cm 7189, 2007)

The Role of The Voluntary and Community Sector in Service Delivery: A Cross Cutting Review (Treasury, 2002)
Working Together: Co-operation between Government and Faith Communities (Home Office Faith Communities Unit, 2004)

Charity Commission Publications

CC – Public Benefit Tests-How We Will Carry Them Out? (2004)
CC – Review of the Register General Key Messages, Questions and Answers (2001)
CC – The Promotion of Human Rights (2002)
CC 9 – Campaigning and Political Activities by Charities (2004)
CC 20 – Charities and Fund-raising (2001)
CC 47 – Complaints about Charities (2003)
[1966] Ch. Com. Annual Report
[1977] Ch. Com. Annual Report
[1978] Ch. Com. Annual Report
[1979] Ch. Com. Annual Report
[1983] Ch. Com. Annual Report
[1985] Ch. Com. Annual Report
[1987] Ch. Com. Annual Report
[1996] Ch. Com. Annual Report
[1998] Ch. Com. Annual Report
[2000/1] Ch. Com. Annual Report
Ch. Com. Dec. Vol. 1 (1993)
Ch. Com. Dec. Vol. 2 (1994)
Ch. Com. Dec. Vol. 5 (1997)
Consultation on Draft Public Benefit Guidance (February 2007)
Consultation Paper: Decision Review-Reconsidering the Commission's Decisions (2007)
Consultation Paper: Review of the Commission's Complaint and Customer Feedback Procedures (2007)
OG 17 Removal of Organisations from the Register (2007)
OG 71 Human Rights Act 1998 (2000)
OG 93 Complaints About the Commission's Standard of Service (2003)
OG 94 Requests For A Decision To Review (2003)
OG 202 Small Charities: Dissolutions and Removals from the Register (2007)
Public Benefit – the Charity Commission's Approach (January 2005)
Public Benefit – The Charity Commission's Position on how Public Benefit is Treated in the Charities Bill (July 2005)
Review of the Register General Key Messages, Questions and Answers (2001)
RR 1 – The Review of the Register of Charities (2001)
RR 1 a – Recognising New Charitable Purposes (2001)
RR 2 – The Promotion of Urban and Rural Regeneration (1999)
RR 3 – The Relief of Unemployment (1999)

RR 5 – The Promotion of Community Capacity Building (2000)
RR 6 – Maintenance of an Accurate Register of Charities (2000)
RR 7 – The Independence of Charities from the State (2001)
RR 8 – The Public Character of Charity (2001)
RR 9 – Preservation and Conservation (2001)
RR 11 – Charitable Status and Sport (2003)
RR 12 – The Promotion of Human Rights (2005)
RS4 a – Collaborative Working and Mergers: Summary (2003)

Index

For EU product safety concerns, contact us at Calle de José Abascal, 56–1°,
28003 Madrid, Spain or eugpsr@cambridge.org.

www.ingramcontent.com/pod-product-compliance
Lightning Source LLC
LaVergne TN
LVHW011813200926
848484LV00005B/1172

* 9 7 8 0 5 2 1 5 1 6 0 3 7 *